D0346257

101 499 732 1

Movies and
Mass Culture

NOT FOR LOAN

REFERENCE

Movies and Mass Culture
Edited by John Belton

The essays in *Movies and Mass Culture* examine the two-way process, of action and reaction, by which films shape the identity of society, its culture and its sense of nationhood; and, in turn, how films are themselves shaped by these forces and matrices. The nation here is America, in which films both effect and reflect changes in the national self-image, the transformation from one kind of nation to another: from an agrarian to an industrial economy; from a nation of producers to one of consumers; from a community of individuals to a mass society.

John Belton is Professor of English at Rutgers University and author of *Widescreen Cinema* and *American Cinema/American Culture*.

0 485 30073 7 pb

Edited and with an introduction by
John Belton

Movies and Mass Culture

ATHLONE
LONDON

SHEFFIELD HALLAM UNIVERSITY LIBRARY
RS
791.430973
BE
PSALTER LANE

First published in Great Britain 1996 by
THE ATHLONE PRESS
1 Park Drive, London NW11 7SG

This collection copyright © 1996 by Rutgers, The State University.
For copyrights to individual pieces, please see first page of each essay.

British Library Cataloguing in Publication Data
A catalogue record for this book is available from the British Library
ISBN 0 485 30073 7

All rights reserved. No part of this publication may be reproduced, stored in a retrieval system, or transmitted in any form or by any means, electronic, mechanical, photocopying or otherwise, without prior permission in writing from the publisher.

Manufactured in the United States

To Jasper Wood and Andrew Sarris

Contents

Mass Production, the Failure of the New, and Reaganite Cinema

Against the Grain

Movies and Mass Culture

John Belton

Introduction

This book looks at the way(s) in which American identity shapes and is shaped by motion pictures. Of course, an American national identity predates the advent of motion pictures. Its construction begins with the first encounters that European, English, and other non-Native Americans had with the American landscape, with one another, and with Native Americans. It is also quite obvious that this identity remains in the process of formation; it is continually coming into being, taking shape, and changing shape. And American identity does this across a cultural horizon that extends beyond the relatively narrow borders of the cinema; the American character is formed within the larger context of American culture as a whole. But aspects of it surface in the movies. The movies play a crucial role in its construction, in its representation/re-presentation, and in its transmission.

The relationship between motion pictures and culture remains complex. The movies are an integral part of mass culture and are embedded within it. One does not produce the other; rather, each interacts with the other, and they mutually determine one another. If films and filmmakers produce culture, they are also produced by it. Thus it is impossible to separate films and filmmakers from the society within which they exist. As Andre Bazin noted in his essay on notions of authorship in the cinema, "The individual transcends society, but society is also and above all *within* him. So there can be no definitive criticism of genius or talent which does not first take into consideration the social determinism, the historical combination of circumstances, and the technical background which to a large extent determine it."[1]

National identity is neither single nor constant in nature; it is not monolithic but complex; and it changes from one period to the next. For example, America's sense of itself shifted in the 1910s and 1920s

1

along with the movement of its population from rural to urban areas. It became an *urban* nation, yet it continued to conceive of itself as an agrarian state. In the early 1950s, white-collar workers began to outnumber blue-collar workers for the first time in U.S. history. By 1956, more than 75 percent of adult Americans—including lower-class, blue-collar workers—began to *think* of themselves as middle class. Again, at mid-century, America's self-image underwent a face-lift of sorts, here in a way that exceeded changes in actual class status. Even today, most Americans—even those with incomes just barely above the poverty level—tend to identify themselves as middle class—in large part because their *values* are middle class. In the 1990s, American demographics shifted yet again as population shifted from the cities to the suburbs. With this move, an urbanized, industrialized America also began to redefine itself as a geographically diverse mass society, built on a service rather than an industrial economy. At the same time, it began to embrace the decentralized structure of a new age—the Age of Information—electronically linked together by means of a communications superhighway of telephones, cables, and computers.

As a cornerstone of the communications industry, the movies have always played a crucial role in the process of this changing identity-formation. They not only serve as texts that document who we think we are or were, but also reflect changes in our self-image, tracing the transformation from one kind of America to another. Contemporary audiences can see in older films different styles of dress, different modes of behavior, and different notions of what it meant to be an American. These differences do not merely consist of the superficial recognition that, in the olden days, women bobbed their hair, men wore double-breasted suits and drove 1948 Packards, and everyone dialed rotary telephones, listened to swing music, and was obsessed with cigarette smoking.

More important, the movies assist audiences in negotiating major changes in identity; they carry them across difficult periods of cultural transition in such a way that a more or less coherent national identity remains in place, spanning the gaps and fissures that threaten to disrupt its movement and to expose its essential disjointedness.

As twentieth-century Americans, we live in and belong to a mass culture. Yet we conceive of ourselves as unique individuals, defined in large part by our intimate relationship to smaller social units or institutions—to our families, our friends, and our local communities—and by our larger identification with a specific class, race, gender, and/or ethnic group. The one way in which we tend *not* to define ourselves is in terms of our alienated relationship to mass society. In other words, we live in a state of denial, acknowledging those aspects of our identity that confirm our uniqueness and repressing those that deny it.

Ideology, or the system(s) of beliefs that individuals hold about the real conditions of their existence, plays a major role in this confirmation of our identity. Those beliefs may be true or false, or a combination of both. It is often difficult to distinguish between beliefs and facts. Even science, which distinguishes itself from ideology in precisely these terms (i.e., science consists of "facts" and ideology of "beliefs"), is necessarily ideological, its assumptions often shaped by individual or social beliefs.[2] The truth of one's beliefs remains secondary to their credibility, to whether or not they are believed. In this sense, ideology determines an individual's or a society's understanding of the world in which he or she or it lives.

As a mass identity within a modern, fully industrialized mass culture, American identity conceives of itself according to certain American myths or systems of cultural beliefs. There is no single myth or system of belief that "explains" American identity. The notion of what it means to be "American" is as diverse as its population; America is and remains a multiethnic mass.[3] Indeed, the American experience includes the unique encounters with America of New England Protestants, Irish or Italian-American Catholics, middle-European Jews, Asian-Americans, African-Americans, women, latinos/Hispanics, gays, and lesbians.

But from one perspective, at least, this multiethnic mass shared one common experience—that of modernity. The experience of modernity for most Americans came in the form of their reactions to the profound changes introduced into the nation's social, cultural, and economic structure by the rapid industrialization and urbanization that took place during the period from the Civil War until World War I. These reactions were complex, combining a positive enthusiasm for the progress and growth associated with these developments and a gnawing fear of the effects these changes might have on traditional American values.

The trauma initiated by this rapid industrialization and urbanization prompted the emergence of two major myths or systems of belief that tended to dominate ways of thinking about the American experience before, during, and after World War I. These systems of belief, with only minor variation, also tended to dominate Hollywood narratives during the crucial period of the development of classical Hollywood cinema (ca. 1896–1917)[4] and have remained significant from that period until the present.[5] These ideologies were themselves dominant during the period in which the cinema itself became a mass art and in which the film-makers who created classical Hollywood cinema were raised.

Individual filmmakers react in a variety of ways to these ideologies, as do specific film genres and film stars. At the same time, each period of American film history provides its own way of understanding American identity in relation to the nation's transformation into a mass society that has been shaped in response to the advent of mass culture. Because motion pictures shape and are shaped by mass culture, they define themselves in terms of these dominant ideologies, sometimes reflecting them and sometimes calling them into question.

From the 1890s until 1914, American political thought was shaped by two major reform movements—populism and progressivism. These ideologies existed within a field of other ideologies with which they interact, but they have emerged as dominant. Indeed, populism achieved such widespread power as a system of beliefs that it has been described by historians as "the American ideology."[6] Populism and progressivism dominated American thought, in large part, because they both identified and confronted problems crucial to an emerging national identity. Both populism and progressivism addressed the nation's anxieties over its cataclysmic transformation from an agrarian to an industrial economy, from a nation of producers to one of consumers, and from a community of individuals to a mass society.

The *politics* of populism and progressivism were short lived, roughly spanning the period between the presidential campaigns of populist William Jennings Bryan (1896) and of two progressives, Theodore Roosevelt (1904/1912) and Woodrow Wilson (1912/1916). But as systems of belief, the *ideologies* of populism and progressivism outlived the rise and fall the Populist and Progressive political parties. It is primarily as myths, or as ideologies, that they found their way into motion picture narratives; thus, it is primarily as ideologies (not as political movements) that they are discussed here.

Populist ideology was rooted in the ideals of the Jeffersonian democratic tradition. Thomas Jefferson envisioned America as "a republic of yeoman farmers, each man working his own land, free to develop in his own way."[7] For Jefferson, the moral virtue of the American citizenry depended on its association with the land. "I think our governments," he wrote, "will remain virtuous for many centuries, as long as they are chiefly agricultural. . . . Cultivators of the earth are most valuable citizens. They are the most vigorous, the most independent, the most virtuous and they are tied to their country and wedded to its liberty and interests by the most lasting bonds."[8]

For Jefferson, the American character was rescued from the corruption and decadence of the Old World through regenerative contact with Nature. But, more important, the land became, for him, the basis on which American democracy was to be built. The availability of free land in the West guaranteed each American an opportunity to own land and, thereby, to have an equal stake in the affairs of the nation. The universal ownership of property would not only empower Americans but ensure their self-sufficiency and independence.

Populist ideology looked back with nostalgia to the "lost Eden" of preindustrial agrarian America, to the nation of shopkeepers, artisans, farmers, and small towns that existed "before the development of industrialism and the commercialization of agriculture."[9] As a reform movement, populism's response to industrialization and mass culture was reactionary rather than revolutionary. "America [did] not need a revolution," writes George McKenna, "for the simple reason that it [had] already had one. What it [did] need [was] a restoration."[10] It needed to return to the values and beliefs of agrarian, small town America. In returning to the original values and beliefs of Revolutionary-era America, populism advocated "democracy, honest and unobtrusive central government, leadership by decent men, equality of opportunity, [and] self-help." Responding to the postindustrial present, populism "opposed big business, the political machine and intellectualism as the things most likely to hamper the individual's pursuit of happiness."[11] However, the populist spirit was, in other ways, undemocratic. Populism attempted to address the interests of farmers, lower-class farm workers, and other elements of the rural population who had become increasingly frustrated by and discontented with the forces of industrialization.[12] To these groups, the nation's fall from grace was seen as the result of "a sustained conspiracy of the international money power" that deliberately oppressed farmers and workers.[13]

In other words, populist thought, as seen here, tended toward a certain paranoia, especially in its treatment of groups with different social or economic interests. Thus, it was anti-intellectual, racist, anti-Semitic, and xenophobic.[14] Populist rhetoric informs the revivalistic fundamentalism of William Jennings Bryan, the anticommunism of Sen. Joseph McCarthy, and the segregationism of Gov. George Wallace.[15]

The racism of D. W. Griffith's *The Birth of a Nation* (1915) has its origins in the populist desire to return to a "lost Eden." According to the film's initial intertitles, the harmony of Eden/America is disrupted by "the bringing of the African to America," which "planted the first seed of disunion." The film ends with a vision of the millennium, in which war, strife, and African-Americans have been banished and in which Christ appears, reinstituting his reign on earth and restoring the "lost Eden."[16]

The popularity of *The Birth of a Nation* gives testimony to the power of Griffith's social and historical vision, but the racist aspects of this vision were rejected by a significant number of Americans, including African-Americans, members of the clergy, intellectuals, and progressive reformers.[17] Today, audiences adamantly refuse to accept the film's racism. It is important to remember that audiences regularly resist and occasionally reject the ideological "messages" present in motion pictures. Certain aspects of populist or progressive thought were clearly *not* embraced by all Americans.

Populist values and beliefs may not necessarily enter the cinema through Griffith, but in him they find one of their most powerful advocates. Griffith's *A Corner in Wheat* (1909), for example, lays bare the exploitation of the rural farmers and the urban poor by the greedy manipulation of a speculator in the grain market. As Tom Gunning has pointed out, the film draws on William Jennings Bryan's famous "Cross of Gold" speech of 1896. Its narrative contrasts "the farmer who goes forth in the morning and toils all day, who begins in the spring and toils all summer, and who by the application of brain and muscle to the natural resources of the country creates wealth" with "the man who goes upon the Board of Trade and bets upon the price of grain."[18] Griffith's narrative weaves scenes of the farmer, idealized within a natural landscape (where he sifts grain through his fingers and sows his fields), and those of the speculator, isolated from the world of nature (and from the honest toil of the working class) in claustrophobic urban interiors.

Griffith's film exposes the corruption and greed of those who manipulate the grain market. And it opposes the rich and the poor, revealing the exploitation by "the haves" of the "have-nots." Yet it is clearly populist, not Marxist. It provides no analysis of the economic relations between capitalists and farmers; it does not explore the ideological underpinnings of the system that governs the production, distribution, and consumption of grain. Instead, it melodramatizes these relations, suggesting that the plight of impoverished farmers and consumers is the result of individual villainy, rather than of any flaw in the capitalist system. Thus, Nature, in the form of the grain in which the speculator is "drowned," destroys the villain. In this way, Nature secures a form of social justice that is eloquently poetic. But, more important, Griffith's logic suggests that the system (capitalist free enterprise) works, if it is only run properly by a benign and morally virtuous individual. The film ends, as it began, with the image of the farmer sowing his field. Although the farmer is left impoverished and exhausted, corruption has been eliminated. The agrarian economy is now free to function naturally, providing an adequate living for the farmer and reasonably priced bread for the consumer.

Within mainstream American thought, capitalism works, but it just sometimes goes a bit crazy. Populists and progressives sought to correct its excesses. Thus, they fought those forces within the economic and social order that abused the system. In this way, both populists and progressives shared common enemies. They both opposed monopolies and trusts; industrial and financial capitalists; railroads and robber barons; large corporations and corrupt political machines. Because they both target the same individuals or groups as villains, it is not always easy to distinguish that which is populist in the cinema from that which is progressive.

Of course, populists and progressives can be distinguished from one another in several ways. Historically, they belonged to different social and geographical groups. Populists, such as the midwesterner Bryan, tended to espouse the moral and religious values of rural, working-class America, whereas Progressives, such as the easterner Teddy Roosevelt, represented the interests of a more privileged, urban class. Progressive reform began in the cities, where the effects of industrialization and urbanization had led to the creation of slums and exploitative labor practices. The Populist movement, which began in the South and the West, sought to regulate the railroads, to protect farmers (and, later, factory workers) from big business interests, and to introduce a graduated income tax that would ensure that corporations and the wealthiest Americans would pay their fair share of taxes. Yet, despite these differences, they share a common cause. The minor features that mark them as unique political movements disappear in the larger process of their transformation into ways of describing the American experience in terms of traditional narrative formats. Thus, to a great extent, American cinema draws on both of them, blurring their differences and fusing them into a common ideological strand.

As a result, many American films combine populist with progressive thinking. Thus, even the populist vision of *A Corner in Wheat* owes much to progressivism.[19] Its narrative is based on the muckraking journalistic fiction of Frank Norris, the author of naturalistic Zolaesque works such as "A Deal in Wheat" (1903), *The Octopus* (1901), and *The Pit* (1902). Norris wrote frequently for *McClure's*, a leading muckraking magazine that published progressive essays by Ida Tarbell, who wrote a famous expose of Standard Oil, and Lincoln Steffens, who wrote about urban political corruption.[20] As historian Richard Hofstadter notes, "The fundamental critical achievement of American Progressivism was the business of exposure. . . . journalism was the chief occupational source of its writers, . . . [and] the muckraker was a central figure."[21]

Progressives such as Norris sought reform through exposure. They believed that public opinion could be educated and that the disclosure of corruption was the first step leading to its elimination.[22] American film has always performed a journalistic function, informing the populace about current events. This was as true of actuality films and newsreels as it was about topical narratives of the 1930s, such as *I Am a Fugitive from a Chain Gang* (1932), which exposed the corruption and brutality of the chain gang system, as well as those of the 1970s and 1980s, such as *The China Syndrome* (1979), which drew attention to the hazardous conditions within contemporary nuclear power plants, and *Wall Street* (1987), which looked at the ruthless practice of insider trading in the New York stock market. In each instance, exposure is understood to lead to reform.

Although it is famous for other reasons, *Citizen Kane* (1941), which focusses on the career of a muckraking newspaper editor, tells the tale of the rise and fall of progressive activism. Kane may be understood as a populist in search of a "lost Eden" (his youth with his mother in rural, preindustrial Colorado, circa 1870). But during the course of the film, he adopts a progressive stance toward the excesses of industry and government. As the editor of a muckraking newspaper, he attempts to expose the traction trust, copper robbers, urban slumlords, and political bosses. He campaigns for governor, as he tells us, "to point out and make public, the dishonesty, the downright villainy of Boss Jim Gettys' political machine." After refusing to be blackmailed into withdrawing from the race, Kane is himself exposed in the press as an adulterer. The film does expose the double standard of the progressive reform movement: the idealism of Kane's attempts at social and political reform is undermined by his own moral hypocrisy. Yet, it also celebrates the energy and enthusiasm of well-intentioned reformers such as Kane. Once he is defeated in the election and retires from politics, Kane and the film lose their idealism and their spirited sense of social mission.

More recently, the progressive spirit has animated the contemporary American documentary. *Roger and Me* (Moore, 1989) investigates the consequences of the closing of a General Motors truck plant in Flint, Michigan, which put 30,000 people out of work. The film intercuts scenes of unemployed auto workers playing basketball or being evicted from their homes with scenes depicting the elite of Flint society at the local country club. A modern muckraker, Moore's target is the CEO of General Motors, Roger Smith, who repeatedly evades the filmmaker's attempts to interview him. The film targets big business as the enemy of working-class America and argues that the excesses of capitalism need to be reformed. In 1994, Moore extended his progressive project to television, adopting a "60 Minutes"-style approach to his lower-middle-class exposé of corporate America in "TV Nation."

To some extent, progressives responded more positively to the industrial revolution than did populists. Progressive narratives featured characters who, through hard work, frugality, and industry, realized the American dream of success, epitomized in the Horatio Alger stories.[23] Progressives believed that within an ideal capitalist state, an individual's integrity and energy would be rewarded with economic success. However, industrial trusts and monopolies had "crooked" the economic wheel in their own favor and prevented the individual entrepreneur from securing an appropriate reward for his or her efforts. Progressives insisted that legislation controlling monopolies and trusts was necessary to ensure that the playing field was kept level.[24] As Hofstadter notes, progressivism attempted "to restore a type of economic individualism and political democracy that was widely believed to have existed earlier in America and to have been destroyed by the great corporation and the corrupt political machine, and with that restoration to bring back a kind of morality and civic purity that was also believed to have been lost."[25]

Unlike populism, which failed to engage with the political realities of postindustrial America, progressive activism was focussed on *legislative* reform. Progressives enacted legislation that regulated railroads, raised corporate taxes, enacted child labor laws, demanded oversight of the food industry, advocated the municipal ownership of public utilities, and campaigned for minimum wage and maximum work hours legislation. Although genuinely interested in the public's welfare, the more extreme progressives sought the passage of restrictive laws that legislated morality. Indeed, Griffith was skeptical of the puritanical nature of Progressive reform, certain factions of which denounced the movies as unwholesome.[26] Later, *The Birth of a Nation* was attacked as racist by many progressives, including Chicago's Jane Addams.[27] Efforts were made to prevent the film from being publicly screened and to force Griffith to delete certain scenes in which African-Americans were depicted as "brutal," "vicious," "grotesque," and "despicable."[28] Griffith viewed this attempt at censorship as an assault on free speech and responded, in the modern story of *Intolerance* (1916), with a denunciation of middle-class reform groups, which he saw as hypocritical busy-bodies who sought to impose their own moral codes on the lower class.

Like Griffith, populists tended to oppose the legislation of morality. In their utopian vision of America, the common people possessed an innate morality that enabled them to tell right from wrong. An inherently virtuous people, Americans knew in their hearts what was right and did not need laws, especially those imposed on them from above, to guide their actions.[29] The populist heroes of Frank Capra and John Ford films enjoyed a special relationship to the truth, which they discovered merely by searching their own hearts.

Laws were what other lesser individuals depended on for their knowledge of what was right and wrong. More important, laws often became the tools that villains used to maintain power. Thus, populist heroes often opposed mundane civil laws, upholding, instead, a more transcendent morality. In *Young Mr. Lincoln* (Ford, 1939), for example, Lincoln (played by Henry Fonda) objects when the mother of his two young clients is on the witness stand and is being forced to reveal to the court which one of her sons was guilty of a murder. Lincoln intervenes with the prosecutor's relentless questioning, declaring that "I may not know much about the law, but I do know what's right and what's wrong. And what you're asking her to do is wrong!" Lincoln knows in his heart what is right and wrong. Thus, he refuses to participate in a legalistic lynching of those whose values, like his own, place them outside of the limited moral vision of the judicial system.

In populist mythology, Lincoln emerges as the archetypal hero.[30] The son of a poor farmer, he maintained the values of agrarian America, remaining humble, honest, God-fearing, and simple. His homespun virtues and dogged attempts at self-betterment were rewarded with the presidency. Populist directors, such as Griffith, Ford, and Capra, are repeatedly drawn to the character of Lincoln. In his first sound film, *Abraham Lincoln* (1930), Griffith portrayed Lincoln as a quasi-messianic saviour of the nation, expanding and humanizing the image of Lincoln as "the Great Heart," which he developed earlier in *The Birth of a Nation*.

Ford returned to the figure of Lincoln throughout his career (*The Iron Horse* [1924]; *Prisoner of Shark Island* [1934]; *Cheyenne Autumn* [1964]).

Capra's heroes, such as Peter Warne (Clark Gable) in *It Happened One Night* (1934), and Jefferson Smith (James Stewart) in *Mr Smith Goes to Washington* (1939), invoke Lincoln as an ideal figure and attempt to model their own behavior on his.[31] Like Ford's young Mr. Lincoln, they know the truth and possess an unshakable moral authority because of that. Indeed, Jeff Smith's filibuster in the Senate, which cites essential populist texts ranging from the Bible to the "Declaration of Independence," represents a tour de force of populist argumentation; it is, perhaps, the best example of what *Cahiers du cinema* referred to as a "moralizing discourse" in the American cinema.[32] It is heartfelt and sincere, and it is delivered with a moral authority that the character has earned over the course of the film.

Populist and progressive ideologies play a crucial role in shaping the notions of individuality, which serve as the foundation on which Hollywood narratives are based. David Bordwell has described classical Hollywood cinema as a character-centered cinema. "The classical Hollywood film," he argues, "presents psychologically defined individuals who struggle to solve a clear-cut problem or to attain specific goals. In the course of this struggle, the characters enter into conflict with others or with external circumstances. The story ends with a decisive victory or defeat. . . . The principal causal agency is thus the character, a distinctive individual endowed with an evident, consistent batch of traits, qualities, and behaviors."[33]

Bordwell does not describe the nature, beliefs, or identity of the individuals who dominate classical Hollywood cinema for the obvious reason that these aspects of individual characters change from film to film. The idea of individuality that underlies Bordwell's description of classical Hollywood cinema draws on the intellectual and political thought of both the Enlightenment and Romanticism, which stressed the primacy of the individual. In the United States, this tradition was appropriated by Jefferson and other founding fathers, who reconceived the concept of individuality within an American (i.e., democratic) context. As we have already seen, Jefferson's theory of the individual's status within a democracy was, in turn, rearticulated in populist and progressive thought. It was this thought that gave form to the uniquely "American" sense of individuality that governs the behavior and agency of the central characters found in American cinema.

This sense of individuality is, however, illusory. It is an idealist construction of the late eighteenth and early nineteenth centuries that survived into the twentieth century (and continues to survive today). It survived because it served a necessary function. It provided individuals with a sense of their uniqueness, autonomy, and agency—traits that were increasingly circumscribed by the mass society within which they lived. Characters in movies were empowered by their individual virtues and were capable of intervening in and possibly even determining the course of events that took place in the films' narratives. This kind of hero appears most frequently in the Western, a populist genre that itself dominated Hollywood, accounting for almost 25 percent of all American films made between 1926 and 1967. But this kind of hero tends to crop up regularly in other films as well.

The hero's sense of agency runs, like a thread, through the body of American cinema. The movies tell us that the individual *can* make a difference, even within modern mass society. The hero can take on those "corporate" forces that would crush integrity and individuality and defeat them. In *It's a Wonderful Life* (Capra, 1946), George Bailey (James Stewart) triumphs over the ruthless banker, Mr. Potter (Lionel Barrymore). The heroes of *Star Wars* (Lucas, 1977) defeat the evil Empire and later convert Darth Vader to the good side of "the Force." Even the corrupt world of insider trading in *Wall Street* (Stone, 1987) can be reformed by the heroic efforts of one man, Bud Fox (Charles Sheen), who prizes his integrity more than he does profit. In the first *Star Wars* film, victory is presented as the triumph of individuality over the machine: Luke Skywalker (Mark Hamill) turns off his computerized gunsight and uses the Force to guide him in the aiming of the missiles that destroy the Death Star. Even in *Schindler's List* (Spielberg, 1993), a film that examines the greatest villainy ever perpetrated by the corporate state—the Holocaust—the individual, Oscar Schindler, can still make a difference.

The innocence and homespun values associated with the rustic heroes of Capra films have tended to give way in recent American films to more worldly, sophisticated, and cynical characters, such as Fox and Schindler. But those values and characters of the past occasionally make a comeback. The central character of *Forrest Gump* (Zemeckis, 1994), a mentally handicapped American version of Voltaire's Candide, embodies the beliefs of the traditional populist hero. The values of the world around Gump change in response to the social and political turmoil of the 1960s (the civil rights movement, drugs, sex, Vietnam), the 1970s (the political corruption symbolized by Watergate), and the 1980s (the AIDS epidemic).

The traditional populist hero transplanted to the 1990s: Forrest Gump (Tom Hanks). Photo courtesy of Paramount.

But Gump's convictions remain constant; he adheres to the simple maxims taught to him by his mother. He is not stupid because he knows that "stupid is as stupid does" and he avoids doing stupid things. His optimism is conveyed through another saying he learned from his mother: "Life is like a box of chocolates: you never know what you're gonna get." His honesty, integrity, sexual innocence, naive optimism, and devoted loyalty to friends and family look back to the utopian small town America envisioned by populist ideology.

Populist and progressive thought constructed an ideal agrarian, small town America, rejecting the reality of an America that was gradually becoming industrialized and urbanized. During the 1940s, that which populist and progressive ideology sought to repress began to return. It came back in the form of film noir, a countercurrent within the mainstream of classical Hollywood cinema. And it reappeared as a nightmarish inversion of the earlier dream, as a distortion of the reality of an industrialized and urbanized America.

The film that best illustrates the rupture that took place in the continuity of American identity at this time is Capra's *It's a Wonderful Life*. The film begins with trouble in populist paradise: George Bailey (James Stewart), a character who epitomizes such traditional values as hard work, frugality, honesty, good-neighborliness, self-sufficiency, egalitarianism, common sense, and moral sincerity, is about to commit suicide. The film reviews Bailey's heroic efforts to combat the evils of big business, special interest groups, commercialism, cynicism, and corruption, and it documents his self-sacrifice on behalf of his community.

Near the end of the film, Capra shows his hero what his hometown, Bedford Falls, would have become if he had never lived. Bedford Falls has now become "Pottersville," named after Bailey's nemesis, the greedy banker, who represents the destructive forces of big business and industrialization. The town has become a monstrous mirror image of its former self and is no longer the populist ideal it once was. There are no families, homes, or small businesses. Its inhabitants are depraved, cynical, bitter, alienated from one another, and depressed. Realizing that his life has made a difference (it has prevented Bedford Falls from becoming "Pottersville"), Bailey abandons his plans to kill himself, Pottersville disappears, and the utopian fantasy world of Bedford Falls returns.

Like the "Pottersville" sequence, film noir was the bad dream of postwar American cinema. The box office hits of the period, such as *Meet Me in St. Louis* (Minnelli, 1944), presented a portrait of an idyllic, small town America. Minnelli's tintype vision of St. Louis in 1903 celebrates a preindustrial community of families and individuals, whose integrity is preserved by a refusal of the modern (instead of moving to New York City, the family remains "right here in our hometown"). The St. Louis World's Fair, which provides a narrative focus for the film, symbolizes the industrial advancement of the twentieth century, with its display of the latest developments in modern technology. Fittingly, the fair itself remains off-screen and unseen.

During the 1970s, America rediscovered film noir, in part, as a result of Paul Schrader's seminal "Notes on Film Noir." In post-Vietnam, post-Watergate America, the social and political vision of film noir spoke to the sense of cynicism and alienation that circulated within popular culture. *Taxi Driver* (Scorsese, 1976), which was written by Schrader, presents a vision of America that is decidedly dark. New York City is portrayed as an urban inferno, inhabited by a disaffected and alienated populace that has surrendered itself to the crime and corruption brought about by industrialization and urbanization. The populist candidate for political office, Sen. Charles Palantine (Leonard Harris), pretends to speak on behalf of the people (his motto is "We Are the People"). But he is seen as phony and opportunistic.

Lacking the coherence of the traditional hero, the film's central character, Vietnam veteran and taxi driver Travis Bickle (Robert De Niro), has no clearly defined goals and does not know what he wants. He is both attracted and repulsed by what he sees. He desires the traditional American ideal—the upper-middle-class, blonde heroine Betsy (Cybill Shepherd); but he then redefines his goal, dedicating himself to the rescue of the teenage prostitute Iris (Jodie Foster). He initially seems intent on assassinating Palantine, yet then abruptly redirects his hostility toward a pimp (Harvey Keitel).

The film ends with an assertion of coherence where there is none. In killing the pimp and his underworld associates, Travis becomes a hero. But his elevation to the status of hero in the media is clearly the result of a misreading of his actions. His incoherent violence is given meaning and coherence by the media. He becomes a progressive reformer despite himself.

Like film noir, films such as *Taxi Driver* represent the dark underside of populist and progressive ideology. They envision the consequences of an industrialization and urbanization that have run amuck; they depict the alienation of the individual within mass society. They turn populist and progressive ideology inside out, providing a realization of its worst nightmares. The boundaries of the American cinema are defined by these two diametrically opposed visions of the American experience. And each of these visions—one utopian, the other dystopian—cannot exist without the other; they are the product of a single, yet nonetheless complex psyche—the American psyche.

Like the flashback structure of *Citizen Kane,* which portrays its central character through the prism of separate and distinct points of view, this anthology is a composite of different perspectives on a single subject—the relationship of American movies to mass culture. Its portrait of this subject is, as a result, fragmentary, but a portrait nonetheless gradually emerges, forming cumulatively as the reader moves from essay to essay.

In "Apocalyptic Cinema," Lary May views Griffith as representative of a nineteenth-century, Protestant, Victorian order that was in danger of collapsing in response to the onslaught of economic and social change. Griffith used the cinema, a form of mass culture, to rescue Victorianism and Anglo-Saxon culture from modernity. Presented as a figure of progressive reform, Griffith used the motion picture to convey moral lessons, to lift "mankind from animality," and to warn his audiences against the threats posed to their moral virtue by the crumbling of the codes and culture of the past.

Nineteenth-century individualism was grounded in a Victorian sense of moral virtue. One person was distinguished from another on the basis of essential worth. In "The Crowd, the Collective, and the Chorus," Martin Rubin examines the way that the notion of individuality changes in American cinema from the 1920s to the 1930s. Looking at *The Crowd* (1928) and a series of Busby Berkeley musicals, Rubin traces the evolution of the relationship between the individual and the mass from the "rugged individualism" of "expansionist, laissez-faire American capitalism of the 1865–1929 period" to the reconfirmation of the individual within the mass by means of a temporary loss of individuality that dominates notions of individualism in the 1930s.

Between 1860 and 1890, the American economy began to shift from that of a society of producers to that of a society of consumers.[34] As Charles Eckert points out in "The Carole Lombard in Macy's Window," motion pictures functioned as transitory display windows for twentieth-century American goods. Film viewers were addressed by the movies as potential consumers who might want to buy the clothing, cosmetics, furniture, and other consumer products featured in Hollywood films. The studios negotiated contracts with major companies such as General Electric, General Motors, Coca-Cola, Lux Soap, and Maxwell

House to plug their products, receiving, in turn, free advertising for their films. At the same time, Hollywood films became increasingly driven by the consumerism that dominated the American economy.

Eckert notes that women enjoy a dominant role in the purchase of consumer items. Mary Ann Doane builds on this notion to reverse notions of the woman as passive commodity and to empower female viewers as active consumers. On one level, female spectators "buy" images of themselves in the form of female stars, thus participating in the commodification of the image of woman. On another, they buy the products that have been placed in motion pictures. On yet another, women consume the stories that classical Hollywood cinema provides them. In all instances, women are sold "a certain image of femininity." This image becomes an object that the female spectator is programmed to desire.

The regulation of desire in classical Hollywood cinema finds its most literal representation in "The Production Code," a list of guidelines adopted by the film industry in 1930 to ensure that the content of motion pictures remained "wholesome" and to forestall, through self-censorship, the threat of federal, state, and/or local censorship. More than any other text, the Production Code dramatizes the potential power of the cinema as an instrument of social reform—at least, as it was perceived by religious and other civic organizations concerned with public morality. Written by Martin Quigley, a Catholic layman and publisher of the trade journal *Motion Picture Herald*, and Rev. Daniel A. Lord, a Jesuit professor at the University of St. Louis, the Production Code established the boundaries for on-screen behavior from 1930 to the mid-1950s when the code was successfully challenged by independent filmmakers who sought to bring a new, more adult content to the screen.

Before it was relaxed, the Production Code played a significant role in the creation of a new kind of cinema, film noir. Writers and directors interested in dealing with forbidden themes, that is, with the "immoral" content prohibited by the code, discovered ways of alluding to taboo material without directly violating the code. Of course, "mature" themes, such as crime, violence, and sexuality, do find their way into serious dramas of the pre-code (i.e., pre-1934) and post-code/prewar (1934–1941) period. But these themes tend to be alluded to tastefully, at least in the post-code period. Film noir, however, sought to *exploit* prohibited material without actually showing it. Thus, acts of sadism or sexual depravity took place off screen, contributing to a sense of fear and paranoia on screen. Low-key lighting and claustrophobic framing concealed and/or disguised taboo subjects. In his seminal essay on film noir, Paul Schrader views noir as the product of postwar American cynicism, pessimism, and disillusionment. Noir emerges as a break with Hollywood tradition: its subject matter was more realistic than that found in the standard 1930s drama. Its stylistic practices were more visible and more intrusive than the transparent lighting, editing, framing, and camera style of classical Hollywood cinema.

Film noir's violation of the narrative and stylistic conventions that dominated classical Hollywood cinema reflect transformations in the social order of postwar America. Sylvia Harvey examines noir in terms of the changing status of women during and after the Second World War. At the start of the war, women moved out of the home and into the workplace, where they filled in for their fathers, husbands, and boyfriends who were in the armed forces. At the end of the war, many women hoped to continue working and to retain their new-found economic and social independence. Men tended to view these new roles for women as a threat to traditional notions of women and to the integrity of the family. This fear surfaces in film noir in the form of femmes fatales, destructive career women, and absent or dysfunctional families.

Eckert and Doane point to the intimate relationship between film audiences and consumerism. In "Postmodernism and Consumer Society," Fredric Jameson looks at American cinema of the 1970s as a postmodern phenomenon that reflects the sense of alienation and fragmentation brought about by late capitalism. Modernist art works responded to the advent of the machine age and mass society, which threatened the uniqueness of the individual with the anonymity of mass production and mass consumption, by asserting the integrity and creativity of the artist. Revolting against tradition, modernist artists sought to say something new and different, to be original in a world dominated by mechanical reproduction(s). Postmodernism represents a reaction to modernism. It refuses to make the traditional distinctions drawn by modernists and premodernists between high culture and popular culture. In terms of stylistic practices, postmodern artists rely on pastiche. Pastiche is a form of imitation of the unique style or content of earlier works that lacks any trace of the satire or parody that characterizes traditional forms of imitation.

Postmodern works also acknowledge the primary obstacle confronting contemporary artists—the inability to say anything that has not already been said. If traditional filmmakers such as D. W. Griffith, Alfred Hitchcock, or Orson Welles invented ways of expressing ideas through the medium of the cinema, postmodern directors such as Brian De Palma could only draw on a pre-existent dictionary of shots, character types, situations, themes, and meanings to express themselves. The "authentic" expression of ideas in the past has thus given way to quotation and allusion to that authentic expression.

Jameson relates this inability to be original, which he refers to as "the failure of the new," to another feature of postmodernism—nostalgia for the past. Nostalgia films, such as *American Graffiti* (Lucas, 1973), return spectators from the incoherence of the present to the coherence of the past. In this idyllic past, the self was whole, not fragmented as it is today, and unified with, not alienated from, a larger community. Postmodern works reflect the schizophrenic breakdown of the normal experience of the world as a continuous, coherent, and meaningful phenomenon. These works consist of a series of "isolated, disconnected, discontinuous material signifiers which fail to link up into a coherent sequence." Postmodern artists thus convey the incoherence that informs the social and cultural reality of contemporary experience.

Robin Wood has written at length about 1970s cinema, noting the incoherence of its "texts" and linking that incoherence to a series of social, political, and cultural events that undermined the stability of traditional authority of patriarchal institutions. Vietnam, Watergate, the black militant movement, feminism, gay liberation, and other protest movements "question[ed] authority, . . . the entire social structure that validated it, . . . patriarchy, . . . social institutions, the family, [and] the Father interiorized as superego."[35] For Wood, this questioning can be seen in "incoherent texts," such as *Taxi Driver* (Scorsese, 1976), *Looking for Mr. Goodbar* (Brooks, 1977), and *Cruising* (Friedkin, 1980).

In "Papering the Cracks," Wood looks at the way in which certain 1970s "coherent texts," such as those films produced and/or directed by George Lucas and Steven Spielberg, address the sociopolitical anxiety of 1970s America to reassure audiences that "the system" of patriarchal capitalism still works. Films of reassurance embrace childishness, providing a regression to infantilism and childlike state of wonder. They dazzle the eyes and the ears with spectacular special effects. Their sense of invention, imagination, and originality is facile. They allay nuclear anxiety and endorse a fascist submission to authority. Most important, they restore and reaffirm the authority of the father.

Hollywood films confirm and/or resist the dominant ideology. But mainstream culture carries within it several subcultures that support more diverse cultural activities. Clyde Taylor situates independent Afro-

American filmmaking of the 1960s and 1970s within the unique traditions of Afro-American art. He identifies a new generation of university-trained, black American filmmakers, who draw on Afro-American oral traditions, black music, and Italian neorealism to produce a cinema that more effectively expresses black experience than was ever possible within classical Hollywood cinema. For Taylor, the work of Charles Burnett, Larry Clark, Haile Gerima, Charles Lane, Ben Caldwell, Warrington Hudlin, and others "has managed a transformation of imaginative possibilities comparable in scope, diversity, and creative verse" to that of the Harlem Renaissance of the 1920s.

 Black audiences can engage with mainstream, white, Hollywood cinema, but that engagement comes at a tremendous cost. In identifying with white characters or with black stereotypes, blacks are disempowered. bell hooks describes what happens to black female spectators as a form of "gaslighting." They are forced to become complicit in their own repression, to deny who they are. Traditionally, blacks have been punished for "looking back" at whites. hooks proposes a form of looking back at the cinema—a look that she refers to as "the oppositional gaze"—which disables the cinema's power by questioning and interrogating it. This oppositional gaze, in turn, can empower not only the black male spectator, who like white males already enjoys possession of the gaze, but also the black female spectator, who is traditionally denied the power of the gaze. Active and critical in her looking, the black female spectator refuses identification with on-screen women, whether black and white. In watching, she resists what she sees; through this resistance, she constructs herself as an active subject. She does not just look; she *looks back.*

 The collection of essays in this anthology is designed not only to look at the phenomenon of American cinema but also to "look back" at it. The book's goal is to provoke thought, to ask questions, and to provide a variety of different perspectives from which various portraits of mainstream American commercial cinema can be constructed and reconstructed. As hooks suggests, empowerment within mass society begins with active and critical engagement with mass culture. If mass culture produces movies that produce us, we, in turn, also produce the mass culture that produces us. Our sense of agency depends on our ability to understand the role that we, as active consumers and engaged audiences, have played (and can play) in the construction of an American identity. The essays in this book attempt to describe the relationship between the movies and mass culture and, by doing this, to give readers a sense of their own place within the operations of this mass medium. This is the first step in the creation of a truly populist and progressive cinema.

NOTES

1. Andre Bazin, "La Politique des Auteurs," in Peter Graham, ed., *The New Wave* (New York: Doubleday, 1968), p. 142.

2. On the way the practice of science remains vulnerable to ideology, see Sandra Harding, *The Science Question in Feminism* (Ithaca, N.Y.: Cornell University Press, 1986); Evelyn Keller, *Reflections on Gender and Science* (New Haven, Conn.: Yale University Press, 1985); Bruno Latour and Steve Woolgar, *Laboratory Life* (Princeton, N.J.: Princeton University Press, 1986 [1979]); or Helen E. Longino, *Science as Social Knowledge* (Princeton, N.J.: Princeton University Press, 1990).

3. Ian Jarvie, *Hollywood's Overseas Campaign: The North Atlantic Movie Trade, 1920–1950* (New York: Cambridge University Press, 1992).

4. David Bordwell dates the dominance of "the classical model" (or the classical Hollywood style) to 1917, by which point it had evolved into an efficient, relatively seamless, coherent, and systematic mode of narration. See David Bordwell, Janet Staiger, and Kristin Thompson, *The Classical Hollywood Cinema: Film Style and Mode of Production to 1960* (New York: Columbia University Press, 1985).

5. Non-Hollywood, non-narrative films (experimental or avant-garde films, documentaries, amateur films, etc.), and certain independently made narrative films (race films, gay and lesbian films, ethnic and minority films, etc.) resist dominant ideologies, drawing on countercurrents within the mainstream. Thus, as David James has argued, certain independent productions of the late 1950s, such as *Shadows* and *Pull My Daisy*, draw on the culture of the Beat Generation rather than on the dominant culture of America in the 1950s. See his *Allegories of Cinema: American Film in the Sixties* (Princeton, N.J.: Princeton University Press, 1989).

6. George McKenna, "Populism: The American Ideology," in George McKenna, ed., *American Populism* (New York: G. P. Putnam's Sons, 1974), pp. xi–ii.

7. Jeffrey Richards, "The Ideology of Populism," in *Visions of Yesterday* (London: Routledge & Kegan Paul, 1973), p. 231.

8. Richards, "Ideology of Populism," p. 223.

9. Richard Hofstadter, *The Age of Reform* (New York: Vintage, 1960), p. 62.

10. McKenna, "Populism," p. xvii.

11. Richards, "Ideology of Populism," p. 231.

12. Sheldon Hackney, "Introduction," in Sheldon Hackney, ed., *Populism: The Critical Issues* (Boston: Little, Brown, 1971), p. xxi.

13. Hofstadter, *Age of Reform*, p. 70.

14. Hackney, "Introduction," vii–iii.

15. McKenna, "Populism," pp. xvii–iii, xxi, xxii.

16. Jeffrey Richards refers to Christ as "the ultimate prototype" of the populist hero. Richards, "Ideology of Populism," pp. 234–5.

17. See Thomas Cripps, "The Year of *The Birth of a Nation*," in *Slow Fade to Black: The Negro in American Film, 1900–1942* (New York: Oxford University Press, 1977), pp. 41–69.

18. Bryan as quoted in Tom Gunning, *D. W. Griffith and the Origins of American Narrative Film* (Urbana: University of Illinois Press, 1991), p. 241.

19. Griffith was intrigued by progressivist thought and, as Gunning has noted, once preferred to describe himself as a "journalist" rather than a "director." Gunning, *D. W. Griffith*, p. 50. For Griffith, film was an agent of reform.

20. Hofstadter, *Age of Reform*, pp. 193–4.

21. Ibid., p. 186.

22. Ibid., p. 202.

23. Ibid., p. 218.

24. Richards, "Ideology of Populism," p. 229.

25. Hofstadter, *Age of Reform*, pp. 5–6.

26. Gunning, *D. W. Griffith*, pp. 151–5.

27. Richard Schickel, *D. W. Griffith: An American Life* (New York: Simon & Schuster/Touchstone, 1985) 283.

28. Schickel, *D. W. Griffith*, pp. 283–93.

29. McKenna, "Populism," p. xiii.

30. Richards, "Ideology of Populism," pp. 234–5.

31. Ibid.

32. The *Cahiers du cinema* essay on *Young Mr. Lincoln* refers to the "moralizing discourse" of Ford's Lincoln. However, this sort of discourse is not unique to Ford—or to Lincoln but emerges as a feature of certain kinds of populist heroes in American cinema. See Editors of *Cahiers du cinema*, "John Ford's *Young Mr. Lincoln*," in Philip Rosen, ed., *Narrative, Apparatus, Ideology* (New York: Columbia University Press, 1986), pp. 456–7.

33. David Bordwell, "Classical Hollywood Cinema: Narrational Principles and Procedures," in Philip Rosen, ed., *Narrative, Apparatus, Ideology* (New York: Columbia University Press, 1986), p. 18.

34. Ann Douglas, *The Feminization of American Culture* (New York: Avon Books, 1977).

35. Robin Wood, "The Incoherent Text: Narrative in the 70s," in *Hollywood from Vietnam to Reagan* (New York: Columbia University Press, 1986), pp. 49–50.

Mass Culture,
the Individual,
and the Mass

Apocalyptic Cinema: D. W. Griffith and the Aesthetics of Reform

> *Do you know that we are playing to the world? What*
> *we film tomorrow will strike the hearts of the world.*
> *And they will know what we are saying. We've gone*
> *beyond Babel, beyond words. We've found a universal*
> *language—a power that can make men brothers and*
> *end wars forever. Remember that, remember that*
> *when you go before the camera.*
> David Wark Griffith, 1914[1]

Six years after McClellan closed the movies, the film industry achieved something that would have been impossible earlier: the approval of the most powerful vice crusader in the city, the Reverend Charles Parkhurst. As the head of the Madison Avenue Presbyterian Church, Parkhurst had sermonized against the decline of a Calvinist tradition. Modern forms of work, he argued, no longer built character. As a result of routinized labor and increased luxury, the masculine conscience, which should work like a "clock," was broken. Even worse, his female peers had become "freaks" by indulging in urban amusements. Initially, Parkhurst's politics had been devoted to defeating Tammany Democrats who allowed unregulated entertainments to exist. In fact, he was McClellan's right-hand man in closing the nickelodeons on Christmas day, 1908. Yet now he was part of the National Board of Review and reflected with satisfaction that all his crusading had reaped rewards. Movies offered an audience of respect-

From *Screening Out the Past: The Birth of Mass Culture and the Motion Picture Industry* by Lary May. Copyright © 1980 by Lary May. Reprinted by permission of Oxford University Press, Inc.

able people healthy recreation. More important, they served as a guide to solving contemporary social problems. Turning movie reviewer, the Reverend Charles Parkhurst even began praising the work of David Wark Griffith, the most popular filmmaker of the day. Indeed, Parkhurst saw that "a boy can learn more pure history and get more atmosphere of the period by sitting down three hours before the films which Mr. Griffith has produced with such artistic skill than by weeks and months of study in the classroom."[2]

Praise for David Wark Griffith has not been uncommon, in his day or ours. Generations of film critics have applauded the countless innovations he pioneered between 1908 and 1915. Yet few have realized that his mastery of the new art was only one reason for his enormous success. His aesthetics were used to dramatize the social and cultural tensions of the era, giving them an explicitly Protestant tone. Reporters referred to him as the "messianic savior of the movie art, a prophet who made shadow sermons more powerful than the pulpit." While creating a style that evoked such metaphors, his films dramatized every major concern of the day: labor-management conflict, white slavery, eugenics, prohibition, women's emancipation, and civic corruption. In all his cinematic dramas, he affirmed a cultural tradition that placed familial values at the heart of political life. Griffith's aims were no mystery. As he wrote,

> Are we not making the world safe for democracy, American democracy, through motion pictures? The increase of knowledge, the shattering of old superstitions, the sense of beauty have all gone forward with the progress of the screen. Our heroes are always democratic. The ordinary virtues of American life triumph. No Toryism. No Socialism.[3]

So closely was this philosophy in tune with national issues that he maintained a lively correspondence with Woodrow Wilson, William Jennings Bryan, and Josephus Daniels, all of whom considered themselves his "great admirers." In testimony to his achievements, his films twice received special showings at the White House.

The merging of politics, vice crusading, and films represented in Griffith's career offers a chance to probe one of the great historical dilemmas of the era. Over the past two decades, scholars have described the Progressive movement as so divided that its central purpose appears unclear. Some claim that the reformers came from many of the same groups that dominated the vice crusading efforts and the censorship boards: the businessmen, professionals, and managers who composed the Republican party and wanted to order rather than destroy the corporate system. Others point to those who composed the early motion picture audience and producers: small propertied men and upwardly mobile workers, usually Democrats, who wanted to resist the new economy in the name of open opportunity. Although historians have correctly observed that the material interests of these two groups were often at odds, the way in which they interacted in the early motion picture industry of 1908 to 1914 suggests that they could unite in a common cultural crusade. At a time when the corporate order seemed to be trapping the individualistic spirit and altering traditional sex roles, this sense of crisis reached far down the social order, binding together people of diverse interests. By looking at D. W. Griffith's work against this backdrop, we might be able to answer a number of questions: How could this reformist crusade take on aesthetic dimensions? Could the rescue of Victorianism unite all groups? Could the quest for moral order take precedence over the need for economic transformation?

Griffith's art does suggest that the movies were beginning to portray the concerns of anxious Victorians. Yet this did not occur in a vacuum. In fact, few would have believed in 1908 that films could project the ideals of vice crusaders and still remain popular. None of the early filmmakers welcomed controls over their creations. Although the major companies were headed by producers who shared a common American Protestant tradition with the reformers, they feared that the antiamusement forces would destroy their businesses. Initially, these filmmakers were not interested in moral crusading. They came from careers in optics, iron making, or electronics, hoping to make money on movies. By making their own improvements on the camera, they skirted Edison's patent rights. They then exploited the immigrant markets as a realm of vice—and were careful to keep their questionable product away from their own families. This proved to be quite lucrative. One early filmmaker acquired a box at the Metropolitan Opera House; another bought an estate on Long Island next to Theodore Roosevelt's. When Edison tried to sue these men for violation of his patent, they militantly resisted, and battled his lawyers from 1900 to 1907. By this time they were in no mood for elite reformers moving in and closing down their prosperous establishments.[4]

Yet one side of vice crusading might work in their interests: the effort to utilize film as a positive social force. After gaining judicial support for reopening the theaters McClellan had closed, these early producers joined with Charles Sprague Smith in creating the National Board of Review. Cooperation promised to provide reasonable guidelines that would define an acceptable film. Not only would this serve their business interests, but it would also protect their own wives and daughters who enjoyed the movies as much as anyone else. As filmmaker George Kline expressed it, films made for "continentals and their colonies" were not suitable for his own Protestant family.[5] Yet now that his daughter went to the movies, he too wanted better films. Furthermore, the early producers saw that censorship might help them monopolize the market. In 1908, they joined with their former foe, Thomas Edison, and formed a patent trust. By consolidating their companies, they hoped to limit the entry of others into the market. Jeremiah Kennedy, head of this trust, noted that with the vice crusades, this "whole mess might turn out working for us." If they could control the censorship board, it would be difficult for competitors to gain the seal of approval that would guarantee a wide distribution. Accordingly, these eight companies paid the entire operating costs of the National Board of Review. At $3.25 a reel, this came to $38,000 a year.[6]

Yet these plans proved naive. Because markets were expanding rapidly, a number of "independents" entered the field with ease. In 1908, the eight patent members were the only ones releasing films; but by 1914 more than forty new producers were also making movies. Like the original trust members, they too purchased their cameras from abroad and made their own innovations. In response, the patent trust itself tried to stamp out these new producers through legal action and economic pressure. Yet the "trust" was not an integrated corporation like those emerging in steel, railroads, or retail chains. As producers only, they had virtually no control over supply, for the players could work for anyone. Most important, films were still sold on an open market to thousands of independent theater owners all over the country. Consequently, as corporations spread in other industries, filmmaking remained an economic "frontier." As *Munsey's* magazine noted,

> With the possible exception of the automobile, no other product of human invention has advanced with such amazing swiftness from a toy to a necessity. . . . It has created a whole new line of millionaires. It has given American enterprise a fresh distinction, and has added a picturesque array to the ever-fascinating drama of the self-made.[7]

The independents were also aware of the potential for tapping markets beyond the immigrant neighborhoods. They saw that censorship would legitimize their product for a national market, bringing the lower and lower-middle classes into the audience. Previously, local censors had banned films, or movies had met resistance in the cities' better neighborhoods. But with the seal of approval and licensed theaters, motion pictures became acceptable to the people who would have shunned them earlier. After 1908, theaters began to spread into the affluent neighborhoods of Boston, New York, Chicago, and Philadelphia. This rapid proliferation was definitely aimed upward, for few new movie houses opened in the poor sections of these cities.[8]

As movies began to move up the class order, producers had to create a product acceptable for an "American audience." In helping to develop appropriate themes, critics in the new trade journals offered abundant advice. They made a direct assault on the importation of hundreds of foreign films that were flooding the market. As one wrote, "We heartily fear that the increased importation of foreign films is luring the director away from the path of cinematic righteousness. . . . Many European features depict sexual problems with a candor and a crudeness intolerable outside a clinic or psychiatric hospital." They also despised the short films made by the domestic producers for the immigrant audience. After viewing forty films released in June 1908, one critic asked, "What is an American subject?" Of the twenty that were made domestically, only ten seemed to be acceptable entertainment. The rest "might have been made in Europe." "After ten years of plugging away, the American subject does not seem to have secured a predominant part in the films of the United States." When producers protested that this was the only way to make money, another critic replied,

> The man, whether he be playwright or producer, who says that our people want to see pictures with vitiating things is ignorant of what is going on around him. The whole country is aroused on the question of race betterment. . . . We do not desire to stimulate what is low in our children, but to train them to exercise self-control, to let their minds dominate their animal natures. We hope to make them better than we are. Moving pictures are now a factor in that evolution.[9]

Ultimately, all the hopes for a higher-quality film came to focus on a longer and more elaborate product, the "photoplay." Unlike the earlier one-reel "shorts," which merely titillated the senses, the photoplay carried a moral lesson. In this, critics saw that film might become an adjunct to libraries, schools, and museums. They argued that a wealthier clientele could be attracted and higher prices charged, provided these feature films told a complete story, with a beginning, middle, and end. All dramas should portray cause and effect, which showed the ethical order lying at the core of the universe. Subject matter should be drawn from "high" art: formal literature and history rather than cheap melodrama or vaudeville. After all, wrote one critic along these lines, the word "*classic* has some meaning because it appeals to the best people in the most enlightened times. The merits of a classic are known to few men. It is the business of the motion picture to make them known to all." Happy endings would show heroes defeating "grafting politicians and other birds of prey" and applaud the "nobility of splendid efforts." Tragic endings were acceptable as long as they portrayed the "disease of bad habits that would befall the dependent and resourceless manhunters of civilized society, the women who rely on sex attraction rather than sex qualification."[10]

As these photoplays began to gain popularity, the industry seemed to be taking on a new face. Foreign films and ribald shorts remained, but the demand for refined entertainment brought more long features into the market. Compared with 1908 when more than half the films came from abroad, by 1913 the efforts of the National Board and the American producers brought the percentage of imports down to 10 percent.[11] Over the same period of time, features that had not existed in the earlier years came to comprise almost half the films produced, with most being made by the independents.[12] Exemplifying the new trend was Harry Aitken's Triangle Company. Aitken, a Midwestern Protestant, advertised himself as a Jacksonian man who managed his own firm and was one of the first to secure the financial backing of Wall Street investors.[13] Following his strict Victorian values, one edition of his trade journal in 1915 called the motion pictures the "world's pulpit." A cartoon portrayed Uncle Sam pointing to a movie theater and saying to "Miss Liberty," "Now, there is a safe and sane amusement."

Expansion, moreover, served to validate reformist hopes. More engrossing photoplays, their Americanization, and national censorship combined to create the beginnings of a truly mass amusement. It will be recalled that before 1908 a movie house could not seat more than 300 people and attracted primarily the lower orders. Yet 4 years after the vice crusades, the Russell Sage Foundation sponsored a study by the People's Institute of New York City's 400 movie houses and found that large, sumptuous theaters seating more than 1,000 had penetrated the lower-middle-class neighborhoods. Laborers still comprised 70 percent of the 1912 audience; but 20 percent were now clerical workers and 5 percent were respectable bourgeois men and women. Without losing the original audience of immigrants, then, the Protestant filmmakers and censors of comfortable Republican backgrounds had created a medium that cut across class, sex, and party lines. In evaluating the type of entertainment appearing at the city's burlesque, cheap melodrama, and expensive Broadway plays, the investigators also concluded that the movies were far and away "the most positive form of entertainment in the entire city."[14]

At the same time, the most innovative filmmakers made the medium the handmaiden of Progressivism. The career of the era's greatest director, David Wark Griffith, illustrates the triumphs as well as the ultimate limitations of this reform spirit. Griffith had come to the industry at precisely that moment in 1908 when the movies were on the verge of being reformed. Working for Biograph company, he began filming classics such as Browning's *Pippa Passes*. Critics pointed to him as a model in the vanguard of filmmaking, and he sparked the *New York Times* to comment, "Since the public has expressed its will through the People's Institute, the public has received a reformed motion picture play." From this auspicious beginning, Griffith made more than 300 films for Biograph. Despite the fact that this company was dedicated to uplifting movies, Griffith soon broke from this trust member to join the independent firm of Harry Aitkin. There Griffith gained control over his product; Aitkin merely handled distribution. Griffith's two masterpieces, *The Birth of a Nation* and *Intolerance*, resulted from this collaboration. Exploring the film art as it had never been utilized before and breaking into the widest markets yet, *The Birth of a Nation* (1915) became the most widely acclaimed and financially successful film of the entire silent era. This film alone grossed more than $13 million, more than any other film before 1934. At the height of Griffith's career, he inspired one critic to write,

> The motion picture is a tremendous uplifting force whose power is not yet measured. Shall we be challenged when we assert that it is the language of democracy which reaches all strata of the population and welds them together? Can it not be made to bring all degrees of people into a coordinated organism, working in harmony for the greater things of the world?[15]

David Wark Griffith could make such an impact not because he was coldly calculating the viewers' tastes but because he saw himself as "above politics" and portraying feelings "bred in the bone." In that statement lies the marrow, for like millions of Americans drawn into the teaming industrial cities at the turn of the century, his roots were deep in small-town rural life. Born in La Grange, Kentucky, he grew up hearing the tales of his father's Civil War exploits as a Confederate soldier. The elder Griffith was appropriately named after the Biblical Jacob and had moved west from meager origins in Virginia. Embodying the tradition of the self-made man, Jacob acquired a small slave plantation in La Grange, a racially divided community. Soon he served in the state legislature as a Jacksonian partisan. But when the Civil War came to this border state, he resigned to fight as a cavalry captain for the Confederacy. After the defeat in 1865, he returned to rebuild the plantation, which "told the world you meant something," and help his fellow whites restore home rule to Dixie. Returning to the legislature as a Democrat, he spent the rest of his days as a struggling farmer, preaching the values of individualism.[16]

In passing on this code to his sons, Jacob enforced strict self-denial. David remembered that Jacob "fought the Indians and anyone who came around" and left a profound impression as to the uses of aggression. One memory that continually reappears in his memoirs was of his "first friend," a yellow dog who "pursued the ladies." But for that indiscretion the friend died at his father's hands. "I didn't like to see it," he wrote, "but I couldn't get out of the report of the gun." A similar precept "ingrained on my memory" was when his brother "wanted to look good for the girls of Louisville" and had an ex-slave cut his hair in the latest style. Jacob saw the result and quickly strapped on his sword, pulled it from the scabbard, and chased the "old uncle around the estate," claiming that the Negro had "ruined my boy." While David recalled that the "nigger liked it," he also learned that the life of a dandy or ladies' man was forbidden. By contrast, his father was a model self-made man. To the young Griffith, Jacob's sword was the "law," for it represented "reason, man's sacrifice for an ideal, for love, a whole world that enters the chaos, reduces it, organizes it." As testimony to his respect for this unifying yet awesome code, he later wrote that "the only person I ever really loved was my father."[17]

Evangelical religion, an influence mainly of Griffith's mother, infused his father's code with significance. In La Grange, all the Griffiths lie buried at the base of a white Methodist church, Mount Tabor, where David went to Sunday school, helped support the minister, and attended with his mother. Mrs. Griffith was the former Mary Oglesby, daughter of a well-to-do Kentucky farmer and, in her son's words, "very religious." The Methodist sect itself had been brought to America as part of the great revivals that spread over the South in the eighteenth and nineteenth centuries. Inspired by a powerful sermon style, Methodist rhetoric appealed to all classes, but in particular to the yeomen farmers, artisans, and small property owners of the rural towns. Never noted for its

originality of thought, or rebellion from authority, the church emphasized a life of self-denial and sinlessness, which would transform not only
the believer, but the entire world as well. In keeping with its doctrines,
Mrs. Griffith warned against the dangers of drink and dissipation. After
one such exhortation, David went for a walk in the forest and saw Christ
appearing in the trees, repeating his mother's admonitions.

Above all, this religious spirit came to rest on women and the
family, which represented the highest values of civilization. In the South
after 1850, the need to create harmony among all whites against inva-
sions from the North and from black rebellion demanded unity around
a common symbol. As yeomen farmers, the Griffiths saw themselves tied
to the upper orders through a reverence for pure womanhood. Among the
elite, recalled David, "even a wink or a bashful nod towards a young lady
would get one a good piece of hot lead or a kick in the pants." The young
Griffith made sure his "conscience was on guard." He recalled a spelling
bee at school that he lost to his girlfriend. Looking at her when called on
to spell the word *desire,* he faltered. Another time, he tried to kiss a young
lady, but her father turned a hose on "me, a poor country jake." In the
broader community, this code ensured that "the line between nice girls
and the other kind was drawn as strictly as possible." Yet the men had
passions that needed some form of outlet. Thus extra- or premarital sex
was tacitly sanctioned, as long as it was removed from their own women.
In river boats or shanty towns, men could find prostitutes and thereby
unleash their lusts far from Victorian homes. As Griffith recalled, "Men
were expected to remain true to their wives only after a fashion. They
claimed their wives considered it beneath them to be jealous of that sort
of thing. If they had an affair with a woman of their own class, there was
the devil to pay, but the other sort of thing was just a part of life. I know
only what the men claimed, how the women felt, I am unable to say."[18]

The coordinates of Griffith's culture, however, began to crumble
at the turn of the century. The first visible wave of disruption came from
the economy. When David was still a young man, creditors confiscated
the ancestral estate after his father's death. Moving to Louisville, Griffith
quit school and secured a job as a clerk and factory laborer. By 1896 he
was thoroughly bored with this work; despite his mother's warning he
followed the "siren" call and joined a traveling theatrical company. But
in the depression of the 1890s, when the nation faced agrarian and labor
unrest, he found himself jobless in California and became a farm laborer
for large growers. Griffith, then, had knocked around in the Jacksonian
style; he was a worker before he was a filmmaker. Yet these experiences

also left him embittered against the new order. He gloried in a past when self-sufficiency was the rule. Later he would write against the tyranny of monopolists who bred labor unrest by thwarting mobility. Things were different in the old days, Griffith argued, when "Bolshevism had small chance of gaining a foothold in America because the worker knew the rich had begun at the bottom and worked their way up. He knew that the rich had begun as he had. As long as the Rockefellers, Schwabs, and Vanderbilts had begun at the bottom, the laboring man could believe he had some chance."[19]

The second source of disruption came from changing sexual roles. They, too, originated in the modern economy and threatened the striving will. Griffith felt this acutely in his own life. Leaving California, he went to New York City where women not only worked but exhibited new sexual behavior. Among the rich along Fifth Avenue in particular, "alluring femininity" could be found "swishing up and down the streets in their carefully gotten-up rigs." Even more alarming, decent girls were in the "hot spots," because there were "no respectable clubs or places of that kind where the two sexes can meet." In Kentucky, "women who smoked and drank and went to bars were not nice girls and that's that." But in the fast northern cities, "new women" might weaken the will of Victorian men. This invasion of sensuality into the urban scene was not lost on Griffith, who wrote,

> New York never seemed like a melting pot to me, it seemed like a boiling pot . . . the flesh of these women was of every color known. They chanted in many languages after the style of the sirens against which Ulysses tied himself to the mast. That was one man who had the right idea. I regretted that I didn't rope myself in on a few occasions. These women chanted in many accents, but they only sang for money. I learned early in life that for all the scheming, busy humanity, money was the king, the devil king.[20]

When Griffith failed to make it in theater, his downward spiral continued. Out of desperation, he sought an acting job in the still unrespectable movies. When he began directing films, he was so ashamed of his work that he did not put his full name on the screen. He also masked his marriage to a motion picture actress, Linda Arvidson, because his mother would have disapproved. Griffith tried to minimize his shame by hiding the fact that he had a working wife. Not even his crew knew. When he was finally able to redeem his self-respect by supporting his spouse, he asked her to stop "working in the street." But Linda Arvidson sought a career for more than money, and when she refused, they separated. The pair remained legally married for the next twenty years, perhaps because divorce was even more unthinkable.[21]

The vice crusades, however, served to turn Griffith's inner turmoil toward regenerating the values of his youth. "Reform was sweeping the country," he recalled of these years, "newspapers were laying down a barrage against gambling, rum and light ladies, particularly light ladies. There were complaints against everything, so I decided to reform the motion picture industry." Although he exaggerated his own role in history, he did see the reformation of amusements as a means not only for the growth of the film audience but for his own improvement. He now put an American Eagle over every caption, placed his full name on the screen, and grounded his new trade firmly on the foundation of his family tradition. Because the movie industry was a marginal realm of the economy, with no unions, corporations, or limitations on production, Griffith saw it as a place where he could revive the frontier spirit of his father. When in 1913 Biograph would not let him make bigger photoplays, he left the "bosses." As an independent, with "no one interfering with my daily commitments," Griffith regarded himself as a typical American working "incessantly" and having "little time for sex."[22]

Throughout these early years, Griffith saw himself infusing Anglo-Saxon culture with a new passion as well. To accomplish this task, his work operated on two very important levels. First, he filmed within an established tradition of Western art. Griffith did not share the concerns of a European or American avant-garde in drama or painting. Rather than rebelling against the values, perceptions, and roles of the bourgeoisie, Griffith saw it as his duty to reinvigorate middle-class mores by spreading the message of high culture to the masses. In order to show how beauty was the hand-maiden of truth, he drew themes from the drama and literature of Anglo-Saxon culture, and the formal subject matter of nineteenth-century novels. Each was clearly presented, with balanced composition that would be understandable to all, so that the audience would learn how the world operated. To heighten the realism, Griffith would draw on the research of scholars, archaeologists, and academic painters for precision and accuracy. Behind this democratizing drive was an effort to depict the truth about the world, and the morals that operated within it.

Yet at the same time these forms gained a new dynamism. In fact, it was Griffith's immersion in the practical, empirical side of life that led to his break from formal ways of viewing the world. Previous directors in Europe and the United States had heightened film drama through a variety of means: close-ups, which showed details of the face with a new intimacy; parallel editing, which moved the scene back and forth across time and space at will and broke from stage traditions; artificial lighting and a mobile camera that were used to help dramatize the story. And moviemaking had taken place in natural surroundings such as city streets, wilderness, and real workplaces. Griffith developed none of these techniques. Each had been utilized before him. Yet he was the first to bring them together in a consistent approach to film, one that made the action on the screen move in entirely new ways. Fortunately, he articulated his motives behind these forms. Ironically, they flowed not from a vision of the future but from a desire to give emotion to the folk culture of American Victorianism. Film was to be a great revival instrument for a threatened culture, inspiring viewers with a new instinctual strength.

Crucial to this endeavor was the film medium itself. Griffith believed that an image projected on a screen could become a tool for completing the great goal of history; lifting mankind from animality. The camera was a God-given means for communicating. Regardless of language, background, or class, everyone could comprehend the universal language of silent pictures. Film not only transcended ethnic or language divisions but also was superior to books, paintings, or the stage. A viewer watching a motion picture saw a production that had been perfected, duplicated, and sent out to the country. When the patrons entered a darkened theater, they saw a standardized creation. They did not look at a unique performance, for it had been completed in advance. Nor did the spectator choose what to look at on the screen. That had been decided by the director. Audiences then could relax much of their active rational minds and let the images penetrate deep into their subconscious. Mesmerized in the darkness and absorbed into the crowd, viewers shed the concerns of social life, and even relinquished their individuality, giving themselves up to the magnified, larger-than-life images that raced across the screen.

At the same time, film transported the viewer to a more spiritual realm of existence, a sphere of the sublime. This was possible, according to Griffith, because the crowd watching a film did not receive its message in traditional ways. Screen images were not transmitted through the ears, like music, or the hands. Instead the medium communicated through the eyes, which he considered nonsensory organs, removed from material reality and closer to the purity of ideas. In other words, the human being was seen as divided into mind and body. Other organs were part of the body, but the eyes were closer to the soul. Silent film worked solely through vision, and like the "hand of God," Griffith saw it lifting people from their "commonplace existence" into a sphere of "poetic simulations." Such a power allowed the director to work like those revivalist preachers he must have heard as a child. Using images of sin and salvation, he might provide an experience that could convert the soul from evil to good. In fact, Griffith saw himself as a secular preacher, spreading the Word far beyond that Methodist church in La Grange. As his favorite actress recalled,

> Griffith told us that we were something new in the world, a great power that had been predicted in the Bible as the universal language. And it was going to end wars and bring about the millennium. Films were going to bring understanding among men—and bring peace to the world. Well those are strong words to teach young people. Therefore we weren't important. It was only the films and sense of family in Mr. Griffith's company.[23]

Idealistic as this vision was, it represented an acute sense of cinematic realism. More than any previous filmmaker, Griffith used the potential of the camera to photograph real people in real settings, avoiding artificial sets. The camera, he argued, was a "cold blooded, truth telling, grim device that registers every gesture . . . every glimmer of emotion." A director should show ordinary people, so that the spirit would be seen as emanating from the democracy. Griffith never used the camera to alter the clarity, balance, and perspective of the world. But he did use realism in the same way as one of his favorite authors, Charles Dickens, to show the way the world ran and inspire the viewers to change it. Through the action of heroes and heroines, the audience learned to identify with their goodness and with hope follow their example. Explaining these aspirations, Griffith wrote that the motion picture would "keep boys and girls along the right lines of conduct. No one need fear it will deviate from the Puritan plane."[24]

Above all, the main players represented the true dynamics of history and progress. In a democratic society, high ideals were found not only in the realm of nobles or the wealthy but also in the daily lives of everyone. Griffith learned early that the movement of the camera could heighten this message. For one thing, the director could discard artificial sets and film characters in favor of real surroundings, capturing spontaneity. Without contrived poses and backdrops, filmmaking reflected natural life rather than stilted artificiality. In this way, film exposed the viewer to whole realms of experience outside his day-to-day world. Yet to evoke idealism from this extended reality, the director used his tools to manipulate the medium and show God's will surfacing in the chaos of material life. No doubt one of the most noted ways of illustrating this was through the "iris." It is not known whether Griffith invented the technique, but the way he used it was unique. On a darkened screen, a small dot would appear. Slowly it opened and a beam of light revealed the action. As the drama unfolded, it was as if the viewer used a spiritual eye to penetrate the truth of life.

Once the iris opened, special lighting would show a world where the demarcations of good and evil were clear. Often heroes and heroines were bathed in light, while villains appeared dark and sinister in the shadows. The audience would have no doubt as to who was among the elect and who among the damned. Griffith instructed his central characters that they, in turn, must radiate the "light within that puts the characterization across." This was clearly a Protestant concept of redemption, and Griffith was well aware of it. He saw his leading players projecting a "divine fluid," which had given men such as Napoleon and Washington their power to transform the world. Faith in these "images of pure and simple beauty," explained Griffith, "allowed us to believe it was done by God himself." Because these characters were to represent universal ideals, Griffith did not believe in the star system. In his company, actors and actresses must "subsume their personalities in the larger endeavor, and forego billing on the screen," for only in that way would they radiate the spirit of a higher destiny.[25]

Griffith fused this idealism to youth and heightened the innocence of his characters. The universal and nameless "boy" and "girl" in his films were incorruptible in the face of economic or political evil. In this he was also in tune with his times. Before the twentieth century, no particular age group was seen as the unique bearer of progress. Youth appealed to the mass audience as an alternative to the "old world," as Griffith phrased it, and also because it was a stage of life that cut across all groups in the society. His stars came "all the way from cooking spaghetti and washing dishes to find themselves famed around the world." Yet most important, youth could be seen as a force outside evil at a time when organized work and new morals seemed to question the old striving independence. Adolescence offered a hiatus before the burdens of economic responsibility and sexual maturity. Youthful heroes and heroines might mingle in dance halls or new entertainments; but at the same time they stayed true to the parental tradition. In this way, they might represent the best potential of the modern age. As Griffith explained,

> It was all nonsense about youth going away from the old morals. Never since the beginning of time have there been so many girls and boys who were clean, so young, their minds are beautiful, they are sweet. Why? To win the dearest thing in the world, love from mankind. That is the motive that separates our civilization from dirty savages.[26]

The prime vessels containing this youthful ideal were female. Women were saints on earth, a vision of Eden before the fall. Griffith believed that no film could be a success without that "pleasing presentation for which all men yearn." We are not likely to understand the tremendous artistry Griffith poured into this vision if we forget the sources of Griffith's emotional stance toward women. He idealized his family, especially his mother, and this admiration infused his attitude toward the female characters in his photoplays. Although he never found a woman "to duplicate the memories of perfection we all have within us," there was one woman whom mankind might love without thoughts of sensuality. "We all know that the beauty of our mothers is no myth." In seeking to revive that memory on the screen, heroines were less objects of passion than reminders of all the spiritual values embodied in the family. No wonder the player who portrayed this type in numerous Griffith films, Lillian Gish, confessed that her mentor was an essentially lonely man who loved his screen images but feared real women. Consequently, his female players were not the "buxom, voluptuous form popular with the Oriental mind," but the frail, innocent girl who was the "very essence of virginity."[27]

It was not just Griffith's camera but the entire environment of filmmaking that infused his heroines with the proper purity. He started by making his studio a Victorian home writ large. Running it like a "stern father," he never allowed his players long hours or even the "taint of scandal." He dismissed potential female players who did not look "clean" or those who had blemishes on their faces, because these skin defects indicated jealousy, greed, or sexual vice. Heroines were usually chaperoned on the set, forbidden to have men in their dressing rooms, and prevented from actually kissing during love scenes. When a passionate embrace did appear in a Griffith film, he suggested that a caption explain that the girl's mother was present. His favorite actress, the thin and frail Lillian Gish, was perfectly cast for this female ideal. As a girl in the

Midwest, she lived in a convent and hoped to become a nun. When working for Griffith, she and her sister Dorothy remained constantly supervised by their mother. She recalled that her director had a "mania" for cleanliness and a body free of germs and lectured to his cast that "women aren't meant for promiscuity. If you're going to be promiscuous, you will end up with some disease."[28]

Griffith used film to make his ideal of saintly womanhood come alive. Whatever taints of the earthly that remained after Griffith's vigorous efforts and exhortations had to be eradicated by the camera itself. First came "exercise, cosmetics, self-denial" and the "right kind of thinking." Then women faced screen tests that magnified the actress's face "twenty times" until he found the look of "perfect health." Through a series of cinematic techniques, this heroine finally became a heavenly vision on the screen. One of the most famous Griffith innovations was "hazy photography," caused by a white sheet beneath the player's feet. A powerful bright light from above would illuminate the body. "We must erase imperfections," he recalled, "and it was in doing this that I invented the hazy photography . . . the camera is a great beauty doctor." With all human imperfections removed, Griffith would then film a scene over and over until he achieved just the right effect. The resulting close-up became one of his most famous technical triumphs. Griffith explained that the goal was

> a face where the skin radiated a smooth soft outline. So with the eyes. . . . Every other physical characteristic is of insignificance compared with the eyes. If they are the window to your soul, your soul must have a window it could see through. The farther the motion picture art progresses, the more important does this become.[29]

At the heart of Griffith's drama was the struggle of humankind to protect this female ideal. He highlighted this tension through a series of masterful editing techniques. In making more than 300 films, he learned that the way in which strips of celluloid were arranged could determine the emotional rhythms of the audience. By alternating between characters lighted "like archangels or devils," the director would personalize the good and evil at work in the world. Building his story around these contrasts, he might arouse the audience to identify with righteousness. Then the director showed the heroine suddenly threatened by men who embodied greed, lust, or tyranny. The climax of his films was the rescue. Cutting back and forth from evil pursuer to endangered innocence, the director built a crescendo of fear and hope as the hero rushes to save her. In one great finale, virtue and sin would struggle in the "battle of human ethics common to all consciousness." As the hero triumphs, the audience sees the "consummation of all romantic and adventurous dreams." To reach this emotional explosion, Griffith explained,

> the pace must be quickened from beginning to end. That is not however a steady ascent. The action must quicken to a height in a minor climax which should be faster than the first, and retard again and build to the third which should be faster than the second, and on to the final climax where the pace should be the fastest. Through all the big moments of the story, the pace should build like an excited pulse.[30]

Ultimately, Griffith saw the struggle between virtue and vice infusing the major political and moral reforms of the day. He did not see his techniques as serving the designs of a master mover manipulating the minds of the lowly. Rather, he identified deeply with his audience, believing that in expressing his own feelings, he expressed theirs as well. Unlike the Republican reformers who had censored the movies, early viewers were workers and small property owners who generally belonged to the Democratic party so dear to Griffith. The director, too, was only one step removed from the experiences of his patrons. He had been a former worker, and an independent businessman, sharing with the moviegoers a hostility to monopolists who thwarted economic autonomy. Although his films were not explicitly political, they did express a broad cultural outlook which appealed to the "producers" of all classes and backgrounds. As Griffith explained, "No matter how contorted, one way or another, the soul may be, the man is still a man, and with recognizable traits common to all men . . . tramps, artists, iron workers, writers, all of us are alike in our souls."[31]

Transcending any artificial barriers was the ability of all peoples to realize the morals embodied in the Victorian home. Griffith used his aesthetics to carry this faith in his films. They were of two general types: lessons and warnings. Either heroes triumphed or they were destroyed by their failure to live up to the ideal. A typical warning film was *The Avenging Conscience* (1914). It opens on an uncle insisting that his nephew prepare himself for a "great career." Yet the boy likes a girl the uncle calls "common" and finds himself attracted to the amusements of Italian immigrants, who are portrayed as having less restrained sexual habits. The patriarch forbids such behavior. In his rage, the boy contemplates murder. Despite an apparition of Christ warning of damnation, the youth kills his uncle. The act is seen by an Italian who blackmails the boy and turns him over to the police. In prison he goes insane, and his girlfriend commits suicide. Yet the film has a happy ending: it is all only a dream.[32]

Nevertheless, the warning is clear: men cannot deviate from the work ethic or indulge in what are perceived as immigrant vices lest they forsake the goals of progress passed on by the fathers. From this parental code came the deeds of his heroes, who carried out a specific historical mission—that of the Anglo-Saxon peoples. This was demonstrated in a classic lesson film, *Man's Genesis* (1912). Dramatizing the eternal struggles that face the human being, Griffith took his audience to the beginning of time. Amid a desolate landscape, a caveman, "Weak Hands," loves a pure girl, "Lily White." But their spiritual union is endangered by an older, lusty villain, "Brute Force." In response, the youth invents humankind's first tool, a club, with which he conquers the villain. He then marries his sweetheart, and they create a community grounded in familial harmony. The hero is the leader of a classless tribe in which love transcends all selfish interests. But the "producers" must strive continually, for Brute Force returns with a mob armed with stolen clubs. To put down this threat to their women, Weak Hands invents an even better weapon, a bow and arrow. Victory once again restores the peaceful community. In the triumph of reason over animality, success is not achieved for money or pleasure but to elevate society above lust and tyranny.[33]

Following creation, this battle informed the dynamics of world history as well. In his films of the French and American Revolutions, westward expansion, and Biblical epics, Brute Force is incarnated in aristocrats, monopolists, or the unruly mob. The struggle is carried into the present, in films of industrial conflict. *A Corner in Wheat* (1909) shows a grain speculator hoarding wheat to increase the price while workers, farmers, and small shopkeepers starve. *The Song of the Shirt* (1908) shows a poor girl suffering at a sewing machine in a sweatshop, while her boss takes the fruits of her labor to live a decadent life. These films condemned the immoral rich; but others condemned the unruly poor. *The Voice of the Violin* (1909) portrays a rich man forbidding his daughter to marry a poor boy. But when the boy turns to a "revolutionary group imbued with the false principles of Karl Marx, the promoter of the communist principles of socialism which in time and under the control of intemperate minds becomes absolute anarchy," he learns that his comrades want to rape his sweetheart and burn her father's factory. In response, he turns against these evil doers and, for his efforts, wins the hand of the girl he loves.[34]

At the same time, the dominant motif for films set in the modern era echoed the beliefs of the vice crusaders: women were in danger and had to be protected. In Griffith's films, heroines moved around the city unchaperoned, working in new tasks as clerks, telephone operators, and laborers. This did not mean they had "fallen." Rather, as heroes guarded them in the public realm, these men were even more inspired to conquer the forces of vice. A film such as *Home Sweet Home* (1914) shows a hero drinking and going to dance halls. When he falls to Hell, his sweetheart becomes an angel with wings, flies into Hades to rescue him, and carries him up to Heaven. On earth, such heroines would not be tempted by saloons, foreigners, or men who offer them empires. Rather than submit, women are willing to die. In several climactic Griffith scenes, heroes, believing that villains are about to overtake them, hold guns to the heads of their pure women—final efforts to protect them from a fate literally worse than death. Final shots of rescue are filled with religious images, such as Christ hovering above the characters.[35]

By 1913, Griffith's art and popularity signaled that the hopes of reformers were at high tide. Instead of movies and mass culture eroding Victorianism, the most advanced filmmaker of the day had reoriented the industry toward social reform. His films depicted historical events and current life, exposing viewers to an expanded realm of experience. At the same time, Anglo-Saxon culture was portrayed as eternal truth. With its values spreading to a growing audience, motion pictures could inspire the population to unite in a crusade against evil. Women might occupy new positions outside the home without losing their virtue; challenges of modern life would spur them on to uphold motherhood and virginity, and inspire men to protect women and liberate themselves from lusty monopolists, vice lords, and corrupt politicians. Griffith gave this historical dynamic power and passion through innovative techniques and made it seem as though all parties and groups could unite to transform modern society, without a great social upheaval. It appeared that reformers of all persuasions could still come together around this battle for a classless and blessed order.

Ironically, the first crack in this consensus came as the result of Griffith's greatest success, the making of his masterpiece and the most popular film of the era, *The Birth of a Nation* (1915). This epic film began when Griffith left Biograph, and Aitken brought him *The Clansman* (1905), a novel that had been made into a hit Broadway play in 1908. The story was written by Thomas Dixon, a former Democratic politician who became a Baptist minister and then quit the clergy for the "wider pulpit" of popular art. *The Clansman*, however, was hardly an original conception. It merely put into story form the Democratic party ideology of the Civil War era. The plot condemns the Radical Republicans, who during Reconstruction imposed a corrupt regime on Dixie. Using the freed slaves' voting power, they disenfranchised the white citizens and unleashed a reign of terror.[36] Although none of these events actually took place, they did express Southerners' fears of what would happen when the corrupt industrial North aligned with Southern blacks.[37] In fact, Griffith's own family included politicians who believed this and doubtless used the same rhetoric to mobilize the South against Northern tyranny in the 1870s. As Griffith meticulously recreated the atmosphere of the Civil War years, he wrote,

> Stronger and stronger came to me the traditions I had learned as a child, all that my father had told me. That sword I told you about became a flashing vision. Gradually came back to my memory the stories one Thurston Griffith had told me of the Ku Klux Klan and the regional impulse that comes to men from the earth where they had their beings stirred. It had all the decisive emotionalism of the highest patriotic sentiment.[38]

The film began its official run at the Liberty Theater in New York and quickly became an enormous financial and critical success. Every crisis of the film revolved around threats to the family. In the opening scenes, Griffith portrays the ideal domestic life on the Cameron plantation. Shot in a soft haze, these scenes show a perfect laissez-faire world. As harmony envelops parents, children, and slaves, neither the state nor hierarchical religions are needed. The Civil War comes, disrupting this ordered paradise. During Reconstruction, a Northern white Radical, Rep. Austin Stoneman, lives with his mulatto mistress, and she spurs him to unleash his lust for gain on the defeated South. He gives the vote to former slaves, who use their power against the good white people of the South. Stripped of their property and political rights, the whites watch helplessly as rowdy blacks pass intermarriage laws. When this culminates in the attempted rape of the Cameron women, the brothers form the Ku Klux Klan, uniting Southerners of all classes. As they ride to the rescue of their "Aryan birthright," the screen comes alive with Griffith's perfected editing techniques. After the climactic battle, the South is liberated. And even the Northerners recognize the folly of miscegenation.

The Klan "tries" Gus (Walter Long), a "renegade Negro," for the "murder" of Flora in D. W. Griffith's The Birth of a Nation *(1915). Photo courtesy of the Museum of Modern Art.*

Symbolizing the return to unity, the Cameron son marries Stoneman's daughter. Now the familial bonds restore order to the stricken land, and Christ rises in the sky to announce the beginning of the millennium in America.[39]

   The Birth of a Nation touched a sensitive political nerve.[40] In its message, the film called for an alliance of the common folk from the formerly warring sections to overthrow a tyranny based on Northern commercial corruption. This was indeed a relevant theme for the Democratic constituency in 1914. As the film was made, the first Southern Democratic president since the Civil War, Woodrow Wilson, had united the various elements of the party—Northern workers, Southerners, small farmers, and property owners—into a crusade for a "New Freedom." These were the same groups that had mobilized against leaders of Radical Reconstruction in 1876. In contrast to the defeated expresident, Theodore Roosevelt, Wilson promised to break up trusts and restore the open economy.[41] True to this spirit, Griffith filled the film with quotations from Wilson's historical writings. No doubt this was done to give credence to the events on the screen. But it was also done to make history relevant to the present. Here was shown what would happen to whites who let monopolists strip them of their property and corrupt the political process. As they fell from grace, they would become vulnerable to tyranny from above and below.[42] Giving power to this metaphor, Thomas Dixon used his friendship with Woodrow Wilson to have the film shown at the White House. Whether or not the President approved of the film, there was no question in Dixon's mind that it would make Northerners "Democrats for life." As Dixon later recalled,

> I told him I had a great motion picture he should see not merely because his classmate had written the story, but because this picture made clear for the first time that a universal language had been invented. That in fact was a process of reasoning which could overwhelm the will with conviction.[43]

Not everyone shared this acclaim, however. In fact, the film generated such a fierce controversy that it practically crippled the National Board of Review and shattered the consensus of reformers who had hailed movies as a beneficial medium. Although people such as Jane Addams and Frederic Howe shared Griffith's sentiments about the Victorian home, they could not tolerate his racial attitudes. Unlike Griffith, most of his critics were heirs to an abolitionist tradition. Mounting a fierce protest, they joined with the National Association for the Advancement of Colored People and convinced the National Board of Review to cut key racist sections of the film. But this did not solve the problem. Frederic Howe was so disturbed by the movie, even after it was censored, that he resigned as president of the board.[44] And Griffith attacked his critics, arguing that he was not a racist, and pointing out that loyal black servants were portrayed heroically whereas others had been corrupted by Northern Radicals. He also correctly pointed out that none of his previous works had been anti-Negro and that his family had always cared for them as "children." Nevertheless, it was clear that Griffith was heir to the white racist beliefs of the South. Although his black characters did not have a monopoly on evil traits—plenty of whites were lustful as well—Negroes were seen as innately dangerous: despite their potential for noble deeds, they could never really be trusted. Griffith thus forbid any "black blood" among the players who might have to touch white actresses. Those actors were always whites in blackface. Likewise, when the NAACP condemned the film, Griffith attacked them in the press as a "pro-intermarriage" group, bent on repealing miscegenation laws.[45]

In Griffith's mind, however, the racial controversy was less important than the economic issue. A common loyalty to domestic values could not overcome this gulf either. The fact that the Board that censored *The Birth of a Nation* included Republican reformers was not lost on Griffith or his audience. Sitting conspicuously in judgment were those very rulers who were often condemned in his films: puritanical paternalists of New England, and industrialists who threatened to make whites into propertyless, dependent men, no better than blacks. Now the evils of Reconstruction had invaded the North, and Griffith saw himself as a chief victim, for the censors were "malignant pygmies" who had grown into "black Calibans" and denied him his rights of free speech and property. Before the people knew it, claimed Griffith, they would lay their hands on "Miss Liberty" and thwart his creativity even further:

> You could not even portray the drama of the days of '49 to '70 in the golden west. If you tell the story of this period, you must show the atrocities committed by the Indians against the whites. Some public-seeking fanatic would protest that it was an injustice to the Indians and might raise feelings against them. . . . These people revel in objections.[46]

To defeat these forces, Griffith felt he had to inspire the masses once again. Using his most powerful weapon, film, he now poured all the money he had made on *The Birth of a Nation* into making the most elaborate and expensive film of his career. His extravaganza coincided with the 1916 election and espoused the ideology that would presumably help Woodrow Wilson and the Democrats defeat the Republicans. *Intolerance* (1916) was a new creation, "from my own head," as the director phrased it. This "sun play of the ages" would carry quotes from Wilson, Emerson, and Mill, relating them to a "universal theme running through the various eras of the race's history . . . events are to flash through the mind seeking to parallel the life of different ages and today. Through all the eras, time brings forth the same passions, the same joys and anxieties."[47] To show this, Griffith alternated three ancient tales that depicted the Medici who ruled sixteenth-century France, the Priests of Baal in Babylon, and the Pharisees of Jerusalem in the time of Christ as greedy men who tyrannized the innocent. In France the Medicis unleashed terror against the Huguenot families, in Jerusalem the Pharisees crucify Christ, in Babylon the priests destroy Belshazzar's benevolent state. Griffith does not condemn power per se, for Belshazzar is shown as a good ruler. He did not inherit his kingdom, nor did he maintain it through privilege. Gaining the loyalty of the people solely through his military prowess, he abolished religious establishments and protected economic independence. Eventually his own spiritual family life radiated through the polity, creating unity. But the priests conspired with a foreign prince and destroyed the kingdom.

Although Griffith believed in progress, the portion of *Intolerance* set in the modern era showed that the sins of the past had been reborn with the "autocratic industrial lords" and their social-worker allies. In scenes designed to duplicate the environs of the New York "Four Hundred," Griffith shows a wealthy manufacturer and his reformer wife policing the innocent amusements of the workers. At the same time, the industrialist cuts wages and uses the proceeds to hold an elaborate "charity ball." In protest, the laborers go out on strike. Now the screen fills with labor management battles modeled on the great strike at Lawrence, Massachusetts. Yet because the rich have the support of the government, they used the national guard to quell the outburst. With the poor impoverished and their families destroyed, the heroic "boy" and "girl," unbeknownst to each other, head for new opportunity in the city. But they find the opposite of their dreams. With few jobs available, the "boy" goes to work in a vice den for a "musketeer of the slums," clearly a machine politician. Although he is attracted to "loose women" and the fast life, redemption comes when he meets the "girl." As they fall in love and marry, the hero quits his old job and begins to "go straight," in the path of upward mobility.

Yet the good home is still not free from evil authorities. His old boss corrupts the judiciary and sends him to jail for a crime he did not commit. As the villain then tries to seduce the hero's wife, social workers attempt to take away her child. Finally the "girl" secures a confession from the real criminal, and the stage is set for Griffith's greatest climactic scene. In accelerating parallel shots, the "girl" chases after the governor's train with the new evidence. Quickly the director interjects scenes depicting the fall of Babylon, the crucifixion of Christ, and the slaughter of the Huguenots. Over and over again, these patterns force the audience to ask, will innocence be crucified again? Is progress doomed to fail? No, for the "girl" catches the governor, just as the noose is being put around the "boy's" head. With the governor's swift pardon, the audience learns that in modern America, law is on the side of the good citizen. The state has proved effective in saving the home. Although the industrial system remains intact, the hero is free to transcend it through individual effort and social mobility. And as he had done in *The Birth of a Nation*, Griffith again hails the millennium with a vision of Christ rising in the sky.[48]

In this elaborate, multilayered film, we can see the full implications of Griffith's art. The hero and heroine were clearly cast as Irish laborers. Yet their universality was not tied to any class or ethnic group. Never were they connected to the Catholic church or the preindustrial culture protected by the urban machine. Nor does Griffith's assault on the industrialists contain a criticism of capitalism. His heroes do not advocate class conflict, unions, or labor parties. Rather, they are in rebellion against selfishness in high places. Presumably, if a self-made man such as Belshazzar rules, the force of his personality would encourage class harmony and open opportunity. In the modern story, the democratic state serves as this just and benevolent ruler, not by overthrowing the factory owners or "moral paternalists" but by saving the virtuous individual. Free labor was not a myth for Griffith but a living reality. In his commitment to autonomy, during the making of the film he aligned himself with Los Angeles reformers to ban unions from the studios. Symbolic of his entire outlook, when the actor who had played Christ was arrested and deported for sexual misconduct, Griffith struck his name from the credits of *Intolerance*.[49]

The film's reception was a great disappointment, for it was Griffith's first critical and financial failure. This was in part because it was 4 hours long and contained four different stories all mixed together. As one critic remarked, viewing was a "real task and the person who tries to find meaning must feel something like dramatic indigestion after seeing the picture."[50] But it was more than this. The tremendous success of *The Birth of a Nation* brought movies squarely into the middle-class market. It was crucial to draw this affluent audience to recoup the enormous financial investment Griffith had poured into *Intolerance*. These new viewers may have liked the opulence displayed on the screen, the magnificent sets, and the historical themes, but they were not receptive to the antagonism toward the rich that the film portrayed. They did not want to see that the "poor are oppressed, and forced into an environment which ruins their lives, and this merely for the purpose of producing additional funds for the wealthy, which the latter uses to advertise themselves as reformers of the poor, who in actuality they repress." As this Philadelphia critic concluded, the "interest of the community will be served by our friends staying away from the theaters where *Intolerance* is shown." Ironically, Griffith recalled being labeled a "communist" for making the film.[51]

Obviously, Griffith was no communist. In fact, as Heywood Broun of the *New Republic* correctly observed, the film advocated "laissez-faire," the "battle cry of a lost cause."[52] Broun suggested that with the failure of *Intolerance,* Griffith's career may have been doomed. Although that prediction was premature, the events surrounding the making of the film shattered the reformist unity. Never again would Griffith produce a film that advocated the transformation of the industrial system through a mass movement. Nor would the National Board of Review, composed of his former allies, have the same strength to impose its will on mass culture. Several members had resigned in the wake of censoring *The Birth of a Nation.* Now the remaining prominent members of the board realized they had lost power; few would agree to serve on its executive committee. Soon other motion picture producers would find it unnecessary to have films sent to the board for its seal, for now that the movies had been legitimized, that seal was no longer needed. As the weakening of the board was reported in the press, the consensus that had existed in the industry prior to 1914 lay in ruins.

Yet the coming of World War I gave rise to a temporary revival. Under the threat of outside attack, reformers called the nation to unite in a crusade that was seen as the peak rather than the end of progressivism. The state drafted the movies into the war effort, making the industry at last a full-fledged partner in patriotism. This allowed Griffith to make a flurry of patriotic films that kept him in the limelight for a few more years. *Hearts of the World* (1918), for example, was a successful propaganda film for the Allies, which he personally dedicated to Woodrow Wilson. This film earned him an invitation to London's 10 Downing Street to meet Prime Minister Lloyd George. Later, when Russia was in communist hands and strikes erupted all over America, Griffith made *Orphans of the Storm* (1921). Using the French Revolution as a metaphor for the modern danger of Bolshevism, this film portrays Reds as lustful and violent, similar to the Huns and blacks of earlier films. This highly political film was shown at Harding's White House. As Griffith said of its message,

> A similar condition exists in Russia today. It is also a great lesson for our own government. Recently here in the United States we find that a small but aggressive minority seems to be able to get almost any kind of laws passed they desire. It is well for us to keep our eyes open, as it is not impossible that we may lose our democratic form of government, just as the people in France did at the time, and come under the tyranny of small but aggressive parties that could hold all government and run things for themselves, while the rest of the people are asleep.[53]

Afterward, Griffith's worst fears materialized in his own life. But the threat did not come from the political world. Industrialists in the postwar period associated Reds with the labor strikes spreading over the country. As the Wilson administration deported radicals and suppressed labor unrest, motion picture producers broke strikes in their own companies. Griffith supported these measures, but this boost to business expansion also paved the way for consolidation. Gradually, eight large firms began to absorb the smaller companies. Griffith tried to resist by establishing his own studio in Long Island and financing his own films. But by the mid-1920s, he too was forced to sell out and come to Los Angeles, a city he hated for its "dissipating" atmosphere. Part of that dislike was due to the fact that Griffith had finally joined what he always fought against, a large firm in which access to the top was closed and employees had to punch a time clock. No longer was the great director autonomous, an artist who supervised his labor force, hired and fired players, and wrote many of his own films. His loyal cameraman Billy Bitzer echoing Griffith's sentiments, explained what it was like:

> Neither Griffith nor I could be his own man. Everything was taken over by efficiency. We belonged to the corporation, the very thing we had fought at Biograph, and the reason we had left there. The business office was on top again.[54]

Not too surprisingly, the master's later films reveal a deepening pessimism. Starting with *True Heart Susie* (1919) and *Broken Blossoms* (1919), the "boy" and "girl" become defenseless against brutal men and women, or they succumb to the temptations of urban nightclubs and sexual allure. In *Dream Street* (1921), a seductive jazz musician rips off his mask to reveal himself as the Devil Lucifer. Now that the spirit of reform had waned, Griffith no longer maintained faith that the evil forces could be conquered. Heroes and heroines in these films had to retreat to small town life for salvation. His last film reveals the source of the problem. *The Struggle* (1931) portrays a man trapped on an automobile assembly line, often out of work and destroying himself and his family by drink and decadence. These themes were not popular in the 1920s, and Griffith had lost his talent for making successful films. This was not so much the result of declining abilities as that he had outlived his era. Explaining why studios no longer hired the great director, one critic noted:

> Mr. Griffith you have reached the point where your abilities are at a standstill. . . . You cannot be the evangelist of the screen. You refuse to

face the world as it is. . . . I'm not recommending that you acquire a set of puttees or a squad of Jap valets. Yet if I had my own way, I would imprison you with Cecil B. DeMille and loan you all of his Hollywood trappings, each and every one of them. Let someone else take charge of your soul for a while.[55]

Needless to say, Griffith never did. The man who dressed like a plain businessman and continually poured profits back into his own works was alienated from the "mad influx of post-War foreign influences." Equally hostile to the political world, he wrote letters to newspapers and politicians arguing that mobility was thwarted by the income tax that confiscated the earnings of the "producing classes," while the rich remained untouched.[56] By the 1930s and 1940s, he appeared as a lonely wanderer often seen inebriated in the bars of Hollywood, presenting roses to female acquaintances.[57] Occasionally, he revived the old spirit. During the 1930s, he finally divorced and then married a young Kentucky woman in the old Mount Tabor Church. He tried his hand at land speculation in Los Angeles. Then in 1934 he built a large marble monument over his parents' graves. On the enormous marker, he inscribed a memorial to his father's Civil War heroism and his mother's service while her husband was in battle. In a remarkable statement, the great director wrote, "I take more pride in this than in anything I have done or as far as I am concerned, anything anyone else has done." In essence, Griffith remained loyal to the past. That familial loyalty generated his earlier creativity, but it ultimately proved to be his cage. When he, too, was buried in that same Methodist cemetery, an old colleague remarked,

> You could tell Mr. Griffith by his conversation. Everything he lived and breathed was his pictures. He was in touch with his times . . . but the box office receipts were indicative of the popularity of his films. They were the things people wanted to see at that particular time. He realized that, and by the same token that may have been his downfall. . . . He pursued that course to where it was no longer popular. At that time he was perhaps outmoded.[58]

Griffith, however, was not the only one who was outmoded. By the 1920s, almost all the early independents and their cinematic themes had disappeared. Yet from 1908 to 1914, Griffith's artistry had expressed the aesthetics and social goals of a great movement, hoping to include elite reformers, an expanding urban audience, and independent Protestant filmmakers. Holding these strange bedfellows together and sparking Griffith's great creativity was a commitment to saving Victorianism in the face of major external threats. In Griffith's hands, this common belief in individualism and family harmony fit his commitment to Wilsonian progressivism. At the same time, it also legitimized movies, bringing the former pariah institution into the American mainstream. However, because the defense of the old culture, particularly sexual ethics, was so strong, it precluded any questioning of nineteenth-century values. What entrepreneurs such as Griffith needed was an alliance with other groups who shared their hostility to big business. But Griffith's art suggests that their antagonism to workers, blacks, or foreigners, who represented group power and sexual chaos, prevented this coalition. Thus Griffith and others who were committed to ascetic individualism watched helplessly as the corporate order emerged in the nation as well as in the motion picture industry. Such was the real tragedy of D. W. Griffith's life. As the world view of the early filmmakers collapsed, something new was already emerging to take its place.

NOTES

1. Lillian Gish, "Interview," *Reel Life* (Winter 1972), unpaginated clipping, Gish File, MOMAFL.

2. The Reverend Dr. Charles H. Parkhurst, "The Birth of a Nation," review reprinted in Fred Silva, ed., *Focus on the Birth of a Nation* (Englewood Cliffs, N.J., 1971), pp. 101–3; Charles Parkhurst, *My Twenty Years in New York* (New York, 1920).

3. On the "savior," see Edward Mott Wooley, "The $100,000 Salary Man of the Movies," *McClure's Magazine* (September 1913), 109–16. Wilson saw *The Birth of a Nation* in 1915, and Harding saw *Orphans of the Storm* in 1921. Both were shown in the White House, unpaginated clippings in Griffith File, MOMAFL. Josephus Daniels to D. W. Griffith, December 1919, and William Jennings Bryan to D. W. Griffith, May 20, 1924, Griffith MSS, MOMAFL. Griffith's admiration for Wilson and the desire to make a film in favor of the League of Nations is in Lillian Gish, *The Movies, Mr. Griffith and Me* (Englewood Cliffs, N.J., 1969), pp. 182–248. For an example of how the formative critics liked his work, see Louis Reeves Harrison, "David Wark Griffith, the Art Director and his Work," *Moving Picture World (hereafter MPW)* (November 22, 1913), 847. The quote is from "Radio Speech," Griffith File, MOMAFL.

4. For the biography of an early producer, see Albert Smith, *Two Reels and a Crank* (New York, 1952), pp. 11, 79–84, 251. On "exceptionally rich," see Isaac Morcosson, "The Magnates of the Motion Picture," *Munsey's* (November 12, 1912), 209–29; and the memoir of John Stuart Blackton, "Lecture," unpublished collection at the Academy of Motion Picture Arts and Science Library, Los Angeles, Calif. See also "The Moving Picture Revolution," *Success Magazine* (April 1910), 238–40; "Big Fortunes Made in Nickles and Dimes," *Theater Magazine* (May 1915), 244.

5. George Kleine, "Testimony," *The Chicago Motion Picture Report* (1918), 42–50.

6. Jeremiah Kennedy to Anonymous, July 8, 1908, National Board of Review Box, LCPA; the cost of running each film was tabulated from the National Board of Review

MSS Box 14, New York Public Library. The theater owners also wanted censorship, see *New York Times*, December 23, 1908, 1.

7. On the "frontier" atmosphere by a contemporary observer, see Terry Ramsaye, *A Million and One Night: A History of the Motion Picture* (New York, 1926), pp. 300–20. Each week the trade journals listed the film companies. In 1906 the future trust members had the market to themselves; see *Views and Film Index* (May 5, 1906), 5. In 1909 the nine trust members still controlled the market; see *Views and Film Index* (January–June 1909), and the same dates for *MPW*. By checking *MPW* for the next 8 years, the figures on new companies were calculated. For the total by 1917, see *MPW* (October 13, 1917), 305–7; Morcosson, "The Magnates," pp. 209–29.

8. See, for example, Russell Merritt, "Nickelodeon Theaters: Building an Audience for the Masses," in Tino Balio, ed., *The American Film Industry* (Madison, Wis., 1976), pp. 59–82.

9. Condemnations of foreign films by journals can be seen in "Our Own Critic," and "Weekly Comments on the Shows," *MPW* (January 1, 1909); "Training the Public Mind," *Views and Film Index* (April 25, 1906), 6; Stephan Bush, "Editorial," *MPW* (March 29, 1913); Louis Reeves Harrison, "Violence and Bloodshed," *MPW* (April 22, 1911); "What Is an American Subject?" *MPW* (January 22, 1910), 82.

10. The best summary of what a "photoplay" should be is Louis Reeves Harrison, *Screencraft* (New York, 1916), pp. 54–70; "Eternal Recurrence," *MPW* (July 8, 1913), 24; "Both Entertaining and Educational," *MPW* (September 7, 1913); "The Art of Criticism," *MPW* (January 31, 1914); and for an exemplary model, see his review of D. W. Griffith's *Ramona, MPW* (June 4, 1910).

11. Early in 1906, half the films released were made by foreign companies, see *Views and Film Index* (December 1, 1906), 5. In 1913, 410 films were released during April, but only 31 came from abroad. See *MPW* (April 5, 1913), 14.

12. See Stephan Bush, "Do Longer Films Make a Better Show," *MPW* (October 18, 1911); "Feature Programs," *MPW* (November 9, 1911), 529; "Is the Nickle Show on the Wane?" *MPW* (November 16, 1914), 1065; Louis Reeves Harrison, "How to Improve the Business," *MPW* (December 24, 1910); "Editorial," *MPW* (October 26, 1912); and for the independents' monopoly of photoplays, see *MPW* (April 5, 1913), 104.

13. Aitkin's life, faith, and morals are described by his brother, Roy Aitkin, *The Birth of a Nation Story* (Middleburg, Va., 1965), pp. 27–28, 46, 65. On his self-advertisement as a "Jacksonian Man," see *Reel Life* (March 4, 1914), 17, and (February 5, 1916), 2, in MOMAFL. On the cartoons and editorials for his company, see *The Triangle* (October 23, 1915), 1; (July 22, 1916), 5–7; February 5, 1916, in Eastman House.

14. Michael Davis, *The Exploitation of Pleasure* (New York, 1911), pp. 21–43.

15. "Browning Given in the Movies," *New York Times*, October 4, 1909, part I, p. 8; the scholarly biography is Robert M. Henderson, *D. W. Griffith: His Life and Work* (New York, 1972); Herbert Francis Sherwood, "Democracy and the Movies," *Bookman* (March 1918), 238–39.

16. Henderson, D. W. Griffith, pp. 16–31; the primary sources for Griffith's upbringing are his "Unfinished Autobiography," in MOMAFL, and a long interview with the director by Henry Stephan Gordon, "The Story of David Wark Griffith," *Photoplay* (June–October 1916). During these years, *Photoplay* was a serious journal, rather than the gossip and fantasy publication it became by the late 1920s. The state history gives the census material for La Grange: the population in 1850 was 612, one-third of the residents were slaves, and there were five Protestant churches. It also contains an account of Jacob Griffith's service in the legislature. See Louis and Richard Collins, *History of Kentucky* (Covington, Kentucky, 1878), pp. 271, 666.

17. Ibid.

18. The mother's piety, teaching, and David's religious experiences are in Griffith, "Autobiography," pp. 1–7. The respect for pure women, vice district allure, and his guilt over early sexual adventures are also in the "Autobiography," pp. 6–10, 13–14, and 39–42. The cemetery, church, and family burial grounds are described first-hand by Seymour Stern, "D. W. Griffith of the Movies," *American Mercury* (March 1949), 308. On the marriage and minister supported by Griffith, see *New York Herald Tribune*, March 3, 1936, unpaginated clipping, in MOMAFL. For the fact that women encouraged success, see Hazel Simpson's interview with Griffith, "The Poet Philosopher of the Photoplay," *Motion Picture Magazine* (September 1919), 28–29.

19. Gordon "Story of Griffith" (June 1916), pp. 35–57; Griffith, "Autobiography," pp. 1–10. D. W. Griffith, "A Criticism of the Income Tax," *Los Angeles Times*, October 26, 1919, 3.

20. Griffith, "Autobiography, pp. 40–43, 55–58.

21. The marriage situation is in Mrs. D. W. Griffith, *When the Movies Were Young* (New York, 1925). Nobody who worked with them knew they were married. See Billy Bitzer, *His Story: The Autobiography of D. W. Griffith's Master Cameraman* (New York, 1973), pp. 63–65.

22. For the quote on reform, see Griffith, "Autobiography," pp. 80–81; Bitzer, *His Story*, pp. 5, 88–89, and 188–90, recalled how he and Griffith saw the need for message films and uplift for the immigrants. On his constant work and little time for sex, see an interview with Griffith by Jim Tully, *Vanity Fair* (November 1928), 80. On the growing acclaim of his films, see "Browning Given the Movies," *New York Times*, October 4, 1909, part I, 8. On reformer's condemnation of monopoly in the industry and hope for trust-busting to improve the art, see *People's Institute Bulletin* (December 23, 1908), 5.

23. Griffith, "A Few Thoughts for the Radio," December 1925, Griffith File, MOMAFL; "Pace in the Movies," *Liberty* (November 13, 1926), 19; "The Future of the Two Dollar Movie," in Silva, *Focus*, pp. 99–101. For Griffith's dislike of sound, see Fred Cox's interview with Griffith, "Screen Pace Setter," *Hollywood Citizen News* (May 7, 1947), and Gish, *The Movies*, p. 241; Gish, *Reel Life* (Winter 1971), 3.

24. "Interview with D. W. Griffith," *New York American*, February 28, 1915, City Life and Dramatic Section, 9; D. W. Griffith, "The Motion Picture and Witch Burners," in Silva, *Focus*, pp. 96–98.

25. Leonard Hall, "Interview with D. W. Griffith," *Stage* (August 1911), unpaginated clipping, Griffith File, MOMAFL; Lillian Gish, "D. W. Griffith," *Harper's Bazaar* (October 1940), 105–6, for the style of handling actors and actresses; see also Gish, *The Movies*, pp. 76, 84, 115, 130, 358. As late as 1948, Griffith was saying that "stars" are unnecessary. See "An Oldtimer Advises Hollywood," *Liberty* (June 7, 1939), 18; D. W. Griffith, "What I Demand of Movie Stars," *Moving Picture Classic* (February 1917), 40–41.

26. D. W. Griffith, "Youth, The Spirit of the Movies," *Illustrated World*, in Geduld, *Focus*, pp. 194–96; Griffith, "What I Demand," pp. 40–41. In his "Radio Talk," Griffith saw youth as the quality for assimilating immigrants.

27. D. W. Griffith, "What Is Beauty," *Liberty* (October 19, 1929), 28–29; Gish, *The Movies*, pp. 45, 100–2, 124–48, 349. One old friend recalled that on his death bed Griffith wondered if he had lived up to his mother's expectations; see Garrett J. Lloyd, "Griffith's Life Story," *Los Angeles Examiner*, July 25, 1948. On the idea that it is woman's "greatest life work" to inspire success in men, see Hazel Simpson's interview with Griffith, "The Poet Philosopher of the Photoplay," *Motion Picture Magazine* (September 1919), pp. 28–29.

28. On the idea that a studio should be free from surrounding corruption, see D. W. Griffith, "Pictures versus One Night Stands," *Independent* (December 11, 1916), 447–48. For the studio atmosphere and its relation to women, health, and morals, see Gish, *The Movies*, pp. 85, 120–28, 206–9, and Bitzer, *His Story*, pp. 208–9.

29. D. W. Griffith, "What is Beauty"; "What I Demand"; "The Real Truth about Breaking into the Movies," *Woman's Home Companion* (February 1924), 16–17; Henry C. Carr, "How Griffith Picks His Leading Ladies," *Photoplay* (December 1918), 24–29; Donald Crisp, "Funeral Eulogy," Griffith File, AMPASL, describes Griffith shooting over and over to attain the right effect. Hall, "Interview," records Griffith as saying, "If we believe in these images of pure and sweet beauty, we must confess it was done by the hand of God himself."

30. Griffith, "Pace," pp. 19–23; "Pictures versus One Night Stands," pp. 447–48; Fox, "Screen Pace Setter," p. 12. For a brilliant discussion of this aesthetic as a liberal bourgeois view of the world versus a Marxist dialectic and synthesis, see Sergei Eisenstein, *Film Form: Essays in Film Theory* (New York, 1949).

31. Gordon, "Story of Griffith" (July 1916), pp. 124–29, 131–32.

32. *The Avenging Conscience* (1914), in MOMAFL.

33. *Man's Genesis* (1912), in MOMAFL.

34. For a few of the historical films, see *Judith of Bethulia* (1914); westward expansion, *The Battle of Elderbush Gulch* (1914); the American Revolution, *America* (1924); the French Revolution, *Orphans of the Storm* (1921), MOMAFL. On contemporary themes, see on labor-capital conflict, *The Voice of the Violin* (1909), which condemns Marxists; on monopolists, *A Corner in Wheat* (1909); on prohibition, *A Drunkard's Reformation* (1909); on vice lords, *Musketeers of Pig Alley* (1912), all in MOMAFL.

35. *Home Sweet Home* (1914); independent, resourceful women appear in nearly every major film. A classic working girl appears in *The Lonedale Operator* (1911), *Musketeers of Pig Alley* (1912), and *The Song of the Shirt* (1908).

36. Raymond J. Cook, "The Man Behind 'The Birth of a Nation,'" *North Carolina Historical Review* 20 (October 1962), 519–40; Thomas Dixon, "Why I Wrote The Clansman," *Theater Magazine* (January 1906), 20–22, in which Dixon explains that his motive was to convert the North to the Southern view of race and miscegenation.

37. See, for example, Alexander Saxton, *The Indispensable Enemy: Labor and the Anti-Chinese Movement in California* (Los Angeles, 1971), pp. 19–30.

38. On Griffith's tremendous enthusiasm on making the film and "Jake Griffith's son fighting the War all over again," see Bitzer, "Interview," in MOMAFL, and *His Story*, p. 107; Gish, *The Movies*, p. 136. The quote is from Gordon, "Story of Griffith" (October 1916), pp. 86–90.

39. *The Birth of a Nation* (1915), in MOMAFL. A detailed shot-by-shot analysis is in Theodore Huff, *Intolerance: The Film by D. W. Griffith, A Shot by Shot Analysis* (New York, 1966). Wagner's "Ride of the Valkyries" was the original music for the ride of the Klan, see Francis Hackett, "Brotherly Love," *New Republic* (March 20, 1915), 185.

40. See *Motion Picture Almanac* (New York, 1934), pp. 16–17. This is the annual trade journal summary.

41. See Arthur Link, *Woodrow Wilson and the Progressive Era, 1910–1917* (New York, 1954), pp. 1–24.

42. *The Birth of a Nation*, especially the titles introducing the Reconstruction story.

43. Dixon, "Southern Horizons," unpublished autobiography, cited in Cook, "The Man," p. 529. Dixon also wrote to Wilson that the "play is transforming the entire population of the North and West into Democratic voters. There will never again be an issue of your segregation policy." See Dixon to Woodrow Wilson, September 5, 1915, in Arthur Link, *Wilson and the New Freedom* (Princeton, N.J., 1956), p. 252.

44. A full examination of the unfavorable response is Thomas Cripps, "The Reaction of the Negro to the Motion Picture, *The Birth of a Nation*," *The Historian* 25 (1963), 344–63; see also W. D. McGuire, "Censoring Motion Pictures," *New Republic* (April 15, 1915), 262–63. For Frederic Howe's and Jane Addams's disapproval, and Howe's resignation from the Board for even allowing its filming, see *The Survey* (April 3, 1915).

45. On Griffith's condemnation of his critics, see D. W. Griffith, "Reply to the *New York Globe*," *New York Globe*, April 10, 1915, in Geduld, *Focus*, pp. 77–80; and "Defense of *The Birth of a Nation* and Attack on the Sullivan Bill," *Boston Herald*, April 26, 1915, in Geduld, *Focus*, pp. 43–45. For no "black blood" in the actors who played leading roles, see Gordon, "Story of Griffith" (October 1916), 79. For Dixon's hatred of race mixing, see Dixon, "Why I Wrote," pp. 20–22; and the producers, see Aitkin, *Birth*, pp. 60–65; and Griffith's denials, see Gish, *The Movies*, pp. 162–63.

46. For his criticism of censors, see D. W. Griffith, *The Rise and Fall of Free Speech in America* (1916), and Griffith, "The Motion Picture and Witch Burners," pp. 96–99.

47. Gordon, "Story of Griffith" (October 1916), pp. 86–90. Quote is from unpaginated undated clipping, Griffith File on *Intolerance*, MOMA.

48. *Intolerance* (1916) MOMAFL. See also Huff, *Intolerance*. The attempt to reproduce each era from exact historical and archeological research is the subject of Bernard Benson, "D. W. Griffith, Some Sources." *Art Bulletin* (December 1972), 493–95. For a discussion of how the charity ball in the modern story was meant to duplicate the New York "Four Hundred," see Joseph Haneberry, the assistant director, interview in Kevin Brownlow, *The Parade's Gone By* (New York, 1969), pp. 55, 68–69. That the coming of Christ and the end to war was the conscious message is discussed in Bitzer, *His Story*, pp. 137–39. Gordon "Story of Griffith" (October 1916), pp. 86–90, has Griffith saying how the film was made from "his head."

49. Howard Gaye was the actor arrested and deported. See Bitzer, *His Story*, p. 142. On locking out the IWW, see Henabery interview in Brownlow, *Parade*, p. 68. For the general struggle against labor, see Louis B. Perry and Richard S. Perry, *A History of the Los Angeles Labor Movement, 1911–1940* (Los Angeles, 1963), pp. 318–40.

50. *New York Sun*, September 6, 1916, unpaginated clipping, Griffith File, *Intolerance* section, MOMA.

51. *Philadelphia North American*, December 30, 1916, unpaginated clipping, Griffith File, *Intolerance* section, MOMA; on being labeled a communist see undated interview, probably 1947, Griffith File, AMPASL. One biographer records that Lenin had the film shown throughout the USSR in 1919, see Iris Berry, *D. W. Griffith: American Film Master* (New York, 1940), p. 26.

52. Heywood Broun, "Intolerance," *New York Tribune*, September 7, 1916.

53. *Hearts of the World* (1918), MOMAFL, is Griffith's propaganda film for the war. It was commissioned by the British government and led to the director's audience with the British Prime Minister, Lloyd George. *Orphans of the Storm* (1921) is Griffith's indirect attack, overtly proclaimed in a long opening title, on the Bolsheviks. On its showing to Harding and the atmosphere of these years, see Gish, *The Movies*, pp. 145–51, 158–61; Playbill, "Orphans of the Storm," Griffith File, MOMA. Griffith of course was not unique in making Red Scare films and applying their meaning to the studios in Hollywood. See *Dangerous Hours* (1919), LCFA.

54. In his final years, Griffith saw himself as the last man to make "one man pictures"; see Otis Guernsey, "A Lively Oldster, D. W. Griffith," *New York Herald Tribune*, October 4, 1942, unpaginated clipping, Griffith File, AMPASL. On his complaints that young men of the new age were being blocked from the top and self-sufficiency, see Griffith, "A Criticism of the Income Tax," p. 3. The quote is from Bitzer, "Interview," MOMAFL. See also Bitzer, *His Story*, p. 235, for a similar sentiment, and Griffith Collection, MOMA, for loan receipts from banks for his 1920s films.

55. See Gish, *The Movies*, p. 324, and "D. W. Griffith" for his alienation from Hollywood and the films he was making. The beginning of his social disillusionment occurred with *Broken Blossoms* (1919). That women were changing and adopting sexual styles that endangered the old masculine code of success, see *True Heart Susie* (1919) and *Way Down East* (1920). The danger of the new cities and the retreat to small towns is in

Dream Street (1921), *Way Down East* (1920), *The White Rose* (1923), and *Sorrows of Satan* (1926). All are in MOMAFL. Some of these films display a growing lack of aesthetic mastery, probably because the director no longer felt the great, socially transforming ideal as relevant. The quote is from "Editorial," *Photoplay* (December 1924), 27. *The Struggle* (1931), in MOMAFL.

56. Griffith, "A Criticism"; letters to Bryan, Josephus Daniels, and other Democrats complaining of the income tax are in Griffith Collection, MOMA.

57. June Glassmeyer, interview, June 22, 1974. She recalled that Griffith drank a great deal but occasionally would leave the bar and come back with a red rose for her.

58. Griffith to Peter Burghard Stone Company, June 6, 1934, Griffith MSS, MOMA. The Methodist cemetery is near where Griffith went to school and worshipped as a youth, see Stern, "D. W. Griffith," p. 308. The quote is from a Griffith assistant, Robert M. Farquar, "Interview," Griffith File, MOMA. On land speculation see interview with his black chauffeur, Richard Reynolds, "Interview," MOMA.

Martin Rubin

The Crowd, the Collective, and the Chorus: Busby Berkeley and the New Deal

Prologue: The Lone Eagle

The highpoint of the first Movietone sound news film, premiered on May 25, 1927, was footage of Charles A. Lindbergh embarking from Roosevelt Field on his historic solo flight across the Atlantic. Unlike in other early talkie milestones, what especially enthralled audiences here was not music or even dialogue. It was a machine: the roar of the motor as the *Spirit of St. Louis* took off.[1]

Lindbergh was perhaps the greatest avatar of a hero-figure closely associated with the 1920s: the rugged individualist. The "Lone Eagle," alone in his flying machine over the Atlantic, riding his airplane like a cowboy rides his horse, Lindbergh was a creature of the Machine Age but not subordinated to the machine. An overnight celebrity through courage, initiative, and luck, Lindbergh was both ordinary and extraordinary, modest and ambitious—a go-getter par excellence.[2]

The great screen stars of the 1920s—Valentino, Bow, Gilbert, Pickford, Fairbanks, Swanson, etc.—were primarily individualists but not quite individuals. They were incarnations of primal forces such as Love, Energy, Innocence, Adventure—sacred monsters standing more or less apart from the society whose ideals they represented.[3]

Copyright © 1996 by Martin Rubin

Chaplin's Little Tramp, first of the great silent comedy personae, exists on the fringe of society, battling for position but never integrated. He is an extraordinary "little man," a universalized eccentric. A semi-Victorian figure, he is never quite at home in the Machine Age, neither its master nor its servant.

Keaton, more aggressive and contemporary than Chaplin, battles the machine, masters it, and ultimately makes it an extension of himself, whether it be a locomotive, a steamboat, or a movie camera. He is at home in the Machine Age, but he retains a freakish, isolated quality that sets him apart from society.

Harold Lloyd, last and most aggressive of the Big Three silent comedians, is both more realistic and more phenomenal than either Chaplin or Keaton, combining elements of ordinary Joe and prodigy. Harold looks like the guy next door. He often works (and seems to belong) in an office or ordinary job. He goes after (and achieves) consensus goals such as romance, popularity, and financial success. At the same time, Harold often seems less like a character than a principle of pure manic energy—the success drive incarnate—with powers and abilities and a mastery of environment that verge on the superhuman.[4]

Like Lindbergh, like the Big Bull Market, Harold's direction is *up*. He battles the skyscraper and turns it into a stage for individual prowess and achievement. Exceptional and representative, he is an embodiment of expansionist, laissez-faire American capitalism of the 1865–1929 period.

Al Jolson, first great star of the talkies, continues the individualist, sacred-monster tradition of the 1920s. Like Lloyd, Keaton, Pickford, Fairbanks, Bow, Gilbert, and Swanson, his career is all but dead by 1930, the year that Busby Berkeley, one of Broadway's most innovative young dance directors, created his first filmed musical number for the Eddie Cantor vehicle *Whoopee!*

One of the Mob

King Vidor's *The Crowd* (1928) is perhaps the first major American film to question the reigning myth of rugged individualism. At the beginning of the film, John Sims, Sr., boasts of his new son (born on July 4, 1900), "There's a little man the world is going to hear from all right." His boy is going to grow up to be "somebody big." The boy's early life emulates those of Washington and Lincoln; in an archetypal rugged individualist myth, he could even grow up to be president.

John Sims, Jr. (James Murray), works in a skyscraper. His face aglow with zeal as he enters New York City, he declares, "All I want is an opportunity." He goes after success by entering brand-name and slogan contests, and he goes after the woman he loves. "I'm the old go-getting kid!" he says. From the top of a bus, he disdainfully surveys the pedestrians below: "Look at that crowd! The poor boobs. . . all in the same rut!" Spotting a juggling clown with an advertising sign-board, John sneers, "The poor sap! And I bet his father thought he would be president!"

Unlike Charles Lindbergh, unlike Harold Lloyd (and unlike Howard Roark, the skyscraper-tamer of Vidor's 1949 film of *The Foun-tainhead*), John Jr.'s lot is not to soar above the crowd. He grows up to be not president of the United States but no. 137 in a sea of identical office workers. He goes on to become one of countless guys who take their girlfriends to Coney Island and honeymoon at Niagara Falls. He ends up as a nonentity in a line of unemployed workers, a juggling clown with an advertising signboard, and finally, an anonymous and indistinguishable figure in a vast theater audience.

The attitude toward the crowd here is deeply ambivalent. To be swallowed up in the crowd is a disheartening experience, but being out of step with it may be even worse.[5] In many of Vidor's films (as in those of such contemporaries as Fritz Lang and Raoul Walsh), the relationship between the individual and the mass is viewed pessimistically, because the interests of both are difficult to reconcile. One or the other must be chosen; attempts at reconciliation and synthesis are usually riddled with strain, contradiction, and instability.

The Irony and the Ecstasy

Vidor's ambivalent and pessimistic attitude toward the individual/mass relationship frequently resolves itself in an ironic stance toward the characters and the story material. In *The Crowd*, an up/down motif functions as an ironic comment on the 1920s—the soaring Roaring Twenties of Lindbergh, the Big Bull Market, and the skyscraper.

The opening shot of the film pans down the facade of the Sims home to reveal a crowd of holiday-makers hurrying by. The camera cranes up the facade of a skyscraper and down over rows of workers at their desks. Leaving work, John descends on a plummeting crowded elevator. He makes a precipitous ascent to the top deck of a bus and looks down on the crowd below. The camera giddily accompanies John and his companions down the shoot-the-chutes at Coney Island. Newlyweds John and Mary climb up a steep hill and view the plunging waters of Niagara Falls. . . . This first section of the film establishes a pattern of upward movements answered by downward movements, imprinting a roller-coaster instability on the galloping optimism of the 1920s.

The irony of the up/down movements in *The Crowd*, applied to the same individual/mass thematic, becomes the ecstasy of the celebrated crane shots in Busby Berkeley's musical numbers of the 1930s. The moment in *The Crowd* that most anticipates Berkeley's numbers is the final one: the series of transcendent high-angle crane shots that dissolve the hero into the crowd at the theater. At the opposite end of the scale in Vidor's filmography is the low-angle crane-up at the end of *The Fountainhead* that shows the hero towering over the crowd. In these films, whether transcendence comes on the level of the individual or the crowd, it is still an either/or proposition. The continuous fields of Berkeley's crane shots represent an attempt to overcome the constraints of either/or.

Raymond Durgnat has pointed out a relationship between *The Crowd* and the mechanized urban motifs of Berkeley numbers such as "42nd Street."[6] It is possible to follow this comparative path much farther. Consider the following parallels between scenes in *The Crowd* and scenes in Berkeley numbers:

1. Sitting in a crowded subway with Mary's head on his shoulder, John looks up and sees a furniture ad: "YOU FURNISH the GIRL—We'll Furnish THE HOME!" This inspires him to propose to her; it also exemplifies John's susceptibility to mass cult and advertising. The next scene shows the couple being seen off on their honeymoon by a group of overly vociferous well-wishers, including John's best friend, who observes as he leaves, "Well, I'll give them a year. . . maybe two."

   In Berkeley's "I Only Have Eyes for You" number (*Dames* [1934]), Dick Powell, sitting on a crowded subway with Ruby Keeler's head on his shoulder, looks up and sees ads for cigarettes, hair conditioner, and cosmetics. The faces of the women in the ads all become the face of Ruby Keeler, inspiring Dick's revery of a nonpareil world endlessly faceted with the faces of Ruby lookalikes.

2. In a Niagara-bound sleeper, honeymooners John and Mary are embarrassed by the Negro porter's suggestion to have their bed made up. Two male travelers watch John preparing for bed, snicker knowingly, and retrieve a marriage manual that has fallen out of his bathrobe. John at first enters the wrong berth. Then, as Mary cowers modestly under the covers, he struggles into the cramped compartment, bumping his head and triggering a small avalanche of toilet articles.

    Similar elements are found in Berkeley's two naughty-nuptials numbers, "Shuffle Off to Buffalo" (*42nd Street* [1933]) and "Honeymoon Hotel" (*Footlight Parade* [1933]). "Shuffle" reshuffles the sleeping-car setting, the Negro porter, the snickering fellow passengers, and even the prediction of divorce ("She'll be wanting alimony in a year or so"). "Honeymoon" emulates the bedtime preparations and the entrance into the wrong bedchamber. Both numbers resolve their coyness and awkwardness into elliptical images of connubial bliss: the bride's outstretched arm sinking languorously in "Shuffle," a baby beaming from the pages of a windblown magazine in "Honeymoon."

3. John and Mary lie down in the grass, overlooking Niagara Falls. He affirms the grandeur and imperishability of their love ("My love will never stop, Mary. It's like these falls."). Rapturous shots of the rushing water are immediately followed by a scene in the newlyweds' ludicrously cramped flat, complete with Murphy bed and window-rattling El. The scene goes on to detail an excruciating visit from the bride's hostile family.

    In Berkeley's "By a Waterfall" (*Footlight Parade*), Dick Powell and Ruby Keeler lie down in the grass. Waterfalls, splashing nearby, trigger Dick's fantasy of Ruby cavorting in the cascades with hordes of water nymphs.

In each case, a situation interpreted ironically by Vidor is interpreted ecstatically by Berkeley. This can be attributed not only to the differing temperaments of the two filmmakers but also to their relationship to a fundamental shift in American socio-political attitudes that occurred in the late 1920s and early 1930s. Vidor's is basically a 1920s outlook, tempered later by his encounter with the 1930s. Berkeley's is basically a 1930s outlook, tempered by his earlier background in the 1920s.

In One Era and Out the Other

Although *The Crowd*, with its depictions of unemployment and poverty and its pessimistic view of individual opportunity, seems uncannily prophetic for a film made at the height of the Big Bull Market, it is in fact related to a rising disillusionment with rugged individualism that began well before the Crash. This type of temporal overlap is not at all unusual. Many of the most important cultural phenomena (cinematic or otherwise) of the early 1930s are precisely those that are overdetermined by belonging both to the late 1920s and the early 1930s, playing both sides of the Crash.

For instance, the gangster film is often interpreted as an outgrowth of the early Depression, but this subgenre actually began its upswing in 1927–28 (*Underworld, The Racket, Lights of New York*, etc.) and can be located more accurately as a hybrid of late 1920s giddiness and early 1930s uncertainty. In a similar way, the early musical film was an outgrowth of 1920s high spirits and Broadway developments, which dovetailed into the frenetic whistling-in-the-dark optimism of the early post-Crash period ("Prosperity Is Just around the Corner," "Happy Days Are Here Again") and then combined with burgeoning Depression consciousness in the classic Warner Bros. musicals of 1933–34. The anarchic/cynical comedy cycle of the early 1930s (The Marx Brothers, W. C. Fields, Wheeler & Woolsey, etc.) combined waning vaudeville traditions and the joyful absurdism of the late silent era with a nihilistic absurdism more suited to the early Depression. The widespread moral revival whose consequences included the Hollywood Production Code was already active in the late 1920s and then was accelerated by the Depression and early 1930s social consciousness.

Obviously, the American public did not wake up on October 30, 1929, and say, "Hey! We're in the Depression! We need a new set of attitudes!" The realization that Old Man Depression was going to stick around for a while did not really sink into the public consciousness until 1931–32.[7] Consciousness may both anticipate and lag behind historical events. The most durable ideas and forms of an era are often those that serve as a bridge during periods of upheaval and social change, which are able to *slide* from one era to another, adapting themselves elastically to historical and ideological shifts.[8]

Disillusionment Is Just around the Corner

In the mid- and late 1920s, at the peak of prosperity, a distinguished minority of writers was expressing an underlying disillusionment with laissez-faire capitalism and its ethos of rugged individualism. These dissenting voices became increasingly concerned that the 1920s cult of prosperity had led to a withering of cultural and spiritual values in favor of materialism and superficiality. Such trends were seen as a betrayal of the high ideals that had characterized turn-of-the-century Progressivism, its Wilsonian sequel, and the United States' intervention in the First World War ("The Great Crusade").[9]

The best-known products of this spearhead movement are the Lost Generation and social-criticism writings of F. Scott Fitzgerald, Sinclair Lewis, Ernest Hemingway, Sherwood Anderson, Elmer Rice, John Dos Passos, Theodore Dreiser, etc. This literary movement also included several lesser novelists whose reputations have declined in later years, such as Floyd Dell, Ben Hecht, Carl Van Vechten, and Glenway Wescott.[10]

Also active in this vein were a small although increasingly influential group of historians, economists, educators, social scientists, and philosophers who explored similar themes in their respective fields.[11] The final, posthumous volume of Vernon Parrington's popular literary survey *Main Currents in American Thought* (1927–30) lamented the decline of a grand tradition of idealistic Jeffersonian liberalism into the cynicism and materialism of the modern industrial age. Joseph Wood Krutch's *The Modern Temper* (1929) stated a similar theme in more generalized terms, painting a gloomy Spenglerian picture of a decadent, science-bound civilization that had lost touch with nature and spirituality. The influential philosopher/educator John Dewey, in *The Public and Its Problems* (1927), saw the individual bewildered and diminished by the decline of rural community life and the increasing corporateness of industrial capitalism.[12]

In the collection *I'll Take My Stand* (1930), a group of leading regional writers known as the Southern Agrarians (Robert Penn Warren, Allen Tate, John Crowe Ransom, Stark Young, etc.) linked the alienation of the individual with northern industrialism and sought a remedy in the southern agrarian tradition based on small yeoman farmers. Among other highly regarded writers who expressed pessimism about the state of American culture from a predominantly conservative viewpoint were the lucid political columnist Walter Lippmann, the "New Humanist" literary scholar Irving Babbitt, the architect turned social critic Ralph Adams Cram, and the caustic essayist/editor H. L. Mencken—the last famously lampooning the era's enshrinement of business and businessmen as a breeding ground for uncultured boobs and Babbitts.[13]

Robert and Helen Lynd's pioneer sociological study *Middletown* (1929) examined the population of Muncie, Indiana, as a barometer of American attitudes at the end of the 1920s. They found that industrialization and mechanization had isolated people from their communities and alienated them from their jobs, where individual personality was subordinated to the assembly line and the large office. To compensate for this weakened sense of community, people turned to consumerism, standardized mass amusements, and conformist activities such as boosterism and club-joining.[14] In many respects, the Lynds were describing a small-city equivalent of the world that had been portrayed the previous year in Vidor's film *The Crowd*.

The Vanishing Individual

The warnings and criticisms of the writers cited above center on the relationship between the individual and the mass. This has been an issue of special and abiding prominence in the ideology of American democracy. Simmering in the late 1920s, the issue was forced to the crisis point by the Crash and the Depression, which intensified a growing critique of individualism and lead eventually to major reconception of its role within American ideology.

The reevaluation of the role of the individual centered on the idea that society was evolving into larger and more interdependent units. This was evidenced by

1. the growth of nationalism. The rise in the power of national states, especially pronounced since the late nineteenth century, had been accompanied by the increasing subordination of the individual to

the state—a trend reaching sinister dimensions in Germany, Italy, and Japan

2. the rise of giant corporations and holding companies, along with the rise of the large factory or large office as the workplace

3. the increasing concentration of population in the cities. The 1920 census revealed that, for the first time, there were more Americans living in cities than in rural areas[15]

4. the rise of the mass media, as represented by the continued growth of the phonograph and motion pictures and, especially, by the rapid expansion in the 1920s of the first broadcast medium: radio[16]

As the structures of civilization became more monolithic and consolidated, the individual was perceived to be in danger of becoming powerless and insignificant—one of the crowd. Picking up where Dewey and the Lynds had left off in the late 1920s, sociologist Henry Pratt Fairchild wrote in 1932, "The gist of the whole matter is that, whether we like it or not, modern life has become so highly integrated, so inextricably socialized, so definitely organic, that the very concept of the individual is becoming obsolete."[17]

Individualism vs. Individuality

The first part of this rising critique was aimed at individualism that was *in danger*—i.e., the diminishing individual who was disappearing into the urban-industrial crowd. The second part of the critique was aimed at individualism that was *dangerous*—i.e., the rugged individualism of capitalism, free enterprise, and unregulated competition. This second type of individualism was linked to the traditional notion that unregulated capitalism worked naturally for the benefit of society, through built-in balances such as Say's Law, the business cycle, and the price system. Progress would then inevitably occur by means of unlimited expansion, competition, and production.

Despite the critical voices raised by Parrington, Dewey, Krutch, etc., a belief in the untrammelled individualism of laissez-faire capitalism was still hegemonic in the late 1920s.[18] In 1927 the influential political pundit Walter Lippmann wrote, "The more or less unconscious and unplanned activities of business men are for once more novel, more daring, and in general more revolutionary, than the theories of the

Progressives."[19] In 1929, even the aging muckraker Lincoln Steffens conceded, "Big business in America is producing what the Socialists held up as their goal: food, shelter, and clothing for all."[20]

With the Crash, the individualism represented by laissez-faire capitalism came under widespread attack. It was increasingly seen as anachronistic, based on a frontier mentality that had been relevant only so long as unlimited expansion was still possible. Now, according to a growing number of historians, economists, political scientists, and politicians, the frontier was closed, the economy was saturated, and growth led only to giant corporations, which subverted the equilibrium of the market by fixing prices and wages.[21]

John Dewey wrote in *Individualism—Old and New* (1930), "The United States has steadily moved from an earlier pioneer individualism to a condition of dominant corporateness."[22] In his essay "The Myth of Rugged American Individualism" (1931), Charles Beard asserted, "The cold truth is that the individualist creed of everybody for himself and the devil take the hindmost is principally responsible for the distress in which Western civilization finds itself."[23] Stuart Chase wrote in his popular economic treatise *A New Deal* (1932), "The American frontier ceased to exist about 1890, but the pioneer tradition continues to color our thought today. Laissez-faire rides well on covered wagons; not so well on conveyor belts and cement roads."[24] During the 1932 presidential campaign, Franklin D. Roosevelt drew on Frederick Jackson Turner's Frontier Thesis and declared, "So began, in American political life, the new day, the day of the individual against the system, the day in which individualism was made the great watchword of American life. The happiest of economic conditions made that day long and splendid. On the Western frontier, land was substantially free.... Our last frontier has long since been reached, and there is practically no more free land.... There is no safety valve in the form of a Western prairie to which those thrown out of work by the Eastern economic machines can go for a new start."[25]

As noted above, there are two different types of individualism involved in this debate. Because writers of the period applied the word *individualism* indiscriminately to both types, it might be useful to devise two separate terms: *individuality* (as in "personal individuality"—the individual citizen *vis-à-vis* society) and *individualism* (as in "rugged individualism"—the guiding self-interest of laissez-faire capitalism).[26]

Both types, individuality and individualism, were increasingly perceived as out-of-date in the early 1930s. Society had become more corporate and interdependent, while its ideology had remained back in the frontier era of rugged individualism. This led to the type of situation covered by the term *cultural lag* (introduced by sociologist William Fielding Ogburn in his 1922 book *Social Change*), a stock phrase in social science writing of the time.[27]

Enter the New Deal

> The problem is seen to be essentially that of creation of a new individualism as significant for modern conditions as the old individualism at its best was for its day and place. The first step in further definition of this problem is realization of the collective age which we have already entered.[28]

In terms of the New Deal, what was needed to correct this cultural lag was a strengthened federal government. This would accomplish two basic goals:

1. It would support and protect individuality—one's personal sense of security and community. It sought to lend strength to this individual, but in an ambivalent way—that is, by attenuating one's individualism, by making one give some of it up and become part of a meaningful larger structure.[29] This could be a community, a labor union, or a government program, whether for workers (such as the CCC) or businessmen (such as the NRA). Pure individualism (the "rugged" type) was discredited as anarchic, a force for fragmentation and disunity. It was replaced by an impure individuality, which was modified or redefined by "collectivism"—another stock phrase of the era.[30]

2. While protecting individuality (by linking it with the seemingly contradictory idea of collectivism), the government would control individualism by regulating the economy. This would be accomplished not so much by breaking up the big corporations as by increasing the power of other institutions—such as labor power, consumer power, and most important, the power of the government itself. In contrast to turn-of-the-century progressivism, antitrust actions were generally a minor part of New Deal strategy.[31] The New Deal was more oriented toward fighting power with power, countering one large unit with another large unit.[32] The most

dramatic and controversial instances of this strategy were the National Recovery Administration (NRA), which could be seen as a government-sanctioned agency of business consolidation, and the Tennessee Valley Authority (TVA), in which the government competed with private enterprise by becoming directly involved in the production and sale of electrical power. In a less spectacular manner, the alphabetical array of New Deal agencies contributed to the increasing role of government planning, regulation, and expertise in the previously sacrosanct business cycle.[33]

Exit Thomas Jefferson (Stage Left)

This shift toward collectivism and government intervention ran against the grain of traditional Jeffersonian liberalism (from which progressivism was descended). The central principle of Jeffersonian liberalism is that the greatest source of civil danger is the power of government, the potential tyranny of the state. Accordingly, the main purpose of laws and governmental structures is to protect the individual from the state, to keep the government out of business and out of the citizen's personal affairs.

This was precisely the position taken by Herbert Hoover during his presidency. When he refused to interfere in the business cycle or to involve the federal government in welfare relief, Hoover (generally considered a liberal throughout his political career) was acting less like a reactionary elitist than like a classic Jeffersonian liberal. For Hoover, America was founded on principles of self-help and individual (or, at most, local) responsibility. In these beliefs, the Republican Hoover stood shoulder-to-shoulder with his 1928 presidential opponent, the Democrat Al Smith, an old-line urban liberal who ultimately found it more difficult to reconcile his beliefs with those of the New Deal than with those of the Liberty League, a millionaire-supported anti-Roosevelt coalition formed in the mid-1930s.[34]

These were the traditions that the New Deal directly opposed. As Arthur Ekrich wrote in his New Deal history, *Ideologies and Utopias:*

> Roosevelt was convinced that American freedom stood in greater danger from vast aggregations of private wealth than from governmental abuse of individual rights. The New Deal philosophy accordingly denied the older American assumption that the people themselves could preserve

their liberties from any type of interference except what might come from a centralized government. The emphasis of the New Deal was on a type of liberty that minimized individual freedom in favor of a greater social security and economic equality of the whole.[35]

In these respects, the New Deal went against the grain of not only post-1865 Republican laissez-faire policies but a system of beliefs that dated back to the beginnings of the Republic and embraced all major political parties. The New Deal constituted, if not a revolution or a new ideology, at least an unprecedented shift in basic American attitudes within the framework of democratic capitalism.[36]

Into the Battle

Even though the New Deal deviated from orthodox American tradition, it did have an important precedent in recent American history: the First World War. During the war, the federal government had regulated prices, industrial production, and the distribution of goods through the War Industries Board and other affiliated programs. Also, it had virtually taken over the national transportation system; it had vastly increased the powers of the presidency; and, for a short while, it had maintained a generally ordered and efficient economy.[37]

Many of those social critics and economists who in the late 1920s were attacking laissez-faire capitalism harked back to the wartime period as a model for a rationally regulated economy. In a 1927 article, Rexford Tugwell (later to become the most radical member of FDR's "Brain Trust") deemed the war "an industrial engineer's utopia" and approvingly cited the War Industries Board as "America's war-time socialism."[38] In the early days of the Depression, a reapplication of wartime policies was called for by popular writers on economics such as Charles Beard, Stuart Chase, George Soule, and William Trufant Foster. The Reconstruction Finance Corporation, the Hoover administration's most ambitious response to the Depression, was modeled on the old War Finance Corporation.[39]

The metaphor of war served both sides of the individualism/individuality relationship. It served as a model for government control of individualism and for the regulation of business. It also served as a model for a meaningful group experience, a unity of national purpose, and an identification of individuality with larger collective goals.

The New Deal was quick to pick up on wartime methods and rhetoric. Raymond Moley, a key member of the Brain Trust, wrote of the heated atmosphere of the first 100 days of the Roosevelt administration, "Official Washington was in the grip of a war psychology as surely as it had been in 1917."[40] The most highly publicized early New Deal agency, the NRA, was patterned after the War Industries Board; it was headed by a former World War I officer, Gen. Hugh Johnson; its supporters wore insignia and badges and frequently staged parades. Another celebrated New Deal program, the Civilian Conservation Corps, applied the war analogy to the labor force, with military-style camps, command structures, discipline, and training.[41]

Roosevelt himself frequently resorted to wartime rhetoric in his public pronouncements. In the "Jefferson Day Dinner" campaign speech of 1932, he contrasted the "considered, relevant measures" of the War Industries Board to the panic-stricken disorganization of the Hoover administration.[42] The loudest applause during his 1932 inaugural speech came when he declared, "I shall ask the Congress for the one remaining instrument to meet the crisis—broad Executive power to wage a war against the emergency, as great as the power that would be given to me if we were in fact invaded by a foreign foe."[43]

FDR's most celebrated speech of the 1932 campaign was a radio address in which he cited the national mobilization of World War I and called for "plans like those of 1917 that . . . put their faith once more in the forgotten man at the bottom of the economic pyramid."[44] The phrase *forgotten man* immediately seized the public imagination, and this became known as the "Forgotten Man" speech.

"Remember My Forgotten Man"

The climactic Busby Berkeley number of *Gold Diggers of 1933* combines two major ideas involved in early 1930s political revisionism:

1. the spirit of the Great Crusade—the high ideals that were aroused by the First World War and later betrayed, first by the materialism of the 1920s, then by the catastrophe of the Crash
2. the New Deal equation between the emergency of the war and the emergency of the Depression, resulting in a call for a revival of wartime spirit and collectivism.

Both ideas converged in an ugly event of the early Depression: the Bonus March of Summer, 1932. An "army" of 15,000 disillusioned, unemployed veterans—complete with uniforms, military discipline, and parades—squatted in Washington, D. C., to demand money and/or jobs. They and their families were finally routed by police, cavalry, and tear gas—one of the most controversial actions of the Hoover administration.

The "Remember My Forgotten Man" number is remarkable both for its explicit reference to the still-warm Bonus Marchers issue and for its wholehearted sympathy for their cause, as attested by the unforgettably withering gaze that saucer-eyed Joan Blondell fixes on a surly cop as he collars a sleeping bum who is wearing a medal beneath his ragged coat. But what is most remarkable (and most Berkeleyesque) about the number is its expansion of the political message to a sexual level.

The number begins on a stark street-corner set. Blondell walks over to a bum, lights her cigarette from his butt, and gives him the fresh cigarette. Wistfully caressing a lamp post, she sings in recitative, "You sent him far away. / You shouted hip-hooray. / But look at him today. . . ." Blondell's lament, later passed on to women of various races and ages in a nearby tenement, is twofold. She wants two things: a job *for* her man and love *from* her man. The latter is dependent on the former: "And once he used to love me, / I was happy then. / He used to take care of me. / Won't you bring him back again? / 'Cause ever since the world began, / A woman's got to have a man. / Forgetting him, you see, / Means you're forgetting me, / Like my, my forgotten man."

The number is based on an equation between economics and sex, a confluence of social and psychological factors. For working men in the Depression, the loss of their jobs or the decrease in their earning power represents a form of impotence.[45] What Blondell and the other women in the number are saying is: because my man can't get a job, he has lost his virility—he can't love me the way he used to.

After this downbeat introduction, there is a rapid fade-out, and the number suddenly opens up to a flashback of men marching off to war, erect, proud, *employed*—images of virility. Blackout: the screen parts to show soldiers marching in the rain and trudging back from battle, wounded, bleeding, sagging—images of castration. Blackout: the screen parts again, this time to reveal a line of unemployed men in a soup kitchen. A series of sliding associations has been made: war/castration/depression.

A cigarette is passed from man to man in the soup line. The sexual connection established in the opening bit of Blondell getting a light from the bum's cigarette butt comes up empty here. Deprived of love and virility, the connection becomes sterile and homoerotic. The social/economic disaster of the Depression has inhibited meaningful sexual congress between man and woman.

After a final blackout, the climactic grand tableau begins with two ranks of civilian men marching toward the foreground. But this apparent resurgence of masculine assertion is quickly qualified. The forward-thrusting line gives way to a circle formed by the men as they turn their backs to the camera, kneel, and face Blondell, who stands alone as she finishes the song. What the men kneel before is both the image of the unattainable woman, in the form of Blondell, and images of their own past glory, in the form of rifle-toting doughboys circling endlessly on a Sisyphean treadmill in the background.

"Remember My Forgotten Man" is the simplest and most straight-forward of Berkeley's big numbers in the classic Warner Bros. musicals. Its directness is a consequence of its political commitment. Its points are punched across for maximum impact, most forcefully by the jarring blackouts that drive home the number's thematic connection more viscerally and vigorously than even a direct cut might do. "Remember My Forgotten Man" is one of Hollywood's most hard-hitting political statements of the 1930s—much more so than the treatment of similar material in Warner Bros.'s *Heroes for Sale* (also 1933).

Fallen Men

One of Hollywood's earliest responses to the emasculating implications of the Crash was the "fallen woman" or "shady lady" cycle, represented by such films as *Morocco* (1930), *Tarnished Lady* (1931), *Susan Lenox: Her Fall and Rise* (1931), *Safe in Hell* (1931), *Blonde Venus* (1932), *Virtue* (1932), and (variations on the theme) *Shanghai Express* (1932) and *Back Street* (1932).

In the typical fallen woman story, the female star, as the result of some unfortunate circumstance (her husband is dying, her marriage was aborted, etc.), turns to prostitution (or a euphemistic equivalent such as dance-hall girl, cabaret singer, etc.). This moral detour often involves a journey south to an exotic tropical locale (equates to "Hell"). The hero eventually finds the heroine and self-righteously spurns her, until, through suffering and self-sacrifice, the fallen woman finally redeems herself in his eyes.

Andrew Bergman, identifying the fallen woman cycle in his book *We're in the Money*, interprets it as an evagination of the gangster film. Whereas gangster films are masculine power fantasies and inverted success stories, the fallen woman melodramas are "failure stories" that demonstrate women's dependence and weakness: "When forced to rely on themselves, the heroines find that only their bodies are marketable. Each picture made evident the fact that no woman could perform work functions not directly related to sex."[46]

Although Bergman's pinpointing of the fallen woman cycle is exemplary, his interpretation of it seems lopsided, perhaps as a result of reading the films too much in terms of plot summary rather than in terms of the way they play on a screen. Certainly, the stories have the heroines degraded and humbled, but in these films the male figures are usually played by bland and unemphatic actors (Donald Cook in *Safe in Hell*, John Boles in *Back Street*), or they are pigheaded and unreasonable (Clark Gable in *Susan Lenox: Her Fall and Rise*, Pat O'Brien in *Virtue*) or old and weak (Herbert Marshall in *Blonde Venus*) or narcissistic and insular (Gary Cooper in *Morocco*).

The heroine, on the other hand, is usually played by a powerful, vibrant, and intensely sympathetic star such as Garbo or Dietrich or Bankhead. Her character suffers from being misunderstood and unjustly tormented by a male-dominated society (these films are chock-full of unsympathetic lawmen, brutal fathers, loutish rapists, slimy seducers). In the final analysis, it is difficult to avoid feeling that this fallen woman towers high above the man of whom she is purportedly so unworthy. Not too far beneath the apparent antifeminism of the fallen woman cycle, one finds frantic distress signals of masculine self-confidence and an implicit indictment of patriarchal society, which, after all, had just laid a large egg called the Depression.

The "Remember My Forgotten Man" number is noteworthy because it makes explicit the implicit subtext of the fallen women films; it sets the record straight. Rather than countering a real fall (the Depression, male unemployment) with a compensatory, mythical fall (the moral status of women), it puts the "fall" back where it belongs. In "Remember My Forgotten Man," it is the men who have fallen—no doubt about it. Sullen, defeated, they skulk in doorways and soup kitchens or shuffle aimlessly down the Depression-blighted streets. Joan Blondell's costume and on-the-street position leave her profession suggestively ambiguous, but there is nothing fallen about her. It is the woman who dominates the song, supplies its voice, stands on the highest step, lights the cigarette, and subdues the club-wielding cop with a withering counterphallic stare.

Even more remarkably, "Remember My Forgotten Man" does not counter the figure of the fallen male with that of the castrating female (in the manner of, say, film noir), nor does it indulge in the sadomasochism of suffering and punishment that underlies the fallen woman cycle. The women in "Remember My Forgotten Man" regard their fallen men with nothing but sympathy and concern, on an equal footing. This is because they view their relationship not as dependent but interdependent. The status of one sex is directly—not inversely—proportional to that of the other: "'Cause ever since the world began, / A woman's got to have a man. / Forgetting him, you see, / Means you're forgetting me."

"Shanghai Lil": Her Fall and Rise

"Shanghai Lil," the finale of the next Berkeley/Warner Bros. musical, *Footlight Parade* (1933), continues the project of ideological rewriting begun in "Remember My Forgotten Man." The number starts out looking very much like a fallen woman melodrama (including an explicit reference in the title to *Shanghai Express*). Tuxedoed Bill (James Cagney), a U.S. Navy sailor who has jumped ship, is seen searching the dives and dens of Shanghai for the notorious Lil, about whom conflicting reports are heard ("That Chinese devil!" / "No, she's on the level."). However, it quickly becomes apparent that, like "Remember My Forgotten Man," this is more a fallen man than a fallen woman number. It begins with Bill literally falling onto the stage, and he is seen in a state of advanced dissolution owing to his inability to forget the errant Lil.

A thuggish sailor insults Lil's name ("She's every sailor's pal! She's anybody's gal!"). Bill slugs him. A free-for-all erupts. The cops raid the joint, and everyone clears out. Bill emerges from behind the bar, clad now in a sailor suit. Lil (an absurdly orientalized Ruby Keeler), in full joy-girl regalia, pops out of a trunk.

The plotty opening might lead one to expect a conventional plot pay-off—perhaps a Frankie-and-Johnnie crime of passion as in *Her Man* (1931), a self-sacrifice as in *Safe in Hell*, a repentance-and-forgiveness outcome as in *Blonde Venus*. Answer: none of the above. Instead, the entire fallen woman plot disappears, evaporates like a dream, along with all its baggage of self-pity, self-righteousness, sadomasochism, and misogyny.

Lil and Bill perform a tap dance on the bar. Suddenly, a bugle sounds. Bill runs outside and joins a parade of marching sailors, cheered by flag-waving spectators. Sailors and chorus-girl/spectators merge together and, in overhead shot, form designs of the U.S. flag, FDR's face, and the NRA eagle, guns firing from its flanks. Lil, now dressed in a sailor suit, joins Bill as he marches off to sea. He fans a deck of cards, which produces an animated image of a departing battleship.

The number moves toward the elimination of plot (the fallen woman melodrama) in favor of pure spectacle (the tap dance, the parade); it also moves in a direction that is progressively more action-oriented, more orderly, and more social. It progresses from (1) the opening scene in the bar (crowded surroundings, personal search, decadent atmosphere, backroom opium den stocked with stupefied blondes) to (2) the fistfight (chaotic action, group activity, masculine display) to (3) the tap dance (orderly action, expressing the union of the heterosexual couple) to (4) the parade (organized drill maneuvers, national symbols, soldiers with rifles).[47]

The overall structure of "Shanghai Lil" is not only linear but also reciprocal. It moves toward resolution, but it also moves toward balance. This balance is twofold: (1) a balance of the sexes, of Lil/Bill, and (2) a balance of the personal/sexual/emotional axis with the social/economic/ideological axis.

The number moves simultaneously in masculine and feminine directions. In their respective introductions, it is the man (Bill) who falls and the woman (Lil) who pops up in the time-honored fashion of the phallic surprise. The tap dancing initiated by Lil is answered by the parading initiated by Bill; he joins in her dance just as she joins in his parade, which alternates rows of marching men and women. The ideological space of military maneuvers and New Deal icons invades the personal space of Bill and Lil, just as Lil somewhat magically invades the ideological space of the Navy and the parade.

As in "Remember My Forgotten Man," sexual partnership is linked with full-fledged economic recovery and national cooperation. Once again, economic recovery is metaphorically equated with the urgency and collective spirit of war (along with a touch of nostalgic imperialism, perhaps harking back to the earlier President Roosevelt).[48] "Shanghai Lil" works toward a nonironic, reconciliatory juxtaposition of such potential contraries as dancing and marching, bedmates and bunkmates, fun and duty, the individual and the collective.

The True Berkeley Trademark

The theme of the individual's relationship to the collective is central to Berkeley's numbers (where it often takes the form of the relationship of the sexual to the social, as illustrated by the preceding discussions of "Remember My Forgotten Man" and "Shanghai Lil"). This theme is also central to New Deal doctrine and to 1930s films in general. It is in the 1930s that the work of several leading American directors crystallizes along the thematic of the individual's integration into a larger entity—which can be national (Capra, DeMille), social (Curtiz, Vidor), professional (Hawks, Wellman), communal/familial (Ford, La Cava), etc.[49]

What makes Berkeley's work distinctive, then, is not this central theme, which is endemic to the 1930s and the early 1940s (at which point the ethos of New Deal cooperation slides into the ethos of wartime cooperation). Nor is it simply his use of specific stylistic devices, such as crane shots or kaleidoscopic overhead shots (the latter are commonly found in several pre-Berkeley movie musicals of the 1929–30 period: *The Hollywood Revue of 1929, Cocoanuts, King of Jazz*, etc.). The true Berkeley trademark is found in the ever-shifting fluidity with which he orchestrates the individual/collective relationship and the ecstatic possibilities that his numbers find in that relationship.

Critiques of Berkeley commonly characterize him as the master of dehumanization, mechanization, and impersonality—a naive abstractionist who reduces human beings to nuts and bolts, mere decorative pieces in a larger formal design.[50] Such interpretations seem incomplete when one takes a closer and more comprehensive look at Berkeley's numbers themselves, which usually develop a much more complex and fluid interplay between the individual and the mass.

The structure of a Berkeley number typically follows this pattern: first, the individual or couple is established. Then the number opens up, and the individual is absorbed into the mass, woven in and out of it, sometimes lost completely (although only momentarily). Finally, the individual returns, intact, but somehow redefined by the experience of having been dissolved into the group.

In Berkeley's numbers, the experience of losing oneself in the group, in the big ensemble, is presented as primarily ecstatic. It is a moment of transcendence and sublimation, analogous to orgasm, but erupting beyond the confines of the ego to fuse self and society, sexuality and politics, emotion and ideology.

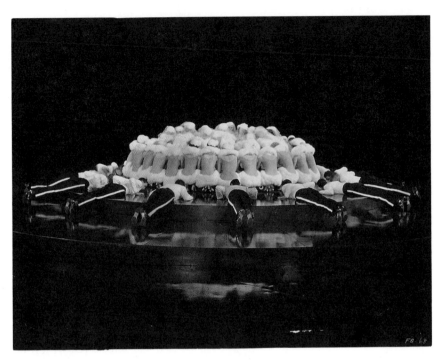

The individual disappears into the mass: the "Young and Healthy" number from 42nd Street *(Bacon/Berkeley, 1933). Photo courtesy of Warner Bros.*

Ev'rything Gets Hazy

One of the methods by which Berkeley evokes this feeling of ecstasy is a distinctive sleight-of-camera that whisks the spectator through a series of ontological and perceptual shifts—shifts of scale, location, tone, matter, image-status, etc. An especially dense example occurs near the end of "I Only Have Eyes for You" (*Dames* [1934]). This section climaxes in a series of astonishing transitions that represent Berkeley's most sustained exercise in controlled disorientation—an orgy of paradox that juggles scales, perspectives, locations, and dimensions to a mind-boggling degree:

In extreme low angle, Ruby Keeler walks toward the camera and (via a glass floor) right over it. (*Shift of matter: one had assumed the floor was opaque.*)

The hem of her long white skirt passes over the camera, transforming the low-angle perspective to extreme high angle, with a sea of chorines seated in rows far below. *(Shift of location and perspective, accomplished with a concealed cut.)*

The chorines stand up, bend over, and lift up the backs of their skirts, to which are attached placards that together form a giant puzzle of Keeler's face. *(Shift of image-status, from live action to still photograph.)*

The camera cranes down into the giant face's right eye, which dilates like a camera lens to disgorge a life-size, live-action Ruby. *(Shift of scale and image-status.)*

Standing in a black space, Ruby walks forward, and the camera pulls back to reveal a circular gold frame around her and, below this frame, sixteen chorines seated in a row on an elongated couch. *(Shift of location.)*

The couch splits in two and slides out of the frame; the chorines form a vertical row beneath the gold frame and are transformed into its handle. *(Shift of matter.)*

An apparently giant-sized Ruby steps into the shot, takes hold of the handle, and turns the frame (now bearing her frozen likeness) to reveal a mirror on its other side, in which Powell and Keeler are seen asleep in the subway car. *(Shift of scale, location, image-status, and dream-to-reality.)* This segues into the low-key, poignant finale, in which Powell and Keeler wake up, discover themselves at the end of the subway line, and slowly cross a rainy, deserted trainyard.

In a sequence like this one, the effect is of space and matter dissolving and reforming so quickly and complexly that it becomes disorienting, dizzying, bedazzling. The mind spins; the world blurs; the line between self and other becomes less distinct.

My Name Is Ruby: For We Are Many

The extraordinary resonance of "I Only Have Eyes for You" serves as a reminder that, although the mode of large-scale spectacle is Berkeley's forte and the quality for which he is best known, his effectiveness is not limited to the spectacular mode. It is more accurate to see his style as being composed of a major key (spectacle, grandiosity, glitter) and a minor key (intimacy, banality, poignancy). One of the most distinctive elements of Berkeley's style is the ability to shift fluidly and even breathtakingly from the spectacular and large scale to the intimate and small scale. The latter qualities are often located in the bathetic and poignant codas of Berkeley's spectacular numbers—e.g., the ersatz bird's nest at the end of "By a Waterfall," the crudely animated ship in the finale of "Shanghai Lil," the rainy trainyard that closes "I Only Have Eyes for You," the neglected kitten near the end of "Lullaby of Broadway," etc.

No Berkeley number demonstrates this double-level principle more vividly than "I Only Have Eyes for You," in which the rich interplay of the personal and the spectacular, the intimate and the grandiose, the individual and the mass is explicitly inscribed in the very subject and design of the number. "I Only Have Eyes for You" sustains a fluid interplay between the central couple and the larger picture: the back-and-forth between the couple and the crowd around them in the opening section, the passing of song lyrics from Dick and Ruby to passersby as they walk down the crowded street, the disappearance and reappearance of the crowd each time Dick sings, "But they all disappear from view. . . ," and the continual reemergence of Ruby, in all her dubious glory, from a chorus of lookalikes.

Like Vidor at the end of *The Crowd*, Berkeley here deals with the idea of the individual disappearing into the crowd. However, the idea is given a special twist, because it is counterpointed by the idea of the crowd disappearing into the individual, into her or his subjectivity ("But they all disappear from view . . ."). This paradox is then extended by the notion that Ruby looks just like every other young woman, and yet she is also absolutely unique and alone in the world with her beloved (". . . And I only have eyes for you").

"I Only Have Eyes for You" is based on the following tautology: if you are like everybody in the crowd, then everybody in the crowd is like you. Should this be considered a loss of individuality or a kind of augmented super-individuality? Such questions and confusions also lie near the heart of New Deal America.

The New Deal Paradox

What we seek is balance in our economic system—balance between agriculture and industry, and balance between the wage earner, the employer and the consumer.[51]

The word that appears most frequently in the writings of New Deal theorists is "balance."[52]

The key word in the vocabulary of the Roosevelt Administration was "balance."[53]

There is a precarious balance at work in the New Deal's revision of American ideology. The New Deal's idealization of the individual's attachment to the group, its idea of losing and finding oneself in the mass, its appeal to militaristic analogies, its use of the requirements of the social whole as the ultimate standard of value—these and similar concepts indicate an authoritarian undertow that could easily lead to repressive conformism (analogous to that of the McCarthy era) and even to outright fascism.

Historians are fond of pointing out that Hitler and FDR took office within a few weeks of each other in 1933. Nazism, Italian Fascism, Stalinism, and New Dealism are commonly interpreted as manifestations of a worldwide movement toward nationalism, social planning, and the restriction of individualism.[54]

Fascistically inclined organizations and demagogues proliferated in the United States in the 1930s: the Khaki Shirts, Silver Shirts, Minute Men, Crusaders, American Nationalists, National Watchmen, Christian Front, German-American Bund, Father Coughlin, Gerald L. K. Smith, Art J. Smith, William Dudley Pelley, Fritz Kuhn, Gerald Winrod, etc. It was not unusual, especially in the last grim days of the Hoover administration, for public officials and popular magazines to call for martial law, homegrown dictatorship, an American Mussolini.[55] Sinclair Lewis's novel *It Can't Happen Here* (1935), describing a fascist takeover of America, was a national best-seller (as well as a widely seen stage production) in 1936.

But it did not happen here. The New Deal sought to avoid the more sinister consequences of collectivism and social planning by maintaining a balance between two sets of values: the traditional American values of individualism and the 1930s values of collectivism. As cultural historian Richard H. Pells points out, these two terms are essentially contradictory; Americans were being asked to "hold two opposing ideals in their minds at the same time."[56]

For a solution to this fundamental contradiction, political and social spokespersons of the 1930s often resorted to paradox. They took the position that the individual self, by submerging itself in the social whole and becoming more aware of values beyond the self, would undergo a transformation of identity that produced a new stronger self.[57] This is similar to the pattern in Berkeley musical numbers of (1) individual established, (2) individual absorbed into the mass, (3) individual emerges redefined.

Social writers of the period frequently envisioned an idealized reciprocity between self and society, a blurring of the distinction between them. In *A Planned Society* (1932), George Soule hypothesized that individuals were subject to both external (i.e., social, environmental) and internal (i.e., biological, psychological) compulsions, which, rather than being in conflict with each other, were bound together as inextricably as the two poles of a magnetic field.[58] Robert Lynd, in his 1939 book *Knowledge for What?*, sought to resolve the Marx vs. Freud antimony with the concept of "culture *in* personality, personality *in* culture."[59] John Dewey's concept of the "plasticity" of human personality, allowing for a mutual interchange between social influence and individual development, had been formulated in his 1922 book *Human Nature and Conduct* and continued to be tremendously influential in the 1930s, especially in the fields of education and psychology. For example, American psychologists such as Harry Stack Sullivan and Karen Horney (whose 1937 *The Neurotic Personality of Our Time* was one of the most popular psychology texts of the period) revised Freud to allow society a greater role in shaping the unconscious. Similar trends characterized the field of anthropology, in which best-selling works by Ruth Benedict and Margaret Mead (who were influenced by Dewey and fellow Columbia professor Franz Boas) stressed both social-cultural determinants *and* individuality.[60]

In the teeth of contradiction, many American writers, artists, and policymakers of the 1930s held to the basic ideas that (1) individual freedom is given up to strengthen it, and (2) the needs of private and public, individual and mass, would naturally merge and reflect each other.[61] These concepts are somewhat idealistic, mystical, and hazy. At the heart of New Deal America is a paradox, and at the heart of that paradox is the individualist/collectivist balance described above. It should be emphasized that this is essentially a balance rather than a synthesis. Two value systems are placed side by side, yoked together in a very steady balance without really coming together—unless one were to attempt to achieve synthesis by resorting to figures of ecstasy and blatant antirealism, as Berkeley's numbers do.

Berkeley in Context

The work of Busby Berkeley can be located in its cultural context, not in terms of identification with a single period or movement but in terms of a *slide* over a certain overlapping sequence of periods and movements.

Berkeley's work is the product of a theatrical background in spectacle-related stage forms dating back to the nineteenth century (the musical extravaganza, the three-ring circus, the Ziegfeldian revue, etc.) and in the 1920s Broadway musical theater where he first gained fame as a dance director.[62] Coming to Hollywood during the talkie conversion period, he attains maturity and reputation as a filmmaker during the 1933–35 advent of the New Deal. He carries a background of late nineteenth/early twentieth-century spectacularism, Roaring 1920s giddiness, and early talkies experimentalism into the ideological project of the early New Deal, whose individual/mass components his numbers seek to resolve on the levels of ecstasy, abstraction, and stylistic excess.

After 1935, however, Berkeley's ability to slide with the times becomes increasingly problematic. The reasons for his post-1935 decline are complex, including personal crises (alcoholism, unsuccessful marriages, a scandalous manslaughter trial), the musical genre's shift from the populist/spectacular Warner Bros. style to the elegant/moderate Astaire/Sandrich/RKO vogue, and Berkeley's career switch from Warner Bros. to M-G-M, a studio ill-suited to his particular talents.

One especially important factor is the disjunction of Berkeley's artistic temperament and his temporal matrix, an increasing difficulty in merging his personal concerns with those of his historical-cultural-ideological-generic context. In the later stages of his career, he often creates numbers that are either au courant but routine and constrained (e.g., "Otchichornya" in *Hollywood Hotel* [1937], "God's Country" in *Babes in Arms* [1939], "La Conga" in *Strike Up the Band* [1940]), or Berkeleyesque but out of touch with the mainstream of the genre (e.g., "All's Fair in Love and War" in *Gold Diggers of 1937* [1936], "I Got Rhythm" in *Girl Crazy* [1943], "Smoke" in *Million Dollar Mermaid* [1952]). Berkeley's most successfully achieved late project, *The Gang's All Here* (1943), is the happy result of his move to a more compatible studio (20th Century-Fox) at the peak of all-night-shift, bombs-away, jumping-jive, Latin-Manhattan wartime delirium.

Putting the Early 1930s to Sleep

The misleadingly titled *Gold Diggers of 1935* represents an abandonment of the relatively realistic, Depression-themed concerns of the cycle of Berkeley/Warner Bros. musicals initiated by *42nd Street*. In *Gold Diggers of 1935,* Berkeley (directing an entire musical for the first time) adopts a style of Sandrichian artificiality, with an emphasis on glitzy, syncopated surfaces and overall consistency of tone.

The "Lullaby of Broadway" number that climaxes the film moves in two apparently contradictory directions. Like the pattern-setting Warner Bros. crime film *G-Men* (also released in 1935), "Lullaby" can be read as a key turning point in its genre, a fulcrum that explicitly inscribes and announces the shift between the early 1930s and the late 1930s.[63]

In its opening scenes of working people on their way to work, "Lullaby of Broadway" harks back to the populist city-streets tradition that informed "42nd Street." Like *The Crowd,* "Lullaby" centers on the theme of the individual out of step with the crowd, but with this crucial difference: in the Bull Market context of *The Crowd,* it is the poor man, the failure, who is out of step with a world oriented (however misleadingly) toward success and individual achievement. In the New Deal context of "Lullaby," on the other hand, it is the high-living swell, the all-night-partier, who is out of step with the shoulder-to-shoulder working world.

While the rest of the world turns in for the night, Dick (Powell) and Wini (Shaw) start stepping out. After snoozing all day, they taxi to a nightclub that initially seems like a cathedral to late 1920s/early 1930s frenzy, feverishness, and excess—as conveyed by the number's vast set, vertiginous angles, stomping feet, and expressionist lighting.

As the number progresses, this excess turns back on itself. The very same elements—vast set, vertiginous angles, expressionist lighting—begin to seem empty, eerie, melancholy, nightmarish. The characteristically large chorus becomes oddly threatening, their stomping feet booming ominously through the cavernous nightclub, which takes on a haunted-house quality. Are Dick and Wini (the huge club's only customers, seated at its only table) the last two swells left on this Depression-battered Earth?

In Berkeley's most startling tone shift, Wini, at the height of her gaiety, plunges off a high balcony. The street below spins, rushes upward, and goes out of focus. This is Berkeley's ultimate kaleidoscopic overhead shot—the eye at the heart of his numbers' ecstatic maelstrom—and it is revealed here to be a void, *la grande mort,* the blur to end all blurs, resolving itself into the mortality-laden image of a spinning clock dial.

"Lullaby of Broadway" is an implicit rejection of late 1920s/early 1930s excess and destabilization, of which Berkeley himself was a key image-maker. "Lullaby" is also a repudiation (albeit an ambivalent one) of hypertrophic individualism. This theme is signaled by the framing shots of Wini's face filling the screen and receding into nothingness, and it is developed in the body of the number by the central opposition between the hedonistic couple and the hard-working crowd.

It is possible to propose a second reading of "Lullaby of Broadway." In this one, what is at issue is not the recent past but the imminent future represented by the ascendent RKO and M-G-M forms of the musical film. In this reading, Dick and Wini become avatars of the debonair Fred and Ginger. The vast nightclub set (atypically deco for Warner Bros.) is Van Nest Polglase with a hangover. The big dance number is "The Continental" gone gothic. Like Berkeley's own career at Warner Bros., "Lullaby of Broadway" moves from populist cityscape (*42nd Street*) to Sandrichian glitz (*Gold Diggers of 1935*)—that is, to the less explicitly social, more polished, and more luxurious world of the Astaire-era musical film.

These two readings appear to contradict each other, but it is not necessary, in either art or ideology, to resolve contradictions. In fact, such a double-edged reading reflects Berkeley's own ambivalent position at this critical juncture in his career. On the one hand, "Lullaby of Broadway" expresses an exhaustion of the pre-New Deal extravagances and early New Deal tensions that came together to nurture the classic Berkeley/Warner Bros. musicals. On the other hand, it expresses a disinclination toward new idioms that signal a resolution (or, perhaps more accurately, a realignment) of those tensions. The uncertainties expressed in "Lullaby of Broadway" mirror those of an artist whose personal concerns are beginning to go out of synch with those of his times. Berkeley's "slide" was coming to an end, but not before he had spun an impressive web of dreams out of the slippery threads of American culture and ideology in the 1930s.

Coda: Singin' in the Waterfall

In the slippery, hyperfluid world of Berkeley's musical numbers, water is a key recurrent image, functioning as an appropriate medium for the emphasis on ecstasy, dissolution of self, and shifting protean forms. A few examples are the rainstorm in "Pettin' in the Park" (*Gold Diggers of 1933*), the rainy trainyard at the end of "I Only Have Eyes for You," the rippling pond in "The Words Are in My Heart" (*Gold Diggers of 1935*), the spray-filled "Fountain" number in *Million Dollar Mermaid* (1952), and the streams, cascades, pools, and fountains of Berkeley's most elaborate water spectacle, "By a Waterfall" (*Footlight Parade*).

It is instructive to compare "By a Waterfall" (and Berkeley's general treatment of the individual/mass relationship) with the "Singin' in the Rain" number from Kelly and Donen's celebrated 1952 musical. Both numbers play on some of the same basic elements: water, ecstasy, high-angle shots. But in terms of the individual/mass thematic, these elements are parlayed to form complementary opposites.

"By a Waterfall" is primarily about getting outside of oneself. "Singin' in the Rain" is about getting into oneself. In "Singin' in the Rain," ecstasy is found inside oneself, in contradiction to the rainy world outside, with Gene Kelly luxuriating in personal gratification to the point of infantile regression. In "By a Waterfall," ecstasy is found outside oneself, in the temporary loss of individuality, with Ruby Keeler being woven in and out of the elaborate settings, the mass of gamboling water nymphs, and the intensely abstract overhead patterns that seem to reduce Ruby and the other nymphs to elemental cellular forms. In "Waterfall" (as in other of Berkeley's socially oriented numbers), the self is redefined in terms of the outer world. In "Singin'" (as in other of Kelly and Donen's mood pieces and exuberant outbursts), the outer world is redefined in terms of the self (It's raining outside? So what? Who cares? *I'm* happy!).

The high-angle shots in "Singin'" have a double-edged function: they serve both as an expression of Kelly's soaring ecstasy and as a benignly ironic comment on its excesses. There is little room for irony in Berkeley's numbers. Excess and paradox are usually transcended not with irony but with more excess—excess extended until it crystallizes into abstract transpersonal forms and then dissolves back again.

The differences between "By a Waterfall" and "Singin' in the Rain" are the differences between not only two styles but two eras. The New Deal balance of the individual and the collective is, by 1952 (the last year of the 20-year Democratic presidency), breaking down into the poles of innerdirection/solipsism on the one hand and conformity/repression on the other. Balance has given way to tension.

NOTES

1. Raymond Fielding, *The American Newsreel, 1911–1967* (Norman: University of Oklahoma Press, 1972), pp. 161–62; Alexander Walker, *The Shattered Silents* (New York: William Morrow, 1979), p. 26.

2. For a classic interpretation of the Lindbergh myth, see John William Ward, "The Meaning of Lindbergh's Flight" (1958), reprinted in Hennig Cohen, ed., *The American Culture: Approaches to the Study of the United States* (Boston: Houghton Mifflin, 1968), pp. 18–29.

3. Edgar Morin characterizes 1920–30 as the era of "great archetypes," after which movie-star images became progressively more realistic and psychological—*The Stars,* trans. Richard Howard (New York: Grove Press, 1961), pp. 12–17. Similar observations can be found in a number of sources, including Richard Dyer, *Stars* (London: BFI Publishing, 1982), pp. 24–25; Alexander Walker, *Stardom: The Hollywood Phenomenon* (New York: Stein and Day, 1970), pp. 235–39; and Godard and Gorin's film-essay, *Letter to Jane* (1972).

4. For similar interpretations of Harold Lloyd and his relationship to the other members of silent comedy's "Big Three," see John Belton, *Cinema Stylists* (Metuchen, N.J.: Scarecrow Press, 1983), pp. 313, 318–19; Len Borger, "Harold Lloyd: The Comic Persona of the All-American Boy," in Adam Reilly, ed., *Harold Lloyd: The King of Daredevil Comedy* (New York: Collier, 1977), p. 184; Walter Kerr, *The Silent Clowns* (New York: Knopf, 1979), pp. 190–91; Andrew Sarris, "Harold Lloyd: A Rediscovery," in Reilly, p. 164.

5. At a low point in John's fortunes, an intertitle reads, "We do not know how big the crowd is, and what opposition it is. . . until we get out of step with it."

6. Raymond Durgnat, "King Vidor," *Film Comment* 9 (July–August 1973), 15–16.

7. Frederick Lewis Allen, *Since Yesterday* (New York: Harper & Brothers, 1940; reprint, New York: Bantam, 1965), pp. 23, 43; Merle Curti, *The Growth of American Thought* (New York: Harper & Brothers, 1943), p. 717; Robert S. Lynd and Helen Merrell Lynd, *Middletown in Transition* (New York: Harcourt, Brace, 1937), p. 16; Richard H. Pells, *Radical Visions and American Dreams* (New York: Harper Torchbooks, 1974), pp. 43–46; Harris Gaylord Warren, *Herbert Hoover and the Great Depression* (New York: W. W. Norton, 1967), p. 133.

8. This is somewhat similar to the phenomenon of cultural persistence noted by William Fielding Ogburn in his influential book *Social Change* (New York: B. W. Huebsch, 1922; reprint, New York: Viking Press, 1938): "The same cultural form or activity may serve different psychological needs at different times" (pp. 157–58).

9. An early forum for these voices of disillusionment was provided by *Civilization in the United States: An Inquiry by 30 Americans* (ed. Harold Stearns, NY: Harcourt, 1922), a collection of essays by thirty authors (including Van Wyck Brooks, H. L. Mencken, and Lewis Mumford) decrying the spiritual impoverishment of modern America.

10. See Frederick J. Hoffman, *The Twenties: American Writing in the Postwar Decade,* rev. ed. (New York: Collier Books, 1962), pp. 115–43, 344–77.

11. For a general overview of these fields, see Robert M. Crunden, *From Self to Society, 1919–1941* (Englewood Cliffs, N.J.: Prentice-Hall, 1972).

12. The American pattern-setter for such pessimistic prognoses of progress was *The Education of Henry Adams,* which, after a small private printing in 1907, received its first public edition in 1918 and reached a peak of influence in the 1920s. Hoffman, *The Twenties,* p. 285; Roderick Nash, *The Nervous Generation: American Thought, 1917–1930* (Chicago: Rand McNally, 1970), p. 42; Pells, *Radical Visions,* p. 27.

13. For a concise summary of this trend, see Nash, *The Nervous Generation,* pp. 55–67.

14. Robert S. Lynd and Helen Merrell Lynd, *Middletown* (New York: Harcourt, Brace & World, 1929), pp. 53–89, 272–312. A classic fictional anticipation of the Lynds' findings is Sinclair Lewis's *Babbitt* (1922): "He beheld, and half admitted that he beheld, his way of life as incredibly mechanical. Mechanical business—a brisk selling of badly built houses. Mechanical religion—a dry, hard church, shut off from the real life of the streets,

inhumanly respectable as a tin hat. Mechanical golf and dinner parties and bridge and conversation" (New York: Signet, 1964), p. 190.

15. The Berkeley/Warner Bros. musicals are usually set in a working-class urban environment, as opposed to the Ruritanian operetta, the college musical, the shipboard/high-society musical, etc.

16. Franklin D. Roosevelt was the first major American political figure to use the power of radio on a wide scale, as demonstrated by the effectiveness of his "fireside chats."

17. Quoted in Arthur A. Ekrich, Jr., *Ideologies and Utopias* (Chicago: Quadrangle Books, 1971), p. 64. Similar sentiments about individualism can also be found in Adolf A. Berle, Jr., and Gardner C. Means, *The Modern Corporation and Private Property* (New York: Macmillan, 1931; reprint, 1948), p. 349; John Dewey, *The Public and Its Problems* (New York: Henry Holt, 1927), pp. 115–16; Harold J. Laski, *Democracy in Crisis* (Chapel Hill: University of North Carolina Press, 1935), pp. 46–47; Robert S. Lynd, *Knowledge for What?: The Place of Social Science in American Culture* (Princeton: Princeton University Press, 1939), pp. 22–23, 214–15; George Soule, *A Planned Society* (New York: Macmillan, 1932), p. 182.

18. For a discussion of the extent to which the principles of laissez-faire capitalism were raised to a quasi-religious level in the 1920s, see Charles R. Hearn, *The American Dream in the Great Depression* (Westport, Conn.: Greenwood Press, 1977), pp. 24–28.

19. Quoted in Arthur M. Schlesinger, Jr., *The Crisis of the Old Order* (Boston: Houghton Mifflin, 1957), p. 142.

20. Ibid., p. 143.

21. Although Frederick Jackson Turner's seminal paper, "The Significance of the Frontier in America History," was written in 1893, the ideas of this influential but sparsely published historian received much wider circulation with the publications of his essay collections, *The Frontier in American History* (1920) and *The Significance of Sections in American History* (1932).

22. John Dewey, *Individualism—Old and New* (New York: G. B. Putnam's Sons, 1930; reprint, New York: Capricorn Books, 1962), p. 36. Dewey's book was substantially expanded from a serialized version that had originally appeared in *The New Republic* in 1929.

23. Charles A. Beard, "The Myth of Rugged American Individualism" (1931), reprinted in Howard Zinn, ed., *New Deal Thought* (Indianapolis: Bobbs-Merrill, 1966), p. 10.

24. Stuart Chase, *A New Deal* (New York: Macmillan, 1932), p. 66. Myths die hard, and the Depression itself was ironically responsible for the biggest revival of the frontier myth since the nineteenth century. Two of the best-known chronicles of this new westward trek are John Steinbeck's novel *The Grapes of Wrath* (1939) and Dorothea Lange and Paul Schuster Taylor's photo/textbook *An American Exodus* (1939), whose cover photo depicts a furniture-laden westbound truck with the caption, "Covered Wagon— 1939 Style."

25. These excerpts are from the "Commonwealth Club" speech of September 23, 1932; *The Public Papers and Addresses of Franklin D. Roosevelt*, 1 (New York: Random House, 1938), pp. 746, 750. In contrast, Roosevelt's predecessor, Herbert Hoover, had declared in the final chapter of his 1922 book *American Individualism*, "There will always be a frontier . . . . The days of the pioneer are not over" (quoted in Nash, *The Nervous Generation*, p. 133).

26. This terminological ambiguity was noted by Chase in *A New Deal*, p. 32; by John Dewey in his 1935 article "The Future of Liberalism" (reprinted in Zinn, *New Deal Thought*), p. 31; and, more recently, by Robert S. McElvaine in his excellent historical overview, *The Great Depression* (New York: Times Books, 1984), pp. 198–202. McElvaine uses the terms *acquisitive individualism* and *cooperative or ethical individualism* in roughly the same way I use *individualism* and *individuality*, respectively.

27. See William F. Ogburn, "Cultural Lag as Theory" (1957) in Otis Dudley, ed., *On Culture and Social Change: Selected Papers* (Chicago: University of Chicago Press, 1964), pp. 86–95; and Ogburn, *Social Change*, pp. 200ff. The phrase *cultural lag* was found in many of the works of the 1920s and 1930s that were sampled for this article, including Stuart Chase, *Government in Business*, (New York: Macmillan, 1935), p. 21; Chase, *A New Deal*, pp. 1, 46; Lewis Corey, *The Decline of American Capitalism* (New York: Covici-Friede, 1934), p. 517; Dewey, *The Public and Its Problems*, p. 114; Lynd, *Knowledge for What?*, pp. 116, 209; Soule, *A Planned Society*, p. 152.

28. Dewey, *Individualism—Old and New*, p. 33.

29. As Roosevelt said in the "Commonwealth Club" speech, "The Government . . . must intervene, not to destroy individualism, but to protect it" (*Public Papers*, 1, p. 746).

30. Charles C. Alexander, *Nationalism in American Thought, 1930–1945* (Chicago: Rand McNally, 1969), pp. 5–7; Chase, *Government in Business*, pp. 3–5; Chase, *A New Deal*, pp. 47–65, 153–54; Curti, *Growth of American Thought*, p. 732; Stuart Kidd, "Collectivist Intellectuals and the Ideal of National Economic Planning, 1929–33," in Stephen W. Baskerville and Ralph Willett, eds., *Nothing Else to Fear: New Perspectives on America in the Thirties* (Manchester, England: Manchester University Press, 1985), pp. 18–27; Lynd, *Knowledge for What?*, pp. 66, 209–17; Robert M. MacIver, "Social Philosophy" (1934), reprinted in Zinn, *New Deal Thought*, p. 59; Warren I. Susman, *Culture as History* (New York: Pantheon, 1984), pp. 172–74; Henry A. Wallace, "America Considers Its Constitution" (1936), reprinted in Zinn, *New Deal Thought*, p. 74.

31. Richard Hofstadter, *The Age of Reform: From Bryan to F.D.R.* (New York: Vintage Books, 1955), pp. 310–13. Hofstadter notes that the New Dealers were equally tolerant of another progressive bête noire: the political machine.

32. This is a major distinction between turn-of-the-century/Wilsonian progressivism (which sought to counter the trend toward increasing aggregation in American society) and the New Deal (which was more inclined to accept the trend and make use of it)—see Hofstadter, *Age of Reform*, pp. 215–17, 224–27, 259–60, 315. This general attitude continued to prevail even when the New Deal turned from the government-sponsored cartelization of the NRA to the trust-busting initiatives of the late 1930s. See Alan Brinkley, "The New Deal and the Idea of the State," in Steve Fraser and Gary Gerstle, eds., *The Rise and Fall of the New Deal Order, 1930–1980* (Princeton, N.J.: Princeton University Press, 1989), pp. 89–91.

33. John A. Garraty, *The Great Depression* (Garden City, N.Y.: Anchor Books, 1987), pp. 140–45; Hofstadter, *Age of Reform*, p. 313; Zinn, *New Deal Thought*, pp. xxxii–xxxiii. Some points in this paragraph merit qualification: (1) although organized labor made unprecedented strides during the New Deal years, FDR's support was somewhat belated and reluctant—see William E. Leuchtenburg, *Franklin D. Roosevelt and the New Deal* (New York: Harper & Row, 1963), p. 108; McElvaine, *The Great Depression*, p. 258. (2) Although Theodore Roosevelt's trust-busting policies were highly publicized, his administration's enforcement of such policies was actually limited and selective—see Sidney Fine, *Laissez Faire and the General-Welfare State* (Ann Arbor: University of Michigan Press, 1956), pp. 387–90; Hofstadter, *Age of Reform*, pp. 246–47, 252–53. (3) After dragging its heels for five years, the FDR administration began to pursue a more aggressive antitrust policy in 1938.

34. Allen, *Since Yesterday*, pp. 191–92; McElvaine, *The Great Depression*, pp. 55–60, 64, 69–70, 275–76; Schlesinger, *Crisis of the Old Order*, pp. 170, 246; Warren, *Herbert Hoover*, pp. 67, 77–78, 114, 256, 264–65.

35. Ekrich, *Ideologies and Utopias*, p. 101.

36. As many historians have noted, the programs of the New Deal were often much more limited in their scope and accomplishments than their reputations warranted; the New Deal was less a coherent ideology than a patchwork of compromises, experiments,

and watered-down policies; and FDR's personal political philosophy was inherently much more conservative than the implications, real or symbolic, of the New Deal as it developed. Nevertheless, the New Deal was widely viewed at the time as representing a major shift in American life; people, whether Columbia professors or dispossessed farmers, saw themselves as being in the midst of an era of great social change. And such perceptions were not completely unsubstantiated: the New Deal introduced class issues into American politics to an unprecedented degree, laid the groundwork for a major reconception of government regulation and intervention, established federal responsibility for public welfare, and advanced the transition to a consumption-based economy. Alexander, *Nationalism*, pp. 1–5; Anthony J. Badger, *The New Deal: The Depression Years, 1933–40* (New York: Farrar, Straus & Giroux, 1989), pp. 3, 299–312; Brinkley, "The New Deal," pp. 86, 93–94; Morton J. Frisch, "An Appraisal of Roosevelt's Legacy: How the Moderate Welfare State Transcended the Tension between Progressivism and Socialism," in Robert Eden, ed., *The New Deal and Its Legacy: Critique and Reappraisal* (New York: Greenwood Press, 1989), pp. 190–98; Hofstadter, *Age of Reform*, pp. 302–5, 307, 317, 325; Leuchtenburg, *Franklin D. Roosevelt*, pp. 326–36; McElvaine, *The Great Depression*, pp. 30, 134, 282; MacIver, "Social Philosophy," pp. 57–59; George Soule, *The Coming American Revolution* (New York: Macmillan, 1934), p. 198; Susman, *Culture as History*, p. 159; John Tipple, *Crisis of the American Dream: A History of American Social Thought 1920–1940* (New York: Pegasus, 1968), pp. 171–76.

37. To avoid overstatement, it should be noted that this fondly recalled wartime economy was not immune in its day to criticism for shortages, corruption, and inefficiency. See Soule, *A Planned Society*, pp. 184–85.

38. Schlesinger, *Crisis of the Old Order*, p. 195.

39. Chase, *Government in Business*, pp. 3–4; Stuart Chase, *The Nemesis of American Business* (New York: Macmillan, 1931), p. 177; Chase, *A New Deal*, pp. 84, 151; Ekrich, *Ideologies and Utopias*, p. 52; Garraty, *The Great Depression*, p. 149; William E. Leuchtenburg, "The New Deal and the Analogue of War," in John Braeman, Robert H. Bremner, and Everett Walters, eds., *Change and Continuity in Twentieth Century America*, vol. 3 (Columbus: Ohio State University Press, 1964), pp. 81–143; McElvaine, *The Great Depression*, p. 89; Soule, *A Planned Society*, pp. 184–203, 231, 271; Warren, *Herbert Hoover*, pp. 141–42.

40. Ekrich, *Ideologies and Utopias*, p. 92.

41. Garraty, *The Great Depression*, pp. 189, 203; McElvaine, *The Great Depression*, pp. 154, 159–160.

42. *Public Papers*, 1, p. 632.

43. Garraty, *The Great Depression*, p. 205; *Public Papers*, 2, p. 15. Walter Lippmann was one of the most prominent figures to question these martial analogies, arguing that measures suitable to the temporary exigencies of wartime could easily lead to despotism when extended to peacetime. "Planning in an Economy of Abundance" (1937), reprinted in Zinn, *New Deal Thought*, pp. 95–102.

44. *Public Papers*, 1, p. 625.

45. For another example of this theme, see Edmund Wilson, *The Thirties: From Notebooks and Diaries of the Period* (New York: Farrar, Straus & Giroux, 1980): "Ideas of impotence were very much in people's minds at this period—on account of the Depression, I think, the difficulty of getting things going" (Entry entitled "New York, 53rd Street, 1932–33," p. 303).

46. Andrew Bergman, *We're in the Money* (New York: Harper Colophon Books, 1972), p. 52.

47. One could also read this progression allegorically as a historical sequence, from (1) the luxury, excess, and decadence of the 1920s, to (2) the chaotic rough-house of the

immediate post-Crash period, to (4) the organized national purpose of the New Deal, with (3) the rise of the musical film inserted in a strategic position between (2) and (4).

48. Meaning Teddy, of course—TR's flexing of national muscle in the round-the-world naval tour of 1908–09 (intended primarily to intimidate the Japanese) is especially relevant here. The mixing of the current President Roosevelt with naval motifs in "Shanghai Lil" also evokes FDR's World War I service as Assistant Secretary of the Navy (a post earlier held by TR).

49. There are certainly major directors of the period who do not fit so neatly into this thematic, such as romantics whose work is more couple-oriented (Borzage, McCarey, Stahl, Stevens) and acknowledged against-the-grain directors whose work derives much of its identity as an alternative to the norm (e.g., Sternberg and Lubitsch, who form a kind of exotic/Continental counterpoint to the mainstream of the 1930s).

50. See, for example, Lucy Fischer, "The Image of Woman as Image: The Optical Politics of *Dames,*" *Film Quarterly* 30 (Fall 1976), pp. 4–5; John Lahr, "On-Stage," *Village Voice* (December 18, 1969); Gerald Mast, *Can't Help Singin': The American Musical on Stage and Screen* (Woodstock, N.Y.: Overlook Press, 1987), pp. 133–34; Pells, *Radical Visions,* p. 282.

51. *Public Papers,* 3, p. 125.

52. Leuchtenburg, *Franklin D. Roosevelt,* p. 35.

53. Pells, *Radical Visions,* p. 79.

54. Garraty, *The Great Depression,* pp. 183, 192, 207; Hofstadter, *Age of Reform,* p. 327; Soule, *The Coming American Revolution,* p. 199.

55. Curti, *Growth of American Thought,* p. 735; Garraty, *The Great Depression,* pp. 210–11; Leuchtenburg, *Franklin D. Roosevelt,* p. 276; McElvaine, *The Great Depression,* pp. 161, 237, 240; Schlesinger, *Crisis of the Old Order,* p. 268; Soule, *The Coming American Revolution,* pp. 293–95.

56. Pells, *Radical Visions,* p. 150.

57. Crunden, *From Self to Society,* p. 80; Ekrich, *Ideologies and Utopias,* p. 113; Pells, *Radical Visions,* p. 113–14. These ideas were anticipated by the concept of "social democracy," espoused in the 1920s by intellectuals such as the biologist Edward Grant Conklin and the philosopher/educator John Dewey and by Populist/Progressive politicians such as Robert La Follette and George W. Norris. See Nash, *The Nervous Generation,* pp. 63–67.

58. Soule, *A Planned Society,* pp. 90–91.

59. Lynd, *Knowledge for What?,* pp. 21–25, 37–41, 51–53, 152–54; Pells, *Radical Visions,* p. 122.

60. Crunden, *From Self to Society,* pp. 6–13, 42–45, 126–31; Lynd, *Knowledge for What?,* p. 162; Pells, *Radical Visions,* p. 114, 120; Susman, *Culture as History,* p. 166; Don M. Wolfe, *The Image of Man in America* (New York: McGraw-Hill, 1963), pp. 307–16.

61. Berle and Means, *The Modern Corporation,* p. 357; Curti, *Growth of American Thought,* p. 736; Fine, *Laissez Faire,* p. 396; John Tipple, *Crisis of the American Dream: A History of American Social Thought 1920–1940* (New York: Pegasus, 1968), p. 170. The latter half of this proposition seems a throwback to the traditional laissez-faire concept of private self-interest inevitably coinciding with the public interest, except that the horse/cart positions of private and public have been reversed.

62. For a more detailed discussion of this aspect of Berkeley's work, see Martin Rubin, *Showstoppers: Busby Berkeley and the Tradition of Spectacle* (New York: Columbia University Press, 1993).

63. In *We're in the Money* (pp. 83–88), Andrew Bergman provides an excellent account of how *G-Men* functions in these terms by spearheading the transition from criminal-centered crime films to crimebuster-centered crime films.

The Regulation of Desire:
From Mass Consumption
to Mass Morality

Charles Eckert

The Carole Lombard in Macy's Window

I

In the last quarter of the nineteenth century, American business was preoccupied with production. Most of its energy went into expanding its physical plant, increasing efficiency, and grinding the face of labor so that greater profits could be extracted and invested in production. In the last five years of the nineteenth century when, coincidentally, motion pictures were invented, American business discovered that it was up to its neck in manufactured goods for which there were no buyers. So it became sales minded. Through the first two decades of this century, sales techniques were developed so intensely that they produced gross excesses, alienating the public and giving impetus to antibusiness and antimaterialist attitudes among intellectuals. About 1915, fixation on sales gave way to an obsession with management, to internal restructuring and systemization. Profits were decisively improved, but the contradiction between production and consumption, between the efficient manufacture and marketing of goods and the capacity of wage-poor workers to buy them, was no closer to solution. Therefore, throughout the 1920s business became consumer-minded.

While American business was going through this process of what a Jungian would call differentiation, evolving from an oral stage in which it was given to eating its young into a rational Apollonian stage in which

Reprinted, with permission, from the *Quarterly Review of Film Studies* 3:1 (Winter 1978).

it stopped thinking of workers as schmoos and began thinking of them as a sort of chicken-lickin', a synthetic substance to be fed with one hand and sliced with the other—while all this was going forward, Hollywood had evolved from a nickel-and-dime business to an entertainment industry funded by the likes of AT&T, Hayden Stone, Dillon Reid, RCA, The House of Morgan, A. P. Giannini's Bank of America, the Rockefellers' Chase National Bank, Goldman Sachs, Lohoran Brothers, Halsey Stuart—in short, all the major banks and investment houses and several of the largest corporations in America. With the representatives of those several economic powers sitting on the directorates of the studio and with the world of business pervaded by the new zeitgeist of consumerism, the conditions were right for Hollywood to assume a role in the phase of capitalism's life history that the emerging philosophy of consumerism was about to give birth to.

All of which brings me to a story, a sort of romance, which I shall begin, as all good storytellers used to, in Medias Res.

II

Awakened by the brakes of the train, Bette Davis pulled aside a window curtain. Beneath a winter moon, the Kansas plains lay gray with late winter snow. The mail clerk glimpsed Bette's face but was too astounded by the pullman car itself to recognize his favorite star. The pullman was totally covered with gold leaf. The rest of the train was brilliantly silvered. From one car, a tall radio aerial emerged mysteriously. Lost in his wonder, the clerk barely noticed that the train was underway again. He would later tell his children about the train with the golden pullman, perhaps fashioned for some Western gold baron, or for a Croesus from a foreign land. But he would never know that the interior of the train held greater wonders still.

As the cars gathered speed, other passengers shifted in their sleep, among them Laura La Plante, Preston Foster, and numerous blond women with muscular legs (was one of them the supernal Toby Wing?). In an adjacent lounge car, Claire Dodd, Lyle Talbot, and Tom Mix were still awake, attending to a reminiscing Leo Carillo. In still another car, a scene as surrealistic as a Dali floated through the Kansas night. Glenda Farrell lay in her Jantzen swimsuit on a miniature Malibu Beach beneath a manufactured California sky made up of banks of General Electric (GE) ultraviolet lamps. The sand on the beach was genuine sand. Everything else was unreal.

The next to the last car held no human occupants. The hum, barely discernable above the clack of the rails, emerged from the GE Monitor-to-refrigerator positioned next to the GE all-electric range. When one grew accustomed to the dark, one saw that this was merely a demonstration kitchen lifted bodily, it seemed, from Macy's or Gimbels, and compressed into the oblong confines of a railway diner. In the last car was a magnificent white horse. An embroidered saddle blanket draped over a rail beside him bore the name "King." The horse was asleep.

The occasion that had gathered this congeries of actresses and appliances, cowboys and miniaturized Malibus, into one passenger train and positioned them in mid-Kansas on a night in February 1933 was the inauguration of Franklin Delano Roosevelt. If the logic of this escapes you, you simply must make the acquaintance of Charles Einfeld, sales manager for Warner Bros.

Charles Einfeld was a dreamer. But unlike yours and mine, his dreams always came true. Charles Einfeld dreamed (and it came true) that Warner's new musical, *42nd Street,* would open in New York on the eve of Roosevelt's inauguration, that the stars of the picture (with other contract stars, if possible) would journey to New York on a train to be called the Better Times Special, and that they would then go to Washington for the inauguration itself. The film, after all, was a boost for the New Deal philosophy of pulling together to whip the depression, and its star, Warner Baxter, played a role that was a patent allegory of F. D. R. Einfeld then sought a tie-up with a large concern that would share the expenses of the train in exchange for a quantity of egregious advertising. GE, already linked with Warner as a supplier of appliances for movie props, rose to the bait.

The gold and silver train was given a definitive name: The Warner-GE Better Times Special. As it crossed North America from Los Angeles to New York, its radio broadcasted Dick Powell's jazzy contralto, GE ad copy, and optimism (GE, as the parent organization of RCA and NBC, was in a position to facilitate hook-ups with local stations). When the train arrived at a major city, the stars and chorus girls motored to the largest available GE showroom and demonstrated whatever appliances they found themselves thrust up against. In the evenings, they appeared at a key theater for a minipremiere. Their *Ultima Thule* was, of course, *42nd Street.*

On March 9, bawdy, gaudy 42nd Street looked as spiffy as a drunkard in church: American flags and red, white, and blue bunting draped the buildings; the ordinary incandescent bulbs were replaced with scintillant "golden" GE lamps; a fleet of Chrysler automobiles (a separate tie-up) and GE automotive equipment was readied for a late afternoon parade that would catch those leaving work. In the North River, a cruiser stood at anchor to fire a salute—a great organ-boom to cap off a roulade of aerial bombs. As the train approached New York from New Rochelle, a pride of small airplanes accompanied it. Once it arrived, the schedule was as exacting as a coronation: a reception at Grand Central by the Forty-Second Street Property Owners and Merchants Association, the parade, a GE sales meeting at the Sam Harris Theatre, and the grand premiere at the Strand.

This stunning synthesis of film, electrical, real estate and transportation exploitation, partisan patrio-politics, and flecked-at-the-mouth starmania did not lurch fully armed from the head of Charles Einfeld, splendid dreamer though he was. It can only be explained in terms of the almost incestuous hegemony that characterized Hollywood's relations with vast reaches of the American economy by the mid-1930s. Like most tales of incest, this one ends badly. By 1950 Hollywood had taken to looking its lover in the neck; the passions of the mid-1930s had become savourless habits. But that is the end of the story. In the beginning, Hollywood was younger than Andy Hardy and the world of industry lived just next door.

When the first movie cameraman shot the first street scene that included a shop sign or a labeled product (Lumiere? 1895?), all the elements of a new advertising form were implicit: a captive audience unlikely to ignore what was placed before it, a manufacturer, a filmmaker, and the Platonic idea of Charles Einfeld. The short dramas and comedies of the first decade of this century, especially those that pictured the contemporary lifestyles of the middle and upper classes, presented innumerable opportunities for product and brand-name tie-ins. But more than this, they functioned as living display windows for all that they contained; windows that were occupied by marvelous mannequins and swathed in a fetish-inducing ambiance of music and emotion.

These films merely had to be shown to Americans who lived away from big cities or to audiences in foreign countries to generate a desire for the cornucopia of material goods they proffered. Around 1912, according to Benjamin Hampton, English and German maufacturers became alarmed at the decline in demand for their goods and an attendant rise in American imports. An investigation disclosed that American movies were responsible: "They began to complain to their governments that audiences saw American sewing machines, typewriters, furniture, clothing, shoes, steam shovels, saddles, automobiles and all sorts of things in the cinema shows, and soon began to want these things. . . ."

From this discovery, a complex chapter of film history arose. The periods immediately preceding and following World War I saw attempts at the establishment of quotas for both American products and films and at shoring up national film industries (especially in England and Germany). This history is tangential to our interests, but the struggle attending it served to alert Hollywood and American industry to the full potential of film as a merchandiser of goods. In 1926 an analyst observed:

> The peoples of many countries now consider America as the arbiter of manners, fashions, sports, customs and standards of living. If it were not for the barrier we have established, there is no doubt that the American movies would be bringing us a flood of immigrants. As it is, in a vast number of instances, the desire to come to this country is thwarted, and the longing to emigrate is changed into a desire to imitate.
>
> The selling influence of this condition is proved by the demand abroad for products the use of which has been confined to this country. Word comes from several countries that swimming pools are being constructed by the wealthier classes, and that the foreign makers of bathing suits have been compelled to adapt their design to the California model. . . .
>
> Not long ago, several large British manufacturers complained that they had been compelled to change the established styles of the shoes they made for their customers in the Far East, and they traced the change directly to the movies from America. Last year, a large demand for sewing machines in China could be credited to no other influence. (James True, *Printer's Ink*, Feb. 4, 1926)

When Joseph Kennedy brought executives of the film industry to Harvard in 1927 for a series of lectures, the topic of film and foreign trade came up again and again. Kennedy had just returned from England where diplomats had told him that American films exerted a "formidable" influence. Kent, Paramount's head of sales, ingenuously informed Harvard's undergraduates: "If you investigate the automobile situation you will find that the American automobiles are making terrific inroads on foreign makes of cars and that the greatest agency for selling American automobiles abroad is the American motion picture. Its influence is working insidiously all the time and even though all this is done without any conscious intent, the effect is that of a direct sales agency."

The demurral on conscious intent was undoubtedly directed at Kent's academic audience. Film executives spoke with another voice before government or industrial groups. William Fox told Upton Sinclair, "I tried to bring government officials to realize that American trade follows American pictures, and not the American flag. . . ." The most prominent spokesman for celluloid imperialism, however, was Will Hays. In a 1930 radio speech sponsored by "Nation's Business," he repeated a theme that he turned to many times:

> Motion pictures perform a service to American business which is greater than the millions in our direct purchases, greater than our buildings. . . . The industry is a new factor in American economic life and gives us a solid basis of hope for the future by creating an increase in demand for our products. The motion picture carries to every American at home, and to millions of potential purchasers abroad, the visual, vivid perception of American manufactured products.

As if to underscore Hays's remarks, a government study published in 1929 revealed that foreign sales of bedroom and bathroom furnishings had increased 100 percent because of movies.

The mid- and late 1920s were also marked by an industrywide attempt to vitiate foreign film industries by hiring away their best stars, directors, and technicians. The logic of this development was very complex: a von Sternberg film made in Hollywood could be expected to stimulate Paramount's film rentals in Europe, to defeat foreign chauvinist critics and quota setters, to undercut foreign competitors, and to keep the doors open for American films and the products they showcased By the early 1930s, the European struggle against Americanization through films had lessened. Trade barriers and a worldwide depression combined to diminish the effects of the process—for a time. From 1931 on, one finds more concern among Hollywood executives with the film industry's relation to the domestic economy. Although I shall concentrate on this economy exclusively for the rest of this essay, we should bear in mind that the foreign market did not drop from Hollywood's consciousness, even though it was seldom publicly discussed. Its continued significance is illustrated in this anecdote recounted by an American fashion buyer just returned from Paris in 1935:

> Even a few years back French dressmakers were still dragging at the leash instead of bounding forward, as now, to get a preview of America's style activities. A certain gown was worn by Crawford in a picture the latter

part of 1932. You will recall it, I am sure, because it is still with us and promises to become a perennial—the one with the big stiff ruffles outlining the shoulders.

No sharp-eyed tipster was on the job then, for that robe swept Paris not only after it had appeared in the film but after it had been sold in New York shops. And when I took ship for America, toward the end of 1934, all the cheap little shops which have sprung up like weeds in the Champs-Elysees, were still gainfully displaying it, with no mention, of course, of its Pacific Coast origin.

The old Paris dressmakers—those with the names which have made history for generations in the annals of French sartorial supremacy—deplore this outcropping of houses with no standards and no reverence for the French traditions. . . .

Worse still, French women are crowding into the places and the streets are filled with the wearers of their output. In the old days, even the Frenchwoman of the petite bourgeoisie managed to achieve a certain chic; if she couldn't, she seemed to prefer to go utterly dowdy.

But all that is changed. "And now," ask the exclusive dressmakers, "are Parisiennes to be caught on their own home grounds going Hollywood, and bad Hollywood at that—Hollywood that is two if not three, years behind the times? Are Joan Crawfords—but Crawfords only five feet tall and without any. . . .—to people the Bois de Bouingne on Sunday afternoon in gowns which will make Paris the laughingstock as a style center?" (*Saturday Evening Post,* May 18, 1935)

The story of Hollywood's plunge into the American marketplace involves two separate histories: that of the showcasing of fashions, furnishings, accessories, cosmetics, and other manufactured items, and that of the establishment of "tie-ups" with brand-name manufacturers, corporations, and industries. The two histories are interpenetrating, but they were distinctive enough to give rise to specialists who worked independently within and without the studio.

The scope of the first history can be set forth in a sentence: at the turn of the century, Hollywood possessed one clothing manufacturer (of shirts) and none of furniture; by 1937 the Associated Apparel Manufacturers of Los Angeles listed 130 members, and the Los Angeles Furniture Manufacturers Association listed 150, with an additional 330 exhibitors. Furthermore, 250 of the largest American department stores kept buyers permanently in Los Angeles.

When those intimately associated with this development reminisced about its origins, they spoke first of Cecil B. De Mille. In his autobiography, De Mille maintained that the form of cinema he pioneered in the late 1910s and 1920s was a response to pressures he received from the publicity and sales people in New York. They wanted few (preferably no) historical "costume" dramas but much "modern stuff with plenty of clothes, rich sets, and action." De Mille brought to Paramount's studios talented architects, designers, artists, costumers, and hairdressers who both drew on the latest styles in fashions and furnishings and created hallmarks of their own. De Mille's "modern photoplays"—films such as *For Better, For Worse* and *Why Change Your Wife?*—guaranteed audiences a display of all that was chic and avant-garde. They also pioneered a cinematic style, the "De Mille style," perfectly tailored to the audience's desire to see the rich detail of furnishings and clothes.

While De Mille perfected a film display aimed at the fashion-conscious, fan magazines and studio publicity photos helped spread an indigenous Hollywood "outdoors" style made up of backless bathing suits, pedal-pushers, slacks, toppers, and skirts. By the early 1930s, these styles had penetrated the smallest of American small towns and had revolutionized recreational and sport dress.

The years 1927 through 1929 saw an explosive expansion of fashion manufacture and wholesaling in Los Angeles. Some of De Mille's designers opened shops that catered to a well-heeled public. The Country Club Manufacturing Company inaugurated copyrighted styles modeled by individual stars and employing their names. It was followed by "Miss Hollywood Junior," which attached to each garment a label bearing the star's name and picture. This line was sold exclusively to one store in each major city, with the proviso that a special floorspace be set aside for display. Soon, 12 cloak and suit manufacturers banded together to form Hollywood Fashion Associates. In addition, the Associated Apparel Manufacturers began to coordinate and give national promotion to dozens of style lines. The latter association took the lead in a form of publicity that became commonplace through the 1930s: it shot thousands of photographs of stars serving as mannequins in such news-editor pleasing locales as the Santa Anita race track, the Rose Bowl, Hollywood swimming pools, and formal film receptions. The photos were distributed free, with appropriate text, to thousands of newspapers and magazines. In a more absurd vein, the association organized bus and airplane style shows, which ferried stars, designers, and buyers to resorts and famous restaurants amid flashbulbs and a contrived sense of occasion.

If one walked into New York's largest department stores toward the end of 1929, one could find abundant evidence of the penetration of Hollywood fashions, as well as a virulent form of moviemania. One store employed uniformed Roxy ushers as its floor managers. Another advertised for sales girls that looked like Janet Gaynor and information clerks that looked like Buddy Rogers. At Saks, Mrs. Pemberton would inform you that she was receiving five orders a day for pajamas identical with the pair that Miriam Hopkins wore in *Camel Thru a Needle's Eye*. She also had received orders for gowns and suits worn by Pauline Lord, Lynne Fontaine, Frieda Innescourt, Sylvia Fields, and Murial Kirkland.

The New York scene became organized, however, only with the advent in 1930 of Bernard Waldman and his Modern Merchandizing Bureau. Waldman's concern soon played the role of fashion middle-man for all the major studios except Warner Bros. (Warners, always a loner, established its own Studio Styles in 1934). By the mid-1930s Waldman's system generally operated as follows: sketches and/or photographs of styles to be worn by specific actresses in specific films were sent from the studios to the bureau (often a year in advance of the film's release). The staff first evaluated these styles and calculated new trends. They then contracted with manufacturers to have the styles produced in time for the film's release. They next secured advertising photos and other materials that would be sent to retail shops. This ad material mentioned the film, stars, and studio as well as the theaters where the film would appear. Waldman's cut of the profits was 5 percent. The studios at first asked for 1 percent, but before 1937 provided their designs free in exchange for abundant advertising.

Waldman's concern also established the best known chain of fashion shops, Cinema Fashions. Macy's contracted for the first of these shops in 1930 and remained a leader in the Hollywood fashion field. By 1934 there were 298 official Cinema Fashions shops (only one permitted in each city). By 1937 there were 400, with about 1,400 other shops willing to handle some of the dozens of the bureau's star-endorsed style lines. Cinema Fashions catered only to women capable of spending $30 and more for a gown. It agreed with the studios that cheaper fashions, even though they would be eagerly received, would destroy the aura of exclusivity that surrounded a Norma Shearer or Loretta Young style. Cheaper lines might also cheapen the stars themselves, imperiling both box-office receipts and the Hollywood fashion industry.

Inevitably, competitors and cheaper lines did appear. Copyrighted styles that had had their run in the Waldman-affiliated shops were passed on to mass production (although seldom if the style was associated with a currently major star). By the later 1930s Waldman had added a line of Cinema shops that sold informal styles at popular prices. The sale of these fashions was tremendously aided by the release of photos to newspapers (they saturated Sunday supplements), major magazines, and the dozens of fan magazines—*Hollywood, Picture Play, Photoplay, Shadowplay, Silver Screen, Screenbook, Movieland, Movie Story, Movie Stories, Modern Movies, Modern Screen, Motion Pictures,* and the rest. In monthly issues of each of these magazines, millions of readers saw Bette Davis, Joan Crawford, Claudette Colbert, and Norma Shearer in a series of roles unique to this period: as mannequins modeling clothes, furs, hats, and accessories that they would wear in forthcoming films. The intent behind these thousands of style photos is epitomized in a 1934 *Shadowplay* caption for a dress modeled by Anita Louise: "You will see the dress in action in Warner's *First Lady.*" Occasionally one was informed that the fashions were "on display in leading department and ready-to-wear stores this month." The names of the leading studio designers, Adrian of M-G-M, Orry-Kelly of Warners, Royer of 20th Century-Fox, Edward Stevenson of RKO, Edith Head of Paramount, Walter Plunkett of Selznick, became as familiar to readers as the stars themselves.

From July 30 to August 4, 1934, Los Angeles presented the first of a twice annual series of trade fairs called, inelegantly, the Combined Market Week. More than 400 local firms displayed women's apparel, millinery, children's and men's wear, dry goods, furniture, flooring, housewares, pottery, machinery, and other lines. More than 7,000 buyers attended. By 1936 the fair attracted more than 10,000 buyers and included 185 women's clothing manufacturers and 260 furniture manufacturers. In less than a decade, Los Angeles had become indisputably first in the fields of sport clothes, street dress, and modern and outdoor furniture, and arguably second to New York and Paris in high fashion.

To all this we must add Hollywood's influence on the cosmetics industry. In a field dominated by Eastern houses such as Helena Rubinstein, Elizabeth Arden, and Richard Hudnut, Hollywood's Max Factor and Perc Westmore were merely two large concerns. But Hollywood seemed to dominate the cosmetics industry because its stars appeared in the hundreds of thousands of ads that saturated the media. In the mid-1930s, cosmetics ranked only second to food products in amount spent on advertising. The cycle of influence made up of films, fashion articles, "beauty hints," columns featuring stars, ads that dutifully mentioned the star's current film, and tie-in advertising in stores, made cosmetics synonymous with Hollywood. The same was true for many brands of soap, deodorants, toothpastes, hair preparations, and other toiletries. No more potent endorsements were possible than those of the women who manifestly possessed the most "radiant" and "scintillant" eyes, teeth, complexions, and hair.

Almost as significant for films as the scope of this merchandizing revolution was the conception of the consumer that underpinned it. As one reads the captions beneath the style photos, the columns of beauty advice, and the articles on the coordination of wardrobes and furnishings, one senses that those who bought these things were not varied as to age, marital status, ethnicity, or any other characteristic. Out there, working as a clerk in a store and living in an apartment with a friend, was *one girl*—single, nineteen years old, Anglo-Saxon, somewhat favoring Janet Gaynor. The thousands of Hollywood-associated designers, publicity men, sales heads, beauty consultants, and merchandizers had internalized her so long ago that her psychic life had become their psychic life. They empathized with her shyness, her social awkwardness, her fear of offending. They understood her slight weight problem and her chagrin at being a trifle too tall. They could tell you what sort of man she hoped to marry and how she spent her leisure time.

They could imagine her, for instance, awakening on a Saturday, realizing that it was her day off, and excitedly preparing to go shopping. After a long soak in a bubble bath (Lux), she prepared herself to meet the critical stares of Fifth Avenue. She first applied successive coats of cleansing (Ponds), lubricating (Jergens), and foundation creams (Richard Hudnut). She then chose a coordinated group of cosmetics keyed to daylight wear and the current fashions of natural flesh tone and heavy lip color. Over a coat of light pink pancake makeup, she applied a light orange rouge high and back on the cheekbones, accentuating the oval effect (Princess Pat). A brown eyebrow pencil, employed to extend the line back along the cheeks, and brown mascara (Lucille Young) was combined with a gray-blue eyeshadow flecked with metallic sheen, appropriate for day wear (Elizabeth Arden). A bright red-orange lipstick, richly applied (Max Factor), and a light dusting of true skintone face powder (Lady Esther) completed her facial. From her several perfumes, she chose a refreshing, outdoor type (Lenheric). She then added a "fingertip-full" of deodorant to each armpit (Mum), massaged her hands (Hinds), and applied a fresh coat of nail enamel (Revlon).

Stepping out of her dressing gown, she lightly dusted herself with a body powder (Luxor) and then, following a hint from Edith Head, taped

Wearing a gown designed by Travis Banton, Carole Lombard dances with George Raft in Rumba *(1935). Photo courtesy of Paramount.*

her ever-so-slightly too large breasts so that they were separated as widely as possible. A Formfit bra, Undikins, a Bonnie Bright Frock (the Frances Dee model from *Of Human Bondage* [RKO, 1934]), silk stockings (Humming Bird), and a pair of Nada White Buck shoes (Enna Jettick) completed her outfit. Donning her Wittnauer watch ("Watches of the Stars") and a simple necklace (the Tecla worn by Barbara Stanwyck in *Gambling Lady* [Warners, 1934]), she picked up her metallic-sheen purse and left.

After several lovely hours of window-shopping, she happened to pass Macy's and was thunder-struck at the sight of the original Travis Banton gown worn by Carole Lombard in her just-released film *Rumba* (also starring—in smaller print—George Raft). Rushing up to Macy's Cinema Fashions Shop, she discovered a $40 copy of the gown, almost as careful in its detail as the original. Her imagination heated by this encounter, she immediately left to catch the early matinee of the film. Three dresses and a fur coat later, the gown entered. Back-lit, descending a stair, vivified by motion and music, it whispered and signed its way into George Raft's roguish arms. Through the alchemy of his caresses, it became libidinous, haunted. It slipped from Carole Lombard's shoulder and had to be lifted back again. It snaked its way across one knee, cascaded from the stair to the floor like liquid light.

From the rear of one theater, two slight moans could be heard. The first small sound, tinged with ecstasy and fulfillment, issued from the girl. The second, somewhat grosser but still redolent with satisfaction, came from Bernard Waldman.

III

Now for our second history, that of the tie-up. In mid-May 1931, a Mr. Tielhet, reporter for the *Outlook and Independent*, sat with a stopwatch in hand viewing a 15-minute "screen-playlet" that a theater was offering as a bonus to its audiences. The next day, he published this report.

> The news reel was run off first. Then the caption, which will be called, for the purpose of this article, "Seduction—featuring Blanche la Belle," was flashed upon the screen. The scene opened in the boudoir of la Belle, and the brassy voice of the dialogue blared forth. The plot was of little importance. I was interested in counting the length in seconds that a bottle of "Seduction Fleur Parfum" was displayed before the audience. The story with unobtrusive cunning brought out the irresistible attracting powers of a seductive perfume. It showed how a comparatively plain woman, deserted by her fiancé, suddenly developed an almost overwhelming charm by the lure of this perfume. Ten times was the square bottle of "Seduction Fleur" displayed before us, for a total of seventy-eight seconds . . . Then a seven-second title was flashed, "This film is

sponsored for your entertainment by the Parfum de Fleurs Company, Paris and London; Levy and Grosstein, New York, sole importers for United States and Canada."

In the lobby the two advertising men from the production company were busy interviewing as many of the audience as possible in order to determine whether the sponsored film had been successful. Next day one of the interviewers gave me his figues. He had talked with 191 men and women. So cunning was the advertising that 54 out of the 191 did not even realize that they had witnessed a sponsored film!

This was but one of a series of advertising shorts shown in early 1931, the first year of catastrophic downturn in box-office receipts. On May 13, *Variety* reported that 50 percent of the theaters were showing advertising films of some sort. Two of the hardest-pressed studios, Paramount and Warners, were seriously committed to these films. In the same month, Paramount revealed that it would produce fifty shorts in response to the favorable receptions accorded to just released *Movie Memories* (Liggett and Myers), *My Merrie Oldsmobile,* and *Jolt for General Germ* (Lysol). Warners projected a dozen or more to follow its *On the Slopes of the Andes* (A&P), *Graduation Day in Bugland* (Listerine), a Chesterfield series, and others. Both studios had many signed contracts in hand. M-G-M was fearful of exhibitor reactions to this development and was a silent spectator. RKO was said to be "on the fence."

If a moviegoer was extremely unlucky, he or she might encounter a Paramount advertising short on the same program with its feature film, *It Pays to Advertise,* starring Carole Lombard and Norman Foster (1931). This comedy, set in an advertising agency, aroused the anger of P. S. Harrison, editor of *Harrison's Reports,* a reviewing service directed at independent exhibitors:

> The Paramount picture, "It Pays to Advertise," is nothing but a billboard of immense size. I have not been able to count all the nationally advertised articles that are spoken of by the characters; but some of them are the following: Boston Garters, Arrow Collars, Manhattan Shirts, Colgate Cream, Gillette Razors, B.V.D.'s, Hart, Shaeffner & Marx clothes, Listerine, Victor phonographs, Murad cigarettes, Florsheim shoes, Dobbs hats, Forhans toothpaste, and others. But the most subtle thing is the brand, "13 Soap, Unlucky for Dirt." A trademark such as this does not, of course, exist; but I understand that Paramount has made the picture for the purpose of making a trademark out of it. My information

is to the effect that Colgate has offered $250,000 for it, and that Paramount is asking $500,000. I understand, in fact, that Paramount has decided to make a regular business out of creating trademarks and then selling them.

Harrison went on in this and subsequent articles to enumerate the brand names he had seen in recent feature films, including ones made by M-G-M, RKO, and United Artists. The response he generated from exhibitors was as angry as his own. Dozens of them supplied his articles to newspapers that were already alert to the threat to their advertising income posed by sponsored shorts.

The offers this man received were part of a reciprocal business between studio publicity people and their counterparts in business advertising agencies. The *New York Times* described the agencies' side of the operation in a 1929 editorial:

> Articles to be advertised are offered as props for films in the making. Automobile manufacturers graciously offer the free use of high-priced cars to studios. Expensive furnishings for a set are willingly supplied by the makers, and even donated as permanent studio property. For kitchen scenes the manufacturers of nationally advertised food products fill cupboard shelves.
>
> *Variety* reports in a Hollywood dispatch that agents eager for publicity for jewelry or wearing apparel approach movie stars directly. If they will agree to wear a certain article in their picture, it is given to them. In cases where an object is "hard to plant," the agency will even offer monetary consideration.

Given the long history behind brand-name props and tie-ups and the deepening of the depression through 1932, it was inevitable that the restraint brought on by the excesses of 1931 would not last. By early 1933, Columbia, a studio not burned by Harrison, had moved aggressively into solicited tie-ups. Prior to the production of *Ann Carver's Profession*, a scene-by-scene breakdown was prepared and mailed to agents for manufacturers of the products that would appear in the film. Example scenes: "Scene No. 4, Bill Graham is seated at a luncheon counter, wheat cakes dominating. General Foods? Dialogue discusses flap-jacks. Ann Carver is cooking, using a griddle, etc. There are a number of important utensil people who might be interested in this. Scene No. 5. Ann Carver looks at her wristwatch. Benrus? Scene No. 68. Main office of a successful law firm. Appears several times throughout the picture. Typewriters, desks—

all kinds of office equipment are here prominently. Remington-Rand?" and so on through over 100 scenes. The intent was not merely to solicit props but to promote on-going tie-ups that would reduce studio overhead and gain advertising for films.

Through the first half of 1931, so much pressure was brought to bear on the major studios that executives were compelled to make public statements. Carl Laemmle of Universal was unequivocally on the exhibitors' side: "I appeal to every producer not to release 'sponsored' moving pictures. . . . Believe me, if you jam advertising down their throats and pack their eyes and ears with it, you will build up a resentment that will in time damn your business." Nicholas Schenck, head of M-G-M, pledged his studio to the crusade. He stated that although Loews had been the first to be offered huge sums to produce "subsidized motion pictures," it had always refused to run commercial ads in its theaters.

When Harrison subsequently revealed that Paramount had threatened to run him out of business, the general reaction was one of shock. By the end of May, both Paramount and Warners were compelled to apologetically disavow their practices and their future plans. Harrison announced Paramount's capitulation coldly but commended Warners for "taking it on the chin."

This early depression development had its antecedents in practices as old as the industry. Product display in films had become common in films prior to World War I. Occasionally, the studios solicited props in exchange for the free advertising they could provide, or they accepted or solicited fees for foregrounding brand names or recognizable articles.

A Los Angeles advertising agent interviewed in late 1933 revealed how extensive the cooperation could become:

> Some time ago I dressed the window of "Toler's Drug Store" on RKO's "Age of Consent" set, using conspicuous showcards and cutouts of Dr. West's products and Bromo-Seltzer (two of my accounts). Considerable action of the drama took place before these windows and that was all to the good. But when the action swung inside the 'store' there were many long shots, hence the counter racks, labels, etc., which I had planted were almost illegible when the picture was projected. On this same set, I had hung a Coca Cola electrolier well to the rear; its lettering was nearly undecipherable; yet the familiar design and trade-mark got across, since it was in full view of the audience for about one-half hour of screening time. (*Sales Management,* Oct. 1, 1933).

In the next year, enough brand names had returned to films to arouse critics—and the interest of manufacturer's agents. "What has particularly heated the industrialists lately," *Variety* said in June 1934, "are the great plug insertions in recent films. Particular bubble in the pot is the reference in that 'Three Little Pigs' cartoon to the Fuller Brush Man, while the three pictures centering around Greyhound buses in the past two months is another thing eating at the hearts of industrial rivals." By 1935 one could see a package of Lucky Strikes flashed in RKO's *Strangers All*, Chesterfields and Wonder Bread in a Laurel and Hardy film, and Donald Cook asking a bartender for a "Clicquot" in RKO's *Gigolette*. And if one attended RKO's *Silver Streak*, one spent 80 minutes on the Burlington's stream-lined "Zephyr," accompanied by Western Union, the company that timed its record run.

All this was small potatoes, however, compared to tie-up schemes fabricated at the two most powerful studios, Warners and M-G-M. Determined not to rekindle the controversies of 1931, these two studios evolved a form of tie-up that revolutionized sales and publicity—and permanently affected the character of films. The keystone of the method was a contractual agreement with a large established manufacturer. If the product would seem blatantly displayed if shown in a film—a bottle of Coca-Cola, for instance—the contract provided merely for a magazine and newspaper campaign that would employ pictures and endorsements of stars, and notice of recent studio releases. M-G-M signed a $500,000 contract with Coca-Cola in March 1933, providing that company with the vaunted "star-power" of the most star-laden studio.

There were other products, however, that could be prominently displayed in films without arousing criticism, except from the most knowledgeable. Warner's tie-up with GE and General Motors (GM) provided both for the use of Warner's stars in magazine ads and for the display of appliances and autos in films. Anyone familiar with the GE Monitor-top refrigerator will recognize it in a number of Warner films of this period. A tie-up with Buick (GM) provided for the display of autos in films and for a national advertising campaign that tied Buick to ten Warner films, among them *Gold Diggers of 1935, Go into Your Dance, The Goose and the Gander, A Night at the Ritz,* and *In Caliente*.

At the end of the campaign, in May 1935, *Variety* reported, "Automobile manufacturers have gone daffy over picture names following the campaign just completed by Buick and Warners. Latter company has tied up to stars on the last 10 pictures with Buick buggies." Among the manufacturers said to be "wild on commercial tie-ups" and anxious to make deals were Auburn, Packard, Dodge, Armour Co., Jantzen Knitting Co., Walkover Shoes, Pure Oil, and Helena Rubinstein.

GM itself was so euphoric that it contemplated raiding the studios for stars, producing its own commercial films, and offering them free to exhibitors. It did, in fact, produce at least five of these, employing such tertiary stars as John Mack Brown, Sheila Manners, and Hedda Hopper. In April 1935, Will Hays spoke out against the return of commercial pictures, scotching GM's plans before they got out of hand. Only twenty exhibitors were actually offered the GM commercials.

42nd Street, discussed at the beginning of this chapter, seems to have inaugurated Warner's new order of tie-up. But major musicals that followed in 1934 and 1935 brought the technique to a refined pitch. For example, one press book (a large magazine-size brochure sent to exhibitors) for a typical musical, Busby Berkeley's *Dames* (1934), offered the following information. The "Exploitation" section announced "9—Count 'em—9" prepared tie-ups. Tie-up number one: Mojud Clair-phane Silk Stockings. The manufacturers were prepared to distribute "ads, posters, die-cut window cards, counter displays, etc." Number two: Dick Powell shirts. The manufacturers placed a cardboard with a photo of Powell and a plug for the film in each shirt. They also would supply window displays, notes and copy for ads, and dealer information. Number three: *Modern Screen* magazine. "Always dependable, this fan magazine tie-up is more extensive on 'Dames' than ever before. . . ." Number four: Bendermade Breeches. "Bender Bros. are all set to work with you on this 'Dames' tie-up." They were supplying window cards, stills, and ads. Number five: Chulla Crepe, "The Fabric of the Stars!" Counter-display cards, blow-ups for windows.

In September 1934, Charles Einfeld explained the Warners' system to *Sales Management:* "Our idea is to prepare with an advertiser a scheme that works just as much to his advantage as it does to ours. Our company has prepared a special department of such tie-ups. It has pursued a definite policy of working with important nationally advertised products. We have religiously avoided the mass of small advertisers who for years have capitalized on the endorsements of movie stars with ultimate injury to both stars and the motion picture industry."

In 1934 Warners also made deals with Quaker Oats ($91,000 worth of cereal and bicycle advertising for a Joe E. Brown film, *Six Day Bike Rider)* and Farrar and Rinehart, publishers of the best-selling *Anthony Adverse.* The book was made into a major film, one that inaugurated a cycle of Warner historical films tied to highly advertised novels.

To further promote *Anthony Adverse,* a $10,000 contest was announced in *Photoplay* with tie-in prizes of five Ford automobiles, A United Air Lines trip to the World's Fair, a Tecla necklace, six Orry-Kelly gowns, and Mojud stockings. *Sales Management* reported that "the merchandise connected with *Anthony Adverse* is expected to develop nearly as great a dollar sales as the picture."

Although Warners probably secured more major tie-ups than any other studio, M-G-M ran it a close race. We can illustrate its exploitational technique by examining the press book for *Dinner at Eight,* the studio's most ambitiously promoted film of 1934. A page of photos of department store displays arranged in many cities was captioned, "The merchandizing value of Jean Harlow's name was never better demonstrated than by the dozens of *Dinner at Eight* fashion and shoe windows." The next page was headed, "Tie Ups A Million Dollars Worth of Promotion" and included this text: "250,000 Coca-Cola dealers will exploit *Dinner at Eight.* First visible evidence of the extensiveness of this national arrangement between the largest selling soft drink in America and M-G-M, which has individually and collectively the greatest star power names in the industry, appeared in September 1933 issues of *Saturday Evening Post, Colliers, Liberty,* and the *Country Gentleman*—full-color pages advertising the rare entertainment qualities of *Dinner at Eight.*" In addition, Coca-Cola delivery trucks would carry side billboards advertising the film. Other tie-ups, accompanied by relevant stills from the film, included Max Factor cosmetics, Lux soap (full-page newspaper ads), Gillette Safety Razor Co., Lord and Taylor hats, *Modern Screen,* A. S. Beck shoes (four-column ads in New York newspapers), and Marconigrams. Dozens of opportunities for local tie-ups were provided by other products appearing in the film: furniture, dinner settings, chocolates, shaving brushes, watches, clocks, and so forth. The dress worn by Madge Evans had been shown in Macy's window and was available in Cinema Shops.

Both studios must have monitored audience reactions carefully and half-expected the epiphany of another P. S. Harrison. But the new formula worked. The audience, after all, was not assailed with brand names, merely by the products themselves. The exhibitor did not feel that his screen was obviously usurped. Perhaps most important, the tie-ups increased the advertising revenues of magazines and newspapers, the most effective critics of the sponsored shorts of 1931. Through the rest of the 1930s, all the major studios adopted and helped to perfect this system. In its classic—or perhaps Hellenistic—form, the head of exploitation supervised an effort that coordinated the creation of the script (tie-ups were often formative influences), the breakdown of the script into categories of products and services, and the search for sponsors. Wilma Freeman of Warners told *Nation's Business* in 1940 that she asked firms to design "a product that conforms with the picture." In return Ms. Freeman offered the sponsor 12,000 theaters and an audience of 80,000,000 each week. When the product came through, a star was posed with it and the press book was made up. The formula, as a mathematician would say, had achieved elegance.

Because this system won wide acceptance in the late 1930s, it became possible to insert some brand names into films again. They were inserted sparingly and as realistically as possible. Examples are: Kay Francis in *First Lady* (Warners, 1937) stating that "Ford always makes good cars"; Spencer Tracy in *Test Pilot* (M-G-M, 1938) asking for "two Coca-Colas, please"; and Barbara Stanwyck in *Always Goodbye* (20th Century-Fox, 1938) asking for a ticket "on the Normandie." The offering of props for films also became highly organized. Two of the largest agencies, the Walter E. Kline Agency and the Stanley-Murphy Service Agency, solicited properties and placed them for a small fee. Certain manufacturers sent their latest models to these agencies as a matter of course.

Before moving on to some conclusions about how all this affected films, there remains another complicity, that of the studio tie-ins with radio, to be discussed. Prior to 1932, the two major networks, CBS and NBC, did not have studio facilities in Hollywood. Warner Bros., however, had acquired their own local station in emulation of Paramount, which owned a half-interest in CBS and used its nationwide facilities to advertise films and to build up stars. RKO, as I noted earlier, considered its affiliate NBC a major resource and used it both to advertise films and as a source of new breed of film star, the radio personality (Amos and Andy were RKO's pride). Typical programs inaugurated prior to 1932 were the *RKO Hour, RKO Theatre,* and the *Paramount Playhouse.* These programs pioneered the plugging of songs from musicals and the production of abbreviated versions of the plots of soon-to-be-released films.

In 1932 NBC opened a studio in Hollywood with only one staff member and originated a modest twelve hours of programming from it. By 1937 the staff had increased to 100, and NBC had constructed a major studio on the old Famous Players-Lasky lot. In this same year, CBS began to build a new studio of its own. More than 700 hours of Hollywood programming issued from both networks in 1937. The studios had done all in their power to woo the major networks to Hollywood, offering them their rosters of stars, their copyrighted music, and advertisers eager to connect their products with star names. The following list suggests the range of programs and sponsors that came to be associated with Hollywood between 1932 and 1937: Rinso Talkie Time, Hollywood Nights (Kissproof), Hollywood Show (Sterling Drugs), Madame Sylvia (Ralston), Hollywood Hotel (Campbell Soups), Lux Radio Theatre, Mary Pickford Dramas (Royal Gelatin), Gigantic Pictures (Tastyeast), Irene Rich Dramas (Welch Juice), Sally of the Talkies (Luxor), Jimmie Fidler (Tangee), Helen Hayes Theatre (Sanka Coffee), Leslie Howard Theatre (Hinds Cream), the Fred Astaire Program (Packard Motors), and Ethel Barrymore Theatre (Bayer Aspirin).

The largest advertisers were, however, associated with the largest names. By 1937 CBS paired Al Jolson and Rinso, Eddie Cantor and Texaco, Jeanette McDonald and Vicks, Jack Oakie and Camels, and Edward G. Robinson and Kraft. NBC followed suit with Rudy Vallee and Royal Gelatin, Bing Crosby and Kraft, Amos and Andy and Pepsodent, and Jack Benny and Jello. This very potent fusion of products and performing stars aroused jealousy in the fields of recording, music publishing, and journalism. Newspaper publishers, in particular, felt that the coalition of Hollywood and radio was drying up their advertising revenue. But the most vocal critics were theater owners. In their trade journals, they protested the use of the stars they relied on for their profits by a medium that gave its product away free. They connected declines in box-office revenue with the increased use of stars by radio, and they saw the studio sales and publicity men as madmen who had created a devouring monster in the foolish belief that they were helping the film industry. The shrewdest critics realized, however, that the tie-ups with radio advertisers gave the studios more than free advertising. Obviously lucrative contracts were involved, similar to those entered into for product tie-ups with films. By 1937 it was, in fact, common knowledge that M-G-M had a major contract with Maxwell House and that all requests for radio appearances and endorsements of its stars were reviewed in consultation with this company. Warners was about to sign a similar contract with Lucky Strike (without which we may never have acquired the phrase "Don't Bogart that joint, my friend"). How many smaller contracts had been entered into over the years only the studios knew. But this oblique penetration of film into a rival medium had been carefully calculated. From about 1934 on, more and more films employed radio personalities, used radio studios as locales, and imitated the variety-show format. Hollywood was not so much aiding the growth of a rival medium as it was attempting to co-opt it.

The result, at least through the mid-1930s, was a kind of symbiosis that blurred the outlines of both media. Fred Astaire became as much a radio personality who performed songs from his pictures and acted out abbreviated versions of film plots over your table model Zenith as he was a dancer and performer on the screen. The products associated with stars in films and radio became subliminally attached to their names and their radio voices. By the late 1930s, the power of film and radio as advertising mediums seemed unlimited. The Hollywood studios, with their rosters of contracted stars, had come to occupy a priviledged position in the advertising industry.

We can gain considerable insight into Hollywood's role in the evolution of consumerism and into many of the characteristics of films of the 1930s and later, by combining this history with all the elements we have so far discussed in isolation. First we have an economy suddenly aware of the importance of the consumer and of the dominant role of women in the purchasing of most consumer items. (Consumer statistics widely disseminated in the late 1920s and early 1930s show that women made 80 to 90 percent of all purchases for family use. They bought 48 percent of drugs, 96 percent of dry goods, 87 percent of raw products, 98 percent of automobiles.) Second we have a film industry committed to schemes for product display and tie-ins, schemes that brought some direct revenue to the studios but more importantly reduced prop and art department and advertising overheads. Add to all this a star system dominated by women—at M-G-M Shearer, Loy, Harlow, Garbo, Russell, Crawford, Goddard, Lombard, Turner, Lamarr; at Warner's Davis, Francis, Stanwyck, Young, Chatterton, and so on—hundreds of women stars and starlets available to the studio publicity, sales tie-in departments as—to use the favored phrase—merchandizing assets.

On one, more local level, the combination of all these factors had some obvious and immediate effects on the kinds of films that were made. There appeared a steady output of films dominated by starlets—those hundreds of "women's films," which are of such interest to feminist critics such as Haskell and Rosen. In addition, Hollywood developed a preference for "modern films," because of the opportunities they offered for product display and tie-ins. In many instances, storylines were reshaped to provide more shooting in locales suitable for tie-ins. Movies were made in fashion salons, department stores, beauty parlors, middle- and upper-class homes with modern kitchens and bathrooms, large living rooms, and so forth.

On another level, the studio tie-ins became important far beyond the influence they exerted on the kinds of films made. It is to this more comprehensive level that I would move as I draw back from the cluttered summary I have led you through, to make some larger suggestions, not just about merchandising's contribution to Hollywood but about Hollywood's contributions to the form and character of consumerism itself. By the early 1930s, market analyses were talking about the sovereignty of the consumer, the importance of women as purchasers, and the necessity of learning more about their tastes and predilections. By the early 1940s, market research had been invented, with its studies of the hidden needs and desires of consumers and its discovery that many products were bought for their images, their associations, or the psychological gratifications they provided. Between these two movements, Hollywood had cooperated in a massive effort to sell products employing a sales method that was essentially covert, associational, and linked to the deeply gratifying and habituating experiences that films provided. Furthermore, the many fine sensibilities of Hollywood's designers, artists, cameramen, lighting men, directors, and composers had lent themselves, even if coincidentally, to the establishment of powerful bonds between the emotional fantasy-generating substance of films and the material objects those films contained.

One can argue only from inference that Hollywood gave consumerism a distinctive bent, but what a massive base this inference can claim. Tens of millions of Americans provided the captive audience for the unique experiments in consumer manipulation that the showcasing of products in films and through star endorsements constituted. And this audience reacted so predictably that every large manufacturer in America would have bought its own small M-G-M had this been possible. Instead they were forced to await the advent of television with its socially acceptable juxtaposition of commercials and entertainment. The form television commercials have taken, their fusion of images augmented by editing and camera techniques, with music, lyrics, and charismatic personalities, is obviously an extension of the techniques pioneered by Hollywood.

But is it equally obvious, as market researchers have claimed, that consumerism is grounded in psychological universals? What should we ascribe to the potent acculturation provided by Hollywood for several decades? Were we, as consumers, such skilled and habituated perceivers of libidinal cues, such receptive audiences for associational complexes, such romanticizers of homes, stores, and highways before Hollywood gave us *Dinner at Eight, The Big Store,* and *The Speed That Kills*? I would suggest that we were not, that Hollywood, drawing on the resources of literature, art, and music, did as much or more than any other force in capitalist culture to smooth the operation of the production-consumption cycle by fetishizing products and putting the libido in libidinally invested advertising.

Mary Ann Doane

The Economy of Desire:
The Commodity Form
in/of the Cinema

Much of feminist theory tends to envisage the woman's relation to the commodity in terms of "being" rather than "having": she is the object of exchange rather than its subject.[1] What is invoked here is the subjectivity of the commodity. The woman's objectification, her susceptibility to processes of fetishization, display, profit and loss, the production of surplus value, all situate her in a relation of resemblance to the commodity form. As Fredric Jameson points out, ". . . by its transformation into a commodity a thing, of whatever type, has been reduced to a means for its own consumption. It no longer has any qualitative value in itself, but only insofar as it can be 'used'. . . ."[2] But the status of the woman as commodity in feminist theory is not merely the result of a striking metaphor or parallel. Its elaboration is a response to Lévi-Strauss's description of the exchange of women as nothing less than the foundation of human society, of culture—the guarantee of an exogamy without which the family, and society along with it, would suffer an incestuous collapse.

The notion of the woman as the Ur-object of exchange has been taken up by theorists such as Luce Irigaray and subjected to a parodic over-writing in essays such as "When the Goods Get Together" and "Women on the Market."[3] From this perspective, Marx's analysis of value and of the commodity as the elementary form of capitalist wealth

Reprinted, with permission, from the *Quarterly Review of Film and Video* 11:1 (1989).

is understood as an accurate although displaced interpretation of the status of women in a patriarchal society.

> In our social order, women are 'products' used and exchanged by men. Their status is that of merchandise, 'commodities'. . . . So women have to remain an 'infrastructure' unrecognized as such by society and our culture. The use, consumption, and circulation of their sexualized bodies underwrite the organization and reproduction of the social order, in which they have never taken part as 'subjects.'[4]

The erasure of female subjectivity by the commodification of the female body is, however, never quite successful. Just as Lévi-Strauss, despite his attempt to compare the exchange of women to the exchange of words, must admit that women also speak, the feminist theorist must acknowledge the fact that women also buy. Not only do they buy but since the early years of the twentieth century the woman has been situated by a capitalist economy as the prototype of the modern consumer. In the theorization of the commodification of the woman, there is, therefore, a hitch—a hitch not unlike the one encountered by Lévi-Strauss. Much to his dismay, the anthropologist discovers that the woman "must be recognized as a generator of signs."[5] But Lévi-Strauss makes an amazing comeback and recoups his losses by attaching the woman's "talent, before and after marriage, for taking her part in a duet"[6] to an intensification of the affective value of sexual relations—to that "affective richness, ardour and mystery" that originally characterized all signs-to-be-exchanged, not just the woman. This leaves the woman with a fairly heavy burden of affect. I would like to argue here that the woman's ability to purchase, her subjectivity as a consumer, is qualified by a relation to commodities that is also ultimately subordinated to that intensification of the affective value of sexual relations that underpins a patriarchal society. In other words, Irigaray's theory of the woman as commodity and the historical analysis of the woman's positioning as consumer—as subject rather than object of the commodity form—are only apparently contradictory. But this involves both rethinking the absoluteness of the dichotomy between subject and object that informs much feminist thinking and analyzing the ways in which the woman is encouraged to actively participate in her own oppression.

Of course, it is only insofar as consumerism is associated with a particularly maligned form of subjectivity or agency that the woman's role in such an exchange is assured. As Jameson points out, ". . . the conception of the mindless consumer, the ultimate commodified 'false consciousness' of shopping-centre capitalism, is a conception of 'other-ness' . . . degraded consumption is assigned to women, to what used to be called 'Mrs. American Housewife.'"[7] The degradation here is linked to the idea of the consumer as a passive subject who is taken in by the lure of advertising, the seduction of the image. In other words, the phenomenon of consumerism is conceptualized in terms that are not far from those used to delineate spectatorship in the cinema. The film frame functions, in this context, not as a "window on the world" as in the Bazinian formulation but as a quite specific kind of window—a shop window. Or, as Charles Eckert points out with reference to the short films of the first decade of the century, ". . . they functioned as living display windows for all that they contained; windows that were occupied by marvelous mannequins and swathed in a fetish-inducing ambiance of music and emotion."[8] The relation between the cinema and consumer-ism is buttressed by the film's capability for representing not merely objects but objects in their fetishized form as commodities. The glamour, the sheen of the cinema, and its stars metonymically infect the objects of the mise-en-scène. As Jeanne Allen claims, the spectator is encouraged to desire the possession of a material environment, an environment that "represented a standard of living promised to the viewer ideologically, but awarded only to the eye."[9] Or, as Will Hays put it in a 1930 radio speech, "The motion picture carries to every American at home, and to millions of potential purchasers abroad, the visual, vivid perception of American manufactured products."[10] It would be quite appropriate, it seems, to apply Laura Mulvey's phrase, "to-be-looked-at-ness," to the filmic object in its transformation into a commodity as well as to the woman as spectacle.

One can isolate at least three instances of the commodity form in its relation to the cinema and the question of the female spectator-consumer. The first is fully consistent with Irigaray's analysis of the woman as commodity in a patriarchal system of exchange and involves the encouragement of the woman's narcissistic apprehension of the image of the woman on the screen. The female spectator is invited to witness her own commodification and, furthermore, to buy an image of herself insofar as the female star is proposed as the ideal of feminine beauty. "Buying" here is belief—the image has a certain amount of currency. This level involves not only the currency of a body but of a space in which to display that body: a car, a house, a room filled with furniture and appliances. The second type of relation between the com-modity form and the cinema is in some ways the most direct—the commodity tie-in, which often involves a contractual agreement between the manufacturer and the studio. The result may be the subtle or not-so-subtle placement of a Coca-Cola logo or other brand name in the background of a scene. As the most explicit link between the commodity form and the cinema, this type of display has historically been subjected to a great deal of criticism. Such criticism is then deflected to some extent away from the movie industry when the commodity is "tied in" in a space off-screen by linking a line of clothing, for instance, to a particular film or associating a star with a specific product. This process serves to mediate the spectator's access to the ideal image on the screen. It disperses the fascination of the cinema onto a multiplicity of products whose function is to allow the spectator to approximate that image. Finally, the third instance of commodity form in the cinematic institution concerns the film itself and its status as a commodity in a circuit of exchange. The film in its commodity form promotes a certain mode of perception that is fully adequate to a consumer society and that, for the female spectator, initiates a particularly complex dialectic of "being," "having," and "appearing." Michèle Le Doeuff has, quite legitimately, warned us about the metaphorical use of the term *economy* in contemporary theory—the resort to phrases such as "libidinal economy," "textual economy," "classical economy," "general economy"—a usage that absolves the theorist from a confrontation with the economy "proper" insofar as it refers to such things as prices, exchanges, markets.[11] However, the injunction negates the profound connections between the different economies, a connection that is, perhaps, most visible in the cinema. The economy of the text, its regulation of spectatorial investments and drives, is linked to the economy of tie-ins, the logic of the female subject's relation to the commodity—her status as consumer of goods and consumer of discourses.

The development of the cinematic institution is frequently associated with the rise of consumerism. Overproduction toward the end of the nineteenth century, together with Henry Ford's development of "line production" in 1910 and the intensification of production during World War I, led to a situation in which there was an excess of material goods and a scarcity of consumers, a condition necessitating the perfection of advertising and marketing strategies geared toward a mass audience. Positioning the laborer as a consumer was also an effective means of countering an emerging resistance to the industrial and corporate structure on the part of workers.[12] As Judith Mayne points out in her study of immigrant audiences, ". . . consumerism offered the image of an homogeneous population pursuing the same goals—'living well' and accumulating goods. The movie theater seemed to offer an ideal space for the exhibition of this image, for workers and eventually middle-class people needed only to pay a small admission price in order to share equally in the spectacle offered on the screen."[13] And it would seem that the spectator-consumer was increasingly envisaged as female. Jeanne Allen notes how, as early as 1916, Paramount's promotional journal printed an article describing "the way in which fashionable women derive ideas for interior decoration by copying the sets presented in films."[14] Furthermore, as Allen points out, the space of the theater itself was conceived as specifically feminine: "A 1927 article in *Theatre Management*, for example, stressed the importance of women as the primary component and motivators of film attendance and argued that the appeal of both the film and the theater must be geared to pleasing women's sensibilities. Art works in the lobbies, attractive fabrics and designs for interior decoration, and subdued and flattering lighting were important appeals to women's tastes and to their desire for comfort and relaxation."[15] Fan magazines in their earliest incarnations are linked with the purportedly female obsession with stars, glamour, gossip, and fashionability. The much sought-after address to the female spectator often seems more readily accessible in the discursive apparatus surrounding the film than in the text itself.

In an article entitled "The Carole Lombard in Macy's Window," Charles Eckert sketches the history of the cinema's links to commodity fetishism, but he is most concerned with what he refers to as "the almost incestuous hegemony that characterized Hollywood's relations with vast reaches of the American economy by the mid-1930s."[16] What is striking about Eckert's account is the amount of space he must devote to the two genres of commodities that are most strongly evocative of female narcissism: fashion and cosmetics. Indeed, Eckert suggests that the projected audience for this "showcasing" of commodities was not at all heterogeneous in relation to such factors as age, sex, ethnicity, or marital status: "Out there, working as a clerk in a store and living in an apartment with a friend, was *one girl*—single, nineteen years old, Anglo-Saxon, somewhat favoring Janet Gaynor."[17] Eckert carefully traces the vicissitudes of fashion's intimate connection with Hollywood, from clothing lines such as "Miss Hollywood Junior," which exploited labels with a star's name and picture, to the brainchild of Bernard Waldman, the chain of Cinema Fashions shops, only one to a city, which sold copies of the gowns worn by stars in specific pictures. Although there were, in addition to such showcasing techniques, a very large number of commodity tie-ups that were not so gender specific—from watches to toothpaste, to desks, typewriters, and cars—the glamour, sheen, and fascination attached to the movie screen seemed most appropriate for the marketing of a certain feminine self-image.

The commodity tie-up or tie-in is usually closely associated with the materials prepared by the studio's publicity department in order to market the movie, materials that are gathered together in a publication referred to as the campaign book or press book and sent to exhibitors. In an article in *The Saturday Evening Post* in 1927, Carl Laemmle speaks of the press book primarily in terms of the marketing of the film itself as a commodity:

> Three departments of advertising, publicity, and exploitation combined first on the preparation of the press book or campaign book. This constitutes a complete and encyclopedic guide to the local theater owner in selling the picture to his public. In effect, it places in the employ of the smallest theater owner in the country the services of the best possible advertising, publicity, and exploitation brains that we can secure.[18]

The press book even goes so far as to provide the "intimate, chatty type of copy so eagerly relished by the screen fans."[19] By the mid-1930s, the press book has been perfected for the promotion not only of the movie itself but of a host of products connected in often extremely tangential ways to the film. In sections entitled "Exploitation," the studio experts isolate a particular scene, condensed onto a publicity still (an arrival scene for example), and suggest its affiliation with the appropriate commodity (in this instance, luggage). Metonymy is the trope of the tie-in. The press book constitutes a detailed reading of the filmic text to produce the conditions of its own marketability as well as the conditions of a general consumerism, which it invites and encourages. It works to disseminate the fetishism of the filmic image in a metonymic chain of commodities.

If the film frame is a kind of display window and spectatorship consequently a form of window-shopping, the intimate association of looking and buying does indeed suggest that the prototype of the spectator-consumer is female. And ultimately Eckert's argument is that the alliance between the cinema and the commodity form in a consumer-conscious society generates a genre of films explicitly addressed to the female spectator. As he points out, "Consumer statistics widely disseminated in the late 1920s and early 1930s show that women made 80 to 90 percent of all purchases for family use. They bought 48 percent of drugs, 96 percent of dry goods, 87 percent of raw products, 98 percent of automobiles."[20] The confluence of three different factors—the expanding awareness of the significant economic role of the female consumer, the industry's commitment to the development of commodity tie-ins, and a star system dominated by women—opened up a space for "a steady output of films dominated by starlets—those hundreds of 'women's films' which are of such interest to feminist critics like Haskell and Rosen."[21] The conditions of possibility of the woman's film as a genre are closely linked to the commodity form.

By the 1940s, the system of tie-ins and press books was fully in place and the machinery of advertising had attained a fairly sophisticated form. Furthermore, the war served to reinforce the view that the spectator to be addressed is female. The film industry tended to operate under the assumption that the audience was composed primarily of women. In addition, audience analysis confirms that women were "usually better versed than men on movie topics."[22] Women were fully immersed in the discursive apparatus surrounding the cinema—fan magazines as well as news columns and articles on or by stars in women's magazines.

Advertising outside the context of the cinema, by this time a highly efficient machine designed to facilitate the circulation of commodities, was frequently subordinated to the ideological imperative of moving women first into and then out of the work force in a fairly short period of time (the "Rosie the Riveter" phenomenon). The commodity was at least a small part of the lure tempting the woman to take a job in the first place—the era of high consumerism had arrived and the new assessment of "economic need" persuaded the woman to work to maintain her standard of living. But the commodity was also activated as the lure back into the domestic space of the home in the postwar years when the threat of male unemployment was great. Even during the war, as Susan M. Hartmann notes, "General Electric predicted that women would welcome their return 'to the old housekeeping routine' because it would be transformed by new appliances. The Eureka Vacuum Cleaner Company praised its women on the assembly line, but promised that at war's end, 'like you, Mrs. America, Eureka will put aside its uniform and return to the ways of peace . . . building household appliances.'"[23] Advertising during the war provoked the reader to fantasize about the various types of commodities that would be available after the war—cars, houses, as well as furniture and household appliances.

What is amazing about advertising in this particular historical conjuncture is that it continues to operate at full force despite the absence of commodities—the scarcity of material goods imposed by a wartime economy. Undoubtedly, this advertising without an object functions to ensure that consumers do not forget brand names, causing advertisers to somehow lose their hold over their audience. But it also demonstrates how advertising, beyond the aim of selling a particular commodity, functions to generate and maintain an aptitude for consumption in the subject. A picture of a woman holding a Revere Copper-Clad Stainless Steel pan in front of a scene depicting an intense military battle is captioned with the apologetic statement, "Mrs. Parker's cooking utensils are making it hot for the Japs." A young woman clad only in a bra and a Lastex Real-Form panty girdle licks a food stamp and looks out provocatively at the reader beneath the phrase "Military Needs Come First."

This objectlessness of the advertising discourse frequently prompts a return to the female body as the prototypical object of commodity fetishism. "Rosie the Riveter" was conceived from the beginning as a temporary phenomenon, active only for the duration, and throughout the war years the female spectator-consumer was sold a certain image of femininity that functioned to sustain the belief that women and work outside the home were basically incompatible. The woman's new role in production was masked by an insistent emphasis on a narcissistic consumption. She was encouraged to view herself as engaged in a constant battle to protect her femininity from the ravages of the workplace with the aid of a host of products: hand lotions, facial creams, mattresses, tampons. Furthermore, it was this idea of femininity that American soldiers were fighting to protect. This notion is most explicit in an ad for Tangee lipstick entitled "War, Women and Lipstick." Alongside a photograph of a glamorous young female pilot emerging from a cockpit is the following text:

> For the first time in history woman-power is a factor in war. Millions of you are fighting and working side by side with your men.
>
> In fact, you are doing double duty—for you are still carrying on your traditional "woman's" work of cooking, and cleaning, and home-making. Yet, somehow, American women are still the loveliest and most spirited in the world. The best dressed, the best informed, the best looking.
>
> It's a reflection of the free democratic way of life that you have succeeded in keeping your femininity—even though you are doing man's work!

> If a symbol were needed of this fine, independent spirit—of this courage and strength—I would choose a lipstick. It is one of those mysterious little essentials that have an importance far beyond their size and cost.
>
> A woman's lipstick is an instrument of personal morale that helps her to conceal heartbreak or sorrow; gives her self-confidence when it's badly needed; heightens her loveliness when she wants to look her loveliest.
>
> No lipstick—ours or anyone else's—will win the war. But it symbolizes one of the reasons why we are fighting . . . the precious right of women to be feminine and lovely—under any circumstances.

Femininity was intimately articulated with a patriotic nationalism. It could also be argued that the Rosie the Riveter image (the original—parodic—Norman Rockwell painting on the cover of *The Saturday Evening Post,* where a Rosie with bulging muscles and a huge riveting gun across her lap crushes a copy of *Mein Kampf* beneath her heel) was chosen precisely for its effectiveness in demarcating the absoluteness of the antithesis between femininity and what continued to be considered as "men's work." Traditional ideas concerning femininity were crucial to the plethora of antifeminist discourses emerging after the war, reaching their apex in Lundberg and Farnham's *Modern Woman: The Lost Sex.*[24]

This aura of a femininity fully contained by a fetishized body image and its corresponding narcissism was also promoted in the press books designed to market and exploit the films of the 1940s.[25] The woman's split subjectivity as worker and wife, or masculinized worker and the embodiment of femininity, is accompanied in the press book by a doubling of female types, subsumed beneath the overpowering category of beauty. A suggested promotional scheme associated with *A Stolen Life,* a film in which Bette Davis plays twin sisters, involves setting the claim "Every Woman Plays a Double Role" next to any one of the following advertisements: "Secretary and Siren—so delightfully *both* with a make-up kit from Maxine's," "You're bright . . . You're blase . . . You're Both with Fashions from Georgia's Dress Shoppe," etc. The press book for *Dark Victory* (1939) is insistent about its potential audience: "*Dark Victory* is definitely a woman's picture and should be exploited as such via the woman's page of your local paper and in cooperation with women's shops." The suggestions include a translation of the film's two female stars, Bette Davis and Geraldine Fitzgerald, into two feminine types with two entirely different make-up needs: medium skin with blonde hair (Bette Davis) and fair skin with dark hair (Geraldine Fitzgerald). The press book for *The Two Mrs. Carrolls* (1947) employs a similar strategy by encouraging exhibitors to set up a contest with the following angle: "All women fall into two general classifications from a beauty-point-of-view. By analyzing the attractions of two beautiful stars of 'The Two Mrs. Carrolls,' contestant should be able to evaluate her own charms at the same time." Another press book exploits the title of Irving Rapper's *Deception* (1946) to sell make-up with the expert's claim that "Most beauty is a delightful deception." The "Exploitation" page of the press book for *In This Our Life* (1942) articulates connections between the different media—magazines, radio, cinema—and underlines the status of the star as an intertextual phenomenon with its headline: "Bette Davis Story in 'Ladies' Home Journal' Cues Campaign for Femme Business!" The story is about how Bette Davis manages to keep a career and hold a husband as well and is entitled "Could Your Husband Take It?"

The very familiarity and banality of such ploys should not blind us to the overwhelming intensity of the injunction to the female specta-tor-consumer to concern herself with her own appearance and position—an appearance that can only be fortified and assured through the purchase of a multiplicity of products. The woman's film as a genre, together with the massive extracinematic discursive apparatus, ensure that what the woman is sold is a certain image of femininity. There is a sense in which the woman's film is not much to look at—the nonstyle or zero degree style of films of the genre has frequently been noted. It is as though there were a condensation of the eroticism of the image onto the figure of the woman—the female star proffered to the female spectator for her imita-tion (and often this took place in extracinematic discourses—outside the context of particular filmic narratives that frequently de-eroticized the female protagonist). The process underlines the tautological nature of the woman's role as consumer: she is the subject of a transaction in which her own commodification is ultimately the object. As Rachel Bowlby points out, "Seducer and seduced, possessor and possessed of one another, women and commodities flaunt their images at one another in an amorous regard which both extends and reinforces the classical picture of the young girl gazing into the mirror in love with herself."[26] Even when consumerism concerns the objects of the space that she inhabits, its tendency is essentially narcissistic. For all consumerism involves the idea of self-image (perhaps this is why the woman is the prototype of the consumer).

Woman as commodity: Jean Harlow in Dinner at Eight *(Cukor, 1933). Photo courtesy of M-G-M.*

Consumerism requires a transformation in modes of perception. Looking and buying are closely linked. Wolfgang Schivelbusch argues that the development of the department store in the latter half of the nineteenth century profoundly altered the notion of the attractiveness of an item, which now ". . . results from the totality of *all* the goods assembled in the salesroom. . . . In the department store, the goods achieve more of their character *as* goods—their appearance as items of exchange value; one might say that their 'commodity-esthetic' aspect becomes ever more dominant."[27] At the cinema, the consumer glance hovers over the surface of the image, isolating details that may be entirely peripheral in relation to the narrative. It is a fixating, obsessive gaze that wanders in and out of the narrative and has a more intimate relation with space—the space of rooms and of bodies—than with the temporal dimension. It is as though there were another text laid over the first—a text with an altogether different mode of address—so that the film becomes something of a palimpsest. In this other text, the desire to possess displaces comprehension as the dominant mechanism of reading. Jameson refers to ". . . a quasi-material 'feeling tone' which floats above the narrative but is only intermittently realized by it: the sense of density in family novels, for instance, or the 'epic' rhythms of the earth or of great movements of 'history' in the various sagas can be seen as so many commodities towards whose consumption the narratives are little more than means, their essential materiality then being confirmed and embodied in the movie music that accompanies their screen versions."[28] It is the sense of the film as spectacle, and desirable in its very appeal to the eye, that is consumed in the viewing.

Walter Benjamin, in his essay "The Work of Art in the Age of Mechanical Reproduction," refers to a possible history of the modes of human sense perception and to the decay of the aura that characterizes contemporary perception. This decay is associated with the development of mass culture and with the "desire of contemporary masses to bring things 'closer' spatially and humanly, which is just as ardent as their bent toward overcoming the uniqueness of every reality by accepting its reproduction."[29] The processes of reproduction and commodification have in common the leveling of differences between things and the promotion of their abstract comparability through the medium of money. Schivelbusch uses Benjamin's claim to argue that the development of the railroad as a new form of transportation and of the circulation of commodities functions in much the same way—bringing geographical locations closer and annihilating the uniqueness of the outlying regions. His argument ultimately links together the railroad, the cinema, the department store, and modernized traffic patterns in the constitution of what he calls, "panoramic perception": "In the filmic perception—i.e., the perception of *montage,* the juxtaposition of the most disparate images into one unit—the new reality of annihilated in-between spaces finds its clearest expression: the film brings things closer to the viewer as well as closer together."[30]

Benjamin's conceptualization of the opposition between the effect of the aura and that of mechanical reproduction is expressed in the spatial terms of *distance* and *closeness*. The aura attached to natural objects is "the unique phenomenon of a distance, however close it may be."[31] And the logic of the consumer's relation to the commodity annihilates this distance: "Every day the urge grows stronger to get hold of an object at very close range by way of its likeness, its reproduction."[32] It is not accidental that the logic of consumerism and mechanical reproduction corresponds to a logic of perception attributed to the female spectator whose nonfetishistic gaze maintains a dangerous intimacy with the image. For the woman, as outlined above, is positioned as the preeminent consumer. What we tend to define, since Marx, as commodity fetishism is in fact more accurately situated as a form of narcissism. Fetishism, in the Freudian paradigm, is a phallic defense that allows the subject to distance himself from the object of desire (or, more precisely, its implications in relation to castration) through the overvaluation of a mediating substitute object. Narcissism confounds the differentiation between subject and object and is one of the few psychical mechanisms Freud associates specifically with female desire.[33]

Having and appearing are closely intertwined in the woman's purportedly narcissistic relation to the commodity. Commodification presupposes that acutely self-conscious relation to the body that is attributed to femininity. The effective operation of the commodity system requires the breakdown of the body into parts—nails, hair, skin, breath—each one of which can constantly be improved through the purchase of a commodity. As Stuart Ewen points out, in relation to this "commodity self," "Each position of the body was to be viewed critically, as a *potential* bauble in a successful assemblage."[34] The ideological effect of commodity logic on a large scale is therefore the deflection of any dissatisfaction with one's life or any critique of the social system onto an intensified concern with a body that is in some way guaranteed to be at fault.[35] The body becomes increasingly *the* stake of late capitalism. *Having* the commodified object—and the initial distance and distinction it presupposes—is displaced by *appearing*, producing a strange constriction of the gap between consumer and commodity. The form of affect that embodies this constriction is also an affect aligned with the feminine—empathy. As Benjamin points out, "If the soul of the commodity which Marx occasionally mentions in jest existed, it would be the most empathetic ever encountered in the realm of souls, for it would have to see in everyone the buyer in whose hand and house it wants to nestle."[36]

Commodity and consumer share the same attributes—appeal to the eye and an empathetic relation to the other—and become indistinguishable. Just as the category of "youth" has been expropriated by the commodity system and, as Guy Debord maintains, "is in no way the property of those who are now young,"[37] "femininity" as a category is not the possession of women—it is not necessarily something we should strive to reclaim. The feminine position has come to exemplify the roles of consumer and spectator in their embodiment of a curiously passive desiring subjectivity.

In her desire to bring the things of the screen closer, to approximate the bodily image of the star and to possess the space in which she dwells, the female spectator experiences the intensity of the image as lure and exemplifies the perception proper to the consumer. The cinematic image for the woman is both shop window and mirror, the one simply a means of access to the other. The mirror/window, then, takes on the aspect of a trap whereby her subjectivity becomes synonymous with her objectification. In the words of Irigaray,

> Man endows the commodities he produces with a narcissism that blurs the seriousness of utility, of use. Desire, as soon as there is exchange, "perverts" need. But that perversion will be attributed to commodities and to their alleged relations. Whereas they can have no relationships except from the perspective of speculating third parties.[38]

The female subject of the consumer look in the cinematic arena becomes, through a series of mediations, the industry's own merchandizing asset. One must ask at this point, "Whose gaze is ultimately addressed?" and "Who profits?"

NOTES

1. This article is drawn from the introductory chapter of my book, *The Desire to Desire: The Woman's Film of the 1940s* (Bloomington: Indiana University Press, 1987).

2. Fredric Jameson, "Reification and Utopia in Mass Culture." *Social Text* 1:1 (Winter 1979), 131.

3. See Elaine Marks and Isabelle de Courtivron, eds., *New French Feminisms* (Amherst: University of Massachusetts Press, 1980), pp. 107–10, and Luce Irigaray, *This Sex Which Is Not One*, trans. Catherine Porter (Ithaca, N.Y.: Cornell University Press, 1985), pp. 170–92.

4. Irigaray, *This Sex Which Is Not One*, p. 84. See also pp. 172–73.

5. Claude Lévi-Strauss, *The Elementary Structures of Kinship*, trans. James Harle Bell, John Richard von Sturmer, and Rodney Needham (Boston: Beacon Press, 1969), p. 496.

6. Ibid.

7. Fredric Jameson, "Pleasure: A Political Issue," in *Formations of Pleasure* (London: Routledge and Kegan Paul, 1983), p. 4.

8. Charles Eckert, "The Carole Lombard in Macy's Window," *Quarterly Review of Film Studies* 3:1 (Winter 1978), 4.

9. Jeanne Allen, "The Film Viewer as Consumer," *Quarterly Review of Film Studies* 5:4 (Fall 1980), 482.

10. Quoted in Eckert, "Carole Lombard," p. 5.

11. Michèle Le Doueff, "Pierre Roussel's Chiasmas: From Imaginary Knowledge to the Learned Imagination," *Ideology and Consciousness* 9 (Winter 1981–82), 46.

12. See Stuart Ewen, *Captains of Consciousness: Advertising and the Social Roots of the Consumer Culture* (New York: McGraw-Hill, 1976).

13. Judith Mayne, "Immigrants and Spectators," *Wide Angle* 5:2 (1982), 34.

14. Allen, "Film Viewer," p. 487.

15. Ibid., p. 486.

16. Eckert, "Carole Lombard," p. 4.

17. Ibid., p. 10.

18. Carl Laemmle, "The Business of Motion Pictures," in Tino Balio, ed., *The American Film Industry* (Madison: University of Wisconsin Press, 1976), p. 163.

19. Ibid., p. 162.

20. Eckert, "Carole Lombard," p. 19. Also, Stuart Ewen claims that, in the 1920s, "The home, the arena of consumption, was central to the woman's world and consequently only a small percentage of advertising appears to have been directed at the male population" (*Captains of Consciousness*, p. 151).

21. Eckert, "Carole Lombard," p. 19–20.

22. Leo A. Handel, *Hollywood Looks at Its Audience: A Report of Film Audience Research* (Urbana: University of Illinois Press, 1950), p. 101.

23. Susan M. Hartmann, *The Home Front and Beyond: American Women in the 1940s* (Boston: Twayne, 1982), p. 200.

24. Ferdinand Lundberg and Marynia F. Farnham, M.D., *Modern Woman: The Lost Sex* (New York: Harper and Brothers, 1947).

25. The press books for 1940s films that I examined are available in the collection of the Doheny Library of the University of Southern California.

26. Rachel Bowlby, *Just Looking: Consumer Culture in Dreiser, Gissing and Zola* (New York: Methuen, 1985), p. 32.

27. Wolfgang Schivelbusch, *The Railway Journey: Trains and Travel in the 19th Century*, trans. Anselm Hollo (New York: Urizen Books, 1977), pp. 184–85.

28. Jameson, "Reification and Utopia in Mass Culture," p. 133.

29. Walter Benjamin, "The Work of Art in the Age of Mechanical Reproduction," in Hannah Arendt, ed., *Illuminations*, trans. Harry Zohn (New York: Schocken Books), p. 223.

30. Schivelbusch, *The Railway Journey*, p. 48.

31. Benjamin, "Work of Art," p. 222.

32. Ibid., p. 223.

33. As Miriam Hansen has pointed out to me, the alignment of the opposition between distance and closeness with that between fetishism and nonfetishism does tend to reduce the dynamics of proximity and distance operating within fetishism itself. One could undoubtedly also argue that narcissism presupposes a similar dialectic, invoking the inevitable distance between the desiring subject and the mirror image. Nevertheless, my point is that fetishism ultimately enables the maintenance of a distance—for the fetishist, "having" and "being" are separable. The fetishist's relation to the object is always doubly mediated: through the constitution of a substitute object and the "knowledge"

that the woman "really" does lack the phallus. Narcissism implies no knowledge whatsoever—rather, it signifies full investment in an illusion.

34. Ewen, *Captains of Consciousness*, p. 47.

35. Ibid., p. 39.

36. Benjamin, *Charles Baudelaire: A Lyric Poet in the Era of High Capitalism*, trans. Harry Zohn (London: New Left Books, 1973), p. 55.

37. Guy Debord, *Society of the Spectacle* (Detroit: Black and Red, 1977), section 62.

38. Irigaray, *This Sex Which Is Not One*, p. 177.

The Production Code

The content of motion pictures has been a subject of public controversy from the age of the peepshow (1894–1896) to the present. Early films made for Edison's Kinetoscope, a small-screen, single-viewer, peepshow device, included relatively racy material. The peepshow provided views of exotic dancers, such as Anabelle in her *Butterfly Dance* and *Serpentine Dance* (1895), whose exposed ankles shocked the sensibilities of middle-class patrons. There were also suggestive films of female acrobats, such as a that of the woman who disrobes while on a trapeze (*Trapeze Disrobing Act* [1901]). Also common were films of women whose skirts were blown upward when they walk over subway gratings (*What Happened on Twenty-Third Street, New York City* [1902]). Several films were set in Chinese opium dens, where unspeakably sinister events presumably took place. Other peepshow items featured a bride who undresses for bed while her husband secretly watches her from behind a screen (*The Bride Retires* [France, 1902]) and a man who spies on a woman undressing in front of her window (*Pull Down the Curtains, Suzie* [1904]).

As more and more middle-class patrons (and women and children) began to frequent the nickelodeons in 1905–1908, both the images on the screen and the physical conditions under which films were viewed in the theaters became an issue of social concern. On December 24, 1908, in response to complaints from clergymen objecting that motion picture shows were breeding grounds for vice, the mayor of New York, George B. McClellan, ordered all the city's nickelodeons to be closed. The motion picture industry placated its would-be city, state, and national censors by instituting a program of self-censorship. In March 1909, the Motion Picture Patents Company, an association of major motion picture producers, established its own board of censorship, which, in October 1909, became the National Board of

135

Censorship (whose name was changed in 1916 to the National Board of Review).

Various states established their own censorship boards in the 1910s and 1920s. In 1915, the U.S. Supreme Court found that motion pictures were not guaranteed the "free speech" protection granted to newspapers and other media under the First Amendment; it was not until 1952 that the court finally ruled that movies were a form of expression protected by the Constitution. In the interim, local and national censorship bodies reviewed the content of motion pictures. In 1922, in the wake of criticism over public scandals involving comedy star Fatty Arbuckle (who was accused of rape and murder), actor Wallace Reid (who died of a drug overdose), and director William Desmond Taylor (who was mysteriously murdered), film producers created a self-regulatory organization, the Motion Picture Producers and Distributors of America (MPPDA), in an attempt to forestall external regulation. They hired Will Hays, Warren Harding's Postmaster General and former Chairman of the Republican National Committee, to clean up Hollywood. In conjunction with the MPPDA, Hays created what would subsequently be known as the "Hays Office," an organization that was charged with guaranteeing to the public that Hollywood movies would be suitable for family consumption.

With the coming of sound, studios began to use screenplays on a regular basis in the production and preproduction process. In 1927, Hays and a group of major Hollywood producers drew up a list of thirty-six specific guidelines for producers, which became known as "The Don'ts and Be Carefuls." The Hays Office also began to review screenplays informally submitted to it by several studios. However, these guidelines were not strictly enforced, and certain major studios, such as Warner Bros., did not routinely submit scripts for review.

In 1930, in response to criticism from religious organizations, a more thorough production code was drafted. Written by Martin Quigley, the (Catholic) publisher of the *Motion Picture Herald*, and Father Daniel A. Lord, S. J., the new code attempted to explain the general moral principles by which motion picture producers should be guided as well as to spell out specific directives regarding the depiction of crimes against the law, sex, dances, religion, vulgarity, "repellant" subjects, and other potentially objectionable material.

However, the 1930 code was ignored as often as it was observed. Indeed, a series of highly successful gangster films, such as *The Public Enemy* (1931), *Little Caesar* (1931), and *Scarface* (1932), in which gangsters were portrayed as tragic heroes, and popular sex comedies starring Mae West (e.g., *I'm No Angel* [1933]; *Belle of the Nineties* [1934]) and Jean Harlow (*Platinum Blonde* [1931]; *Red Dust* [1932]; *Bombshell* [1933]) prompted the Catholic Bishops of the United States to form the Legion of Decency in 1934. Insisting that industry self-regulation was not working, the legion, under the direction of Joseph I. Breen, threatened a nationwide boycott of motion pictures unless teeth were put into the 1930 code or a new code was written and strictly enforced. This threat led to the creation of the Production Code Administration (PCA), headed by Joe Breen, on July 1, 1934. The PCA was empowered by the studios to enforce the 1930 code.

The code remained in effect until the 1950s, when it was challenged by independent producer-director Otto Preminger, who successfully released two films, *The Moon Is Blue* (1953) and *The Man with the Golden Arm* (1955), without a PCA seal of approval. The PCA had objected to the use of the words *professional virgin* and *pregnant* in *Moon* and to the subject matter of *Golden Arm*, which dealt openly with the problem of drug addiction. The major studios, however, continued to submit scripts and finished films to the PCA for approval.

During the 1960s, controversial topics that tested the flexibility of the code became increasingly popular with Hollywood producers. In 1966, a major studio (Warner Bros.) released director Mike Nichols' screen adaptation of Edward Albee's play, *Who's Afraid of Virginia Woolf?* Its stars, Richard Burton and Elizabeth Taylor, traded expletives back and forth that had never been heard before in first-run American theaters, including *goddam, son of a bitch, bastard, screw you,* and *up yours.* The PCA responded with a revision of the code, expanding it to include a new category, "Suggested for Mature Audiences." In November 1968, the industry had abandoned the restrictive code for a more flexible ratings system, administered by the Motion Picture Association of America and the National Association of Theater Owners. Under the ratings system, motion pictures were "graded" in an attempt to identity the particular age group for which a film had been deemed appropriate. "G" meant that a film was suitable for general audiences of all ages; an "M" (which was subsequently changed to "PG") identified a film as suitable for mature audiences (i.e., adults) and, subject to the guidance of their parents or to "parental guidance," for children. An "R" indicated that a film was restricted to adults; children younger than the age of sixteen (later changed to seventeen) were admitted only if accompanied by an adult. In the case of an "X" rating, no one younger than the age of sixteen (later seventeen) was admitted. After the release of *Indiana Jones and the Temple of Doom* (1984), which contained graphic violence deemed unsuitable for children younger than age thirteen, the PG rating was modified, broken down into PG and PG-13. In 1990, a new rating—"NC-17" (no children younger than seventeen)—was introduced to distinguish "serious" films with mature themes from X-rated pornographic films.—Editor.

The Production Code

Code to Govern the Making of Talking, Synchronized and Silent Motion Pictures

Formulated by Association of Motion Picture Producers, Inc., and the Motion Picture Producers and Distributors of America, Inc.

Motion picture producers recognize the high trust and confidence which have been placed in them by the people of the world and which have made motion pictures a universal form of entertainment.

They recognize their responsibility to the public because of this trust and because entertainment and art are important influences in the life of a nation.

Hence, through regarding motion pictures primarily as entertainment without any explicit purpose of teaching or propaganda, they know that the motion picture within its own field of entertainment may be directly responsible for spiritual or moral progress, for higher types of social life, and for much correct thinking.

During the rapid transition from silent to talking pictures they have realized the necessity and the opportunity of subscribing to a Code to govern the production of talking pictures and of reacknowledging this responsibility.

On their part, they ask from the public and from public leaders a sympathetic understanding of their purposes and problems and a spirit of cooperation that will allow them the freedom and opportunity necessary to bring the motion picture to a still higher level of wholesome entertainment for all the people.

General Principles

1. No picture shall be produced which will lower the moral standards of those who see it. Hence the sympathy of the audience shall never be thrown to the side of crime, wrong-doing, evil or sin.

2. Correct standards of life, subject only to the requirements of drama and entertainment, shall be presented.

3. Law, natural or human, shall not be ridiculed, nor shall sympathy be created for its violation.

Particular Applications

I. CRIMES AGAINST THE LAW

These shall never be presented in such a way as to throw sympathy with the crime as against law and justice or to inspire others with a desire for imitation.

    1. *Murder*
        a. The technique of murder must be presented in a way that will not inspire imitation.
        b. Brutal killings are not to be presented in detail.
        c. Revenge in modern times shall not be justified.
    2. *Methods of Crime* should not be explicitly presented.
        a. Theft, robbery, safe-cracking, and dynamiting of trains, mines, building, etc., should not be detailed in method.
        b. Arson must be subject to the same safeguards.
        c. The use of firearms should be restricted to essentials.
        d. Methods of smuggling should not be presented.
    3. *Illegal drug traffic* must never be presented.
    4. *The use of liquor* in American life, when not required by the plot or for proper characterization, will not be shown.

II. SEX

The sanctity of the institution of marriage and the home shall be upheld. Pictures shall not infer that low forms of sex relationship are the accepted or common thing.

    1. *Adultery*, sometimes necessary plot material, must not be explicitly treated or justified or presented attractively.
    2. *Scenes of Passion*
        a. They should not be introduced when not essential to the plot.
        b. Excessive and lustful kissing, lustful embraces, suggestive postures and gestures, are not to be shown.
        c. In general passion should so be treated that these scenes do not stimulate the lower and baser elements.

3. *Seduction or Rape*
   a. They should never be more than suggested, and only when essential for the plot, and even then never shown by explicit method.
   b. They are never the proper subject for comedy.
4. *Sex perversion* or any inference to it is forbidden.
5. *White slavery* shall not be treated.
6. *Miscegenation* (sex relationship between white and black races) is forbidden.
7. *Sex Hygiene* and venereal disease are not subjects for motion pictures.
8. Scenes of *actual child birth*, in fact or in silhouette, are never to be presented.
9. *Children's sex organs* are never to be exposed.

III. VULGARITY

The treatment of low, disgusting, unpleasant, though not necessarily evil, subjects should be subject always to the dictate of good taste and a regard for the sensibilities of the audience.

IV. OBSCENITY

Obscenity in word, gesture, references, song, joke, or by suggestion (even when likely to be understood only by part of the audience) is forbidden.

V. PROFANITY

Pointed profanity (this includes the words, God, Lord, Jesus, Christ—unless used reverently—Hell, S.O.B., damn, Gawd), or every other profane or vulgar expression however used, is forbidden.

VI. COSTUME

1. *Complete nudity* is never permitted. This includes nudity in fact or in silhouette, or any lecherous or licentious notice thereof by other characters in the pictures.
2. *Undressing scenes* should be avoided, and never used save where essential to the plot.
3. *Indecent or undue exposure* is forbidden.
4. *Dancing costumes* intended to permit undue exposure or indecent movements in the dance are forbidden.

VII. DANCES

1. Dances suggesting or representing sexual actions or indecent passion are forbidden.
2. Dances which emphasize indecent movements are to be regarded as obscene.

VIII. RELIGION
1. No film or episode may throw *ridicule* on any religious faith.
2. *Ministers of religion* in their character as ministers of religion should not be used as comic characters or as villains.
3. *Ceremonies* of any definite religion should be carefully and respectfully handled.

IX. LOCATIONS

The treatment of bedrooms must be governed by good taste and delicacy.

X. NATIONAL FEELINGS
1. *The use of the Flag* shall be consistently respectful.
2. The history, institutions, prominent people and citizenry of other nations shall be represented fairly.

XI. TITLES

Salacious, indecent, or obscene titles shall not be used.

XII. REPELLENT SUBJECTS

The following subjects must be treated within the careful limits of good taste:
1. *Actual hangings* or electrocutions as legal punishments for crime.
2. *Third degree* methods.
3. *Brutality* and possible gruesomeness.
4. *Branding* of people or animals.
5. *Apparent cruelty* to children or animals.
6. *The sale of women,* or a woman selling her virtue.
7. *Surgical operations.*

The Reasons Supporting Preamble of Code

1. Theatrical motion pictures, that is, pictures intended for the theatre as distinct from pictures intended for churches, schools, lecture halls, educational movements, social reform movements, etc., are primarily to be regarded as ENTERTAINMENT.

Mankind has always recognized the importance of entertainment and its value in rebuilding the bodies and souls of human beings.

But it has always recognized that entertainment can be of a character either HELPFUL or HARMFUL to the human race, and in consequence has clearly distinguished between:

   a. *Entertainment which tends to improve* the race, or at least to re-create and rebuild human beings exhausted with the realities of life; and
   b. *Entertainment which tends to degrade* human beings, or to lower their standards of life and living.

Hence the MORAL IMPORTANCE of entertainment is something which has been universally recognized. It enters intimately into the lives of men and women and affects them closely; it occupies their minds and affections during leisure hours; and ultimately touches the whole of their lives. A man may be judged by his standard of entertainment as easily as by the standard of his work.

So *correct entertainment raises* the whole of a nation.

Wrong entertainment lowers the whole living conditions and moral ideas of a race.

   Note, for example, the healthy reactions to healthful, moral sports, like baseball, golf; the unhealthy reactions to sports like cock-fighting, bull-fighting, bear baiting, etc.

   Note, too, the effect on ancient nations of gladiatorial combats, the obscene plays of Roman times, etc.

2. Motion pictures are very important as art.

Though a new art, possibly a combination art, it has the same object as the other arts, the presentation of human thought, emotion, and experience, in terms of an appeal to the soul through the senses.

   Here, as in entertainment:

   Art *enters intimately* into the lives of human beings.

   Art can be *morally good,* lifting men to higher levels. This has been done through good music, great painting, authentic fiction, poetry, drama.

   Art can be *morally* evil in its effects. This is the case clearly enough with unclean art, indecent books, suggestive drama. The effect on the lives of men and women is obvious.

   Note: It has often been argued that art in itself is unmoral, neither good nor bad. This is perhaps true of the THING which is music, painting, poetry, etc. But the thing is the PRODUCT of some person's mind, and the intention of that mind was either good or bad morally when it produced the thing. Besides, the thing has its EFFECT upon those who come into contact with it. In both these ways, that is, as a product of a mind and as the cause of definite effects, it has a deep moral significance and an unmistakable moral quality.

Hence: The motion pictures, which are the most popular of modern arts for the masses, have their moral quality from the intention of the minds which produce them and from their effects on the moral lives and reactions of their audiences. This gives them a most important morality.

> 1. They *reproduce* the morality of the men who use the pictures as a medium for the expression of their ideas and ideals.
> 2. They *affect* the moral standards of those who through the screen take in these ideas and ideals.

In the case of the motion pictures, this effect may be particularly emphasized because no art has so quick and so widespread an appeal to the masses. It has become in an incredibly short period *the art of the multitudes.*

3. The motion picture, because of its importance as an entertainment and because of the trust placed in it by the peoples of the world, has special MORAL OBLIGATIONS.

> A. Most arts appeal to the mature. This art appeals at once to *every class,* immature, developed, undeveloped, law abiding, criminal. Music has its grades for different classes; so has literature and drama. This art of the motion picture, combining as it does the two fundamental appeals of looking at a *picture* and *listening to a story,* at once reaches every class of society.
>
> B. By reason of the mobility of a film and the ease of picture distribution, and because of the possibility of duplicating positives in large quantities, this art *reaches places* unpenetrated by other forms of art.
>
> C. Because of these two facts, it is difficult to produce films intended for only certain classes of people. The exhibitor's theatres are built for the masses, for the cultivated and the rude, the mature and the immature, the self-respecting and the criminal. Films, unlike books and music, can with difficulty be confined to certain selected groups.
>
> D. The latitude given to film material cannot, in consequence, be as wide as the latitude given to *book material.* In addition:
>
> > a. A book describes; a film vividly presents. One presents on a cold page; the other by apparently living people.

    b. A book reaches the mind through words merely; a film reaches the eyes and ears through the reproduction of actual events.

    c. The reaction of a reader to a book depends largely on the keenness of the reader's imagination; the reaction to a film depends on the vividness of presentation.

    Hence many things which might be described or suggested in a book could not possibly be presented in a film.

E. This is also true when comparing the film with the newspaper.

    a. Newspapers present by description, films by actual presentation.

    b. Newspapers are after the fact and present things as having taken place; the film gives the events in the process of enactment and with the apparent reality of life.

F. Everything possible in a *play* is not possible in a film.

    a. Because of the *larger audience of the film* and its consequential mixed character. Psychologically, the larger the audience, the lower the moral mass resistance to suggestion.

    b. Because through light, enlargement of character, presentation, scenic emphasis, etc., the screen story is *brought closer* to the audience than the play.

    c. The enthusiasm for and interest in the film actors and actresses, developed beyond anything of the sort in history, makes the audience largely sympathetic toward the characters they portray and the stories in which they figure. Hence the audience is more ready to confuse actor and actress and the characters they portray, and it is most receptive of the emotions and ideals presented by their favorite stars.

G. *Small communities*, remote from sophistication and from the hardening process which often takes place in the ethical and moral standards of groups in larger cities, are easily and readily reached by any sort of film.

H. The grandeur of mass settings, large action, spectacular features, etc., affects and arouses more intensely the emotional side of the audience.

In general, the mobility, popularity, accessibility, emotional appeal, vividness, straightforward presentation of fact in the film make for more intimate contact with a larger audience and for greater emotional appeal. Hence the larger moral responsibilities of the motion pictures.

Reasons Supporting the General Principles

1. No picture shall be produced which will lower the moral standards of those who see it. Hence, the sympathy of the audience should never be thrown on the side of crime, wrong-doing, evil or sin.

This is done:

1. When *evil* is made to appear *attractive* or *alluring* and good is made to appear *unattractive*.
2. When the *sympathy* of the audience is thrown on the side of crime, wrong-doing, evil, sin. The same thing is true of a film that would throw sympathy against goodness, honor, innocence, purity or honesty.

Note: Sympathy with a person who sins is not the same as sympathy with the sin or crime of which he is guilty. We may feel sorry for the plight of the murderer or even understand the circumstances which led him to his crime. We may not feel sympathy for the wrong which he has done.

The *presentation of evil* is often essential for art or fiction or drama.

This in itself is not wrong provided:

a. That evil is *not presented alluringly*. Even if later in the film the evil is condemned or punished, it must not be allowed to appear so attractive that the audience's emotions are drawn to desire or approve so strongly that later the condemnation is forgotten and only the apparent joy of the sin remembered.
b. That throughout, the audience feels sure that *evil is wrong* and *good is right*.

2. Correct standards of life shall, as far as possible, be presented.

A *wide knowledge of life and living* is made possible through the film. When right standards are consistently presented, the motion picture exercises the most powerful influences. It builds character, develops right ideals, inculcates correct principles, and all this in the attractive story form.

If motion pictures consistently *hold up for admiration high types of characters* and present stories that will affect lives for the better, they can become the most powerful and natural force for the improvement of mankind.

3. Law, natural or human, shall not be ridiculed, nor shall sympathy be created for its violation.

> By *natural law* is understood the law which is written in the hearts of all mankind, the great underlying principles of right and justice dictated by conscience.
>
> By *human law* is understood the law written by civilized nations.
>
>> 1. *The presentation of crimes* against the law is *often necessary* for the carrying out of the plot. But the presentation must not throw sympathy with the crime as against the law nor with the criminal as against those who punish him.
>>
>> 2. *The courts of the land* should not be presented as unjust. This does not mean that a single court may not be represented as unjust, much less that a single court official must not be presented this way. But the court system of the country must not suffer as a result of this presentation.

Reasons Underlying Particular Applications
Preliminary:

1. *Sin and evil* enter into the story of human beings and hence in themselves *are dramatic material.*

2. In the use of this material, it must be distinguished between *sin which repels* by its very nature, and *sins which often attract.*

> a. In the first class come murder, most theft, many legal crimes, lying, hypocrisy, cruelty, etc.
>
> b. In the second class come sex sins, sins and crimes of apparent heroism, such as banditry, daring thefts, leadership in evil, organized crime, revenge, etc.

The first class needs far less care in treatment, as sins and crimes of this class are naturally unattractive. The audience instinctively condemns and is repelled. Hence the important objective must be to avoid the hardening of the audience, especially of those who are young and impressionable, to the thought and fact of crime. People can become accustomed even to murder, cruelty, brutality, and repellent crimes, if these are sufficiently repeated. The second class needs real care in handling, as the response of human natures to their appeal is obvious. This is treated more fully below.

3. A careful distinction can be made between films intended for *general distribution*, and films intended for use in theatres restricted to a *limited audience*. Themes and plots quite appropriate for the latter would be altogether out of place and dangerous in the former.

> Note: In general the practice of using a general theatre and limiting its patronage during the showing of a certain film to "Adults Only" is not completely satisfactory and is only partially effective.
>
> However, maturer minds may easily understand and accept without harm subject matter in plots which do younger people positive harm.
>
> Hence: If there should be created a special type of theatre, catering exclusively to an adult audience, for plays of this character (plays with problem themes, difficult discussions and maturer treatment) it would seem to afford an outlet, which does not now exist, for pictures unsuitable for general distribution but permissible for exhibitions to a restricted audience.

I. CRIMES AGAINST THE LAW

The treatment of crimes against the law must not:

> 1. *Teach methods* of crime.
> 2. *Inspire potential criminals* with a desire for imitation.
> 3. *Make criminals seem heroic* and justified.

Revenge in modern times shall not be justified. In lands and ages of less developed civilization and moral principles, revenge may sometimes be presented. This would be the case especially in places where no law exists to cover the crime because of which revenge is committed.

Because of its evil consequences, the drug traffic should not be presented in any form. The existence of the trade should not be brought to the attention of audiences.

The use of liquor should never be excessively presented even in picturing countries where its use is legal. In scenes from American life, the necessities of plot and proper characterization alone justify its use. And in this case, it should be shown with moderation.

II. SEX

Out of regard to the sanctity of marriage and the home, the *triangle*, that is, the love of a third party for one already married, needs careful handling.

The treatment should not throw sympathy against marriage as an institution. *Scenes of passion* must be treated with an honest acknowledgment of human nature and its normal reactions. Many scenes cannot be presented without arousing dangerous emotions on the part of immature, the young or the *criminal classes.*

Even within the limits of *pure love,* certain facts have been universally regarded by lawmakers as outside the limits of safe presentation.

In the case of *impure love,* the love which society has always regarded as wrong and which has been banned by divine law, the following are important:

1. Impure love must *not* be presented as *attractive and beautiful.*
2. It must *not* be the subject of *comedy or farce,* or treated as material for *laughter.*
3. It must *not* be presented in such a way as to *arouse passion* or morbid curiosity on the part of the audience.
4. It must *not* be made to seem *right and permissible.*
5. In general, it must *not* be *detailed* in method and manner.

III. VULGARITY; IV OBSCENTIY; V. PROFANITY, hardly need further explanation than is contained in the Code.

VI. COSTUME

General Principles:

1. The effect of nudity or semi-nudity upon the normal man or woman, and much more upon the young and upon the immature persons, has been honestly recognized by all lawmakers and moralists.
2. Hence the fact that the nude or semi-nude body may be *beautiful* does not make its use in the films moral. For, in addition to its beauty, the effect of the nude or semi-nude body on the normal individual must be taken into consideration.
3. Nudity or semi-nudity used simply to put a *"punch"* into a picture comes under the head of immoral actions. It is immoral in its effect on the average audience.
4. Nudity can never be permitted as being *necessary for the plot.* Semi-nudity must not result in undue or indecent exposure.
5. *Transparent* or *translucent materials* and silhouettes are frequently more suggestive than actual exposure.

VII. DANCES

Dancing in general is recognized as an *art* and as a *beautiful* form of expressing human emotions.

But dances which suggest or represent sexual actions, whether preformed solo or with two or more, dances intended to excite the emotional reaction of an audience, dances with movement of the breasts, excessive body movements while the feet are stationary, violate decency and are wrong.

VIII. RELIGION

The reason why ministers of religion may not be comic characters or villains is simply because the attitude taken toward them may easily become the attitude taken toward religion in general. Religion is lowered in the minds of the audience because of the lowering of the audience's respect for a minister.

IX. LOCATIONS

Certain places are so closely and thoroughly associated with sexual life or with sexual sin that their use must be carefully limited.

X. NATIONAL FEELINGS

The just rights, history, and feelings of any nation are entitled to consideration and respectful treatment.

XI. TITLES

As the title of a picture is the brand on that particular type of goods, it must conform to the ethical practices of all such honest business.

XII. REPELLENT SUBJECTS

Such subjects are occasionally necessary for the plot. Their treatment must never offend good taste or injure the sensibilities of an audience.

The Dark Side of Mass
Culture: Film Noir

Paul Schrader

Notes on Film Noir

In 1946 French critics, seeing the American films they had missed during the war, noticed the new mood of cynicism, pessimism, and darkness that had crept into the American cinema. The darkening stain was most evident in routine crime thrillers but was also apparent in prestigious melodramas.

The French cinéastes soon realized they had seen only the tip of the iceberg: as the years went by, Hollywood lighting grew darker, characters more corrupt, themes more fatalistic, and the tone more hopeless. By 1949 American movies were in the throes of their deepest and most creative funk. Never before had films dared to take such a harsh uncomplimentary look at American life, and they would not dare to do so again for 20 years.

Hollywood's film noir has recently become the subject of renewed interest among moviegoers and critics. The fascination film noir holds for today's young filmgoers and film students reflects recent trends in American cinema: American movies are again taking a look at the underside of the American character, but compared to such relentlessly cynical film noir as *Kiss Me Deadly* or *Kiss Tomorrow Goodbye*, the new self-hate cinema of *Easy Rider* and *Medium Cool* seems naive and romantic. As the current political mood hardens, filmgoers and filmmakers will find the film noir of the late 1940s increasingly attractive. The 1940s may be to the 1970s what the 1930s were to the 1960s.

Film noir is equally interesting to critics. It offers writers a cache of excellent, little-known films (film noir is oddly both one of Hollywood's best periods and least known) and gives auteur-weary critics an

Originally published 1971 (pamphlet to accompany short season programmed by Schrader for Los Angeles Film Festival); *Film Comment*, 8:1 (Spring 1972); reprinted, with the permission of the author, from *Schrader on Schrader* (London: Faber & Faber, 1992).

opportunity to apply themselves to the newer questions of classification and transdirectorial style. After all, what is a film noir?

Film noir is not a genre (as Raymond Durgnat has helpfully pointed out over the objections of Higham and Greenberg's *Hollywood in the Forties*). It is not defined, as are the Western and gangster genres, by conventions of setting and conflict, but rather by the more subtle qualities of tone and mood. It is a film "noir," as opposed to the possible variants of film grey or film off-white.

Film noir is also a specific period of film history, such as German Expressionism or the French New Wave. In general, film noir refers to those Hollywood films of the 1940s and early 1950s that portrayed the world of dark, slick city streets, crime, and corruption.

Film noir is an extremely unwieldy period. It harks back to many previous periods: Warners' 1930s gangster films, the French "poetic realism" of Carné and Duvivier, Von Sternbergian melodrama, and, farthest back, German Expressionist crime films (Lang's Mabuse cycle). Film noir can stretch at its outer limits from *The Maltese Falcon* (1941) to *Touch of Evil* (1958), and almost every dramatic Hollywood film from 1941 to 1953 contains some noir elements. There are also foreign off-shoots of film noir, such as *The Third Man, Breathless*, and *Le Doulos*.

Almost every critic has his own definition of film noir and a personal list of film titles and dates to back it up. Personal and descriptive definitions, however, can get a bit sticky. A film of urban nightlife is not necessarily a film noir, and a film noir need not necessarily concern crime and corruption. Because film noir is defined by tone rather than genre, it is almost impossible to argue one critic's descriptive definition against another's. How many noir elements does it take to make a film noir noir?

Rather than haggle definitions, I would attempt to reduce film noir to its primary colours (all shades of black), those cultural and stylistic elements to which any definition must return.

At the risk of sounding like Arthur Knight, I would suggest that there were four conditions in Hollywood in the 1940s that brought about the film noir. (The danger of Knight's *Liveliest Art* method is that it makes film history less a matter of structural analysis and more a case of artistic and social forces magically interacting and coalescing.) Each of the following four catalytic elements, however, can define the film noir; the distinctly noir tonality draws from each of these elements.

War and postwar disillusionment. The acute downer that hit the United States after the Second World War was, in fact, a delayed reaction to the 1930s. All through the Depression, movies were needed to keep people's spirits up, and for the most part, they did. The crime films of this period were Horatio Algerish and socially conscious. Toward the end of the 1930s, a darker crime film began to appear (*You Only Live Once, The Roaring Twenties*), and were it not for the war, film noir would have been at full steam by the early 1940s.

The need to produce Allied propaganda abroad and promote patriotism at home blunted the fledgling moves toward a dark cinema, and the film noir thrashed about in the studio system, not quite able to come into full prominence. During the war, the first uniquely film noirs appeared: *The Maltese Falcon, The Glass Key, This Gun for Hire,* and *Laura,* but these films lacked the distinctly noir bite the end of the war would bring.

As soon as the war was over, however, American films became markedly more sardonic—and there was a boom in the crime film. For fifteen years, the pressures against America's amelioristic cinema had been building up, and given the freedom, audiences and artists were now eager to take a less optimistic view of things. The disillusionment many soldiers, small businessmen, and housewife/factory employees felt in returning to a peacetime economy was directly mirrored in the sordidness of the urban crime film.

This immediate postwar disillusionment was directly demonstrated in films such as *Cornered, The Blue Dahlia, Dead Reckoning,* and *Ride a Pink Horse,* in which a serviceman returns from the war to find his sweetheart unfaithful or dead, or his business partner cheating him, or the whole society something less than worth fighting for. The war continues, but now the antagonism turns with a new viciousness toward the American society itself.

Postwar realism. Shortly after the war, every film-producing country had a resurgence of realism. In America it first took the form of films by such producers as Louis de Rochemont (*House on 92nd Street, Call Northside 777*) and Mark Hellinger (*The Killers, Brute Force*), and directors such as Henry Hathaway and Jules Dassin. "Every scene was filmed on the actual location depicted," the 1947 de Rochemont-Hathaway *Kiss of Death* proudly proclaimed. Even after de Rochemont's particular "March of Time" authenticity fell from vogue, realistic exteriors remained a permanent fixture of film noir.

The realistic movement also suited America's postwar mood; the public's desire for a more honest and harsh view of America would not be satisfied by the same studio streets they had been watching for a dozen years. The postwar realistic trend succeeded in breaking film noir away from the domain of the high-class melodrama, placing it where it more properly belonged, in the streets with everyday people. In retrospect, the pre-de Rochemont films noirs look definitely tamer than the postwar realistic films. The studio look of films such as *The Big Sleep* and *The Mask of Dimitrios* blunts their sting, making them seem polite and conventional in contrast to their later, more realistic counterparts.

The German influence. Hollywood played host to an influx of German expatriates in the 1920s and 1930s, and these filmmakers and technicians had, for the most part, integrated themselves into the American film establishment. Hollywood never experienced the "Germanization" some civic-minded natives feared, and there is a danger of overemphasizing the German influence in film noir.

But when, in the late 1940s, Hollywood decided to paint it black, there were no greater masters of chiaroscuro than the Germans. The influence of Expressionist lighting has always been just beneath the surface of Hollywood films, and it is not surprising, in film noir, to find it bursting out full bloom. Neither is it surprising to find a large number of Germans and East Europeans working in film noir: Fritz Lang, Robert Siodmak, Billy Wilder, Franz Waxman, Otto Preminger, John Brahm, Anatole Litvak, Karl Freund, Max Ophüls, John Alton, Douglas Sirk, Fred Zinnemann, William Dieterle, Max Steiner, Edgar G. Ulmer, Curtis Bernhardt, and Rudolph Maté.

On the surface, the German Expressionist influence, with its reliance on artificial studio lighting, seems incompatible with postwar realism, with its harsh unadorned exteriors; but it is the unique quality of film noir that it was able to weld seemingly contradictory elements into a uniform style. The best noir technicians simply made all the world a sound stage, directing unnatural and Expressionistic lighting on to realistic settings. In films such as *Union Station, They Live by Night*, and *The Killers*, there is an uneasy, exhilarating combination of realism and Expressionism.

Perhaps the greatest master of noir was Hungarian-born John Alton, an Expressionist cinematographer who could relight Times Square at noon if necessary. No cinematographer better adapted the old Expressionist techniques to the new desire for realism, and his black-and-white photography in such gritty films noirs as *T-Men, Raw Deal, I the Jury*, and *The Big Combo* equals that of such German Expressionist masters as Fritz Wagner and Karl Freund.

The hard-boiled tradition. Another stylistic influence waiting in the wings was the "hard-boiled" school of writers. In the 1930s, authors such as Ernest Hemingway, Dashiell Hammett, Raymond Chandler, James M. Cain, Horace McCoy, and John O'Hara created the "tough," a cynical way of acting and thinking that separated one from the world of everyday emotions— romanticism with a protective shell. The hard-boiled writers had their roots in pulp fiction or journalism, and their protagonists lived out a narcissistic, defeatist code. The hard-boiled hero was, in reality, a soft egg compared with his existential counterpart (Camus is said to have based *The Stranger* on McCoy), but they were a good deal tougher than anything American fiction had seen.

When the movies of the 1940s turned to the American tough moral understrata, the hard-boiled school was waiting with preset conventions of heroes, minor characters, plots, dialogue, and themes. Like the German expatriates, the hard-boiled writers had a style made to order for film noir; and, in turn, they influenced noir screenwriting as much as the Germans influenced noir cinematography.

The most hard-boiled of Hollywood's writers was Raymond Chandler himself, whose script of *Double Indemnity* (from a James M. Cain story) was the best written and most characteristically noir of the period. *Double Indemnity* was the first film that played film noir for what it essentially was: small-time, unredeemed, unheroic; it made a break from the romantic noir cinema of *Mildred Pierce* and *The Big Sleep.*

(In its final stages, however, film noir adapted then bypassed the hard-boiled school. Manic, neurotic, post-1949 films such as *Kiss Tomorrow Goodbye, D.O.A., Where the Sidewalk Ends, White Heat,* and *The Big Heat* are all post-hard-boiled: the air in these regions was even too thin for old-time cynics like Chandler.)

Stylistics. There is not yet a study of the stylistics of film noir, and the task is certainly too large to be attempted here. Like all film movements, film noir drew on a reservoir of film techniques, and given the time, one could correlate its techniques, themes, and causal elements into a stylistic schemata. For the present, however, I'd like to point out some of film noir's recurring techniques.

The majority of scenes are lit for night. Gangsters sit in the offices at midday with the shades pulled and the lights off. Ceiling lights are hung low, and floor lamps are seldom more than 5 feet high. One always has the suspicion that if the lights were all suddenly flipped on, the characters would shrink from the scene like Count Dracula at noontime.

As in German Expressionism, oblique and vertical lines are preferred to horizontal. Obliquity adheres to the choreography of the city and is in direct opposition to the horizontal American tradition of Griffith and Ford. Oblique lines tend to splinter a screen, making it restless and unstable. Light enters the dingy rooms of film noir in such odd shapes—jagged trapezoids, obtuse triangles, vertical slits—that one suspects the windows were cut out with a penknife. No character can speak authoritatively from a space which is being continually cut into ribbons of light. The Anthony

Mann/John Alton *T-Men* is the most dramatic but far from the only example of oblique noir choreography.

The actors and setting are often given equal lighting emphasis. The actors are often hidden in the realistic tableau of the city at night, and more obviously, their faces are often blacked out by shadow as they speak. These shadow effects are unlike the famous Warner Bros. lighting of the 1930s in which the central character was accentuated by a heavy shadow; in film noir, the central character is likely to be standing *in* the shadow. When the environment is given an equal or greater weight than the actor, it, of course, creates a fatalistic, hopeless mood. There is nothing the protagonist can do; the city will outlast and negate even his or her best efforts.

Compositional tension is preferred to physical action. A typical film noir would rather move the scene cinematographically around the actor than have the actor control the scene by physical action. The beating of Robert Ryan in *The Set-Up,* the gunning down of Farley Granger in *They Live by Night,* and the execution of the taxi driver in *The Enforcer* and of Brian Donlevy in *The Big Combo* are all marked by measured pacing, restrained anger, and oppressive compositions and seem much closer to the film noir spirit than the rat-tat-tat and screeching tires of *Scarface* twenty years before or the violent expression actions of *Underworld U.S.A.* ten years later.

There seems to be an almost Freudian attachment to water. The empty noir streets are almost always glistening with fresh evening rain (even in Los Angeles), and the rainfall tends to increase in direct proportion to the drama. Docks and piers are second only to alleyways as the most popular rendezvous points.

There is a love of romantic narration. In such films as *The Postman Always Rings Twice, Laura, Double Indemnity, The Lady from Shanghai, Out of the Past,* and *Sunset Boulevard,* the narration creates a mood of temps perdu: an irretrievable past, a predetermined fate, and an all-enveloping hopelessness. In *Out of the*

Past, Robert Mitchum relates his history with such pathetic relish that it is obvious there is no hope for any future: one can only take pleasure in reliving a doomed past.

A complex chronological order is frequently used to reinforce the feelings of hopelessness and lost time. Such films as *The Enforcer, The Killers, Mildred Pierce, The Dark Past, Chicago Deadline, Out of the Past,* and *The Killing* use a convoluted time sequence to immerse the viewer in a time-disoriented but highly stylized world. The manipulation of time, whether slight or complex, is often used to reinforce a noir principle: the how is always more important than the what.

Themes. Raymond Durgnat has delineated the themes of film noir in an excellent article in British *Cinema* magazine ("The Family Tree of *Film Noir,*" August 1970), and it would be foolish for me to attempt to redo his thorough work in this short space. Durgnat divides film noir into eleven thematic categories, and although one might criticize some of his specific groupings, he does cover the whole gamut of noir production (thematically categorizing more than 300 films).

In each of Durgnat's noir themes (whether Black Widow, Killers-on-the-run, *Doppelgängers*), one finds that the upwardly mobile forces of the 1930s have halted; frontierism has turned to paranoia and claustrophobia. The small-time gangster has now made it big and sits in the mayor's chair, the private eye has quit the police force in disgust, and the young heroine, sick of going along for the ride, is taking others for a ride.

Durgnat, however, does not touch on what is perhaps the most overriding noir theme: there is a passion for the past and present, but a fear of the future. The noir hero dreads to look ahead but instead tries to survive by the day, and if unsuccessful at that, he retreats to the past. Thus film noir's techniques emphasize loss, nostalgia, lack of clear priorities, insecurity; then submerge these self-doubts in mannerism and style. In such a world, style becomes paramount; it is all that separates one from meaninglessness. Chandler described this fundamental noir theme when he described his own fictional world: "It is not a very fragrant world, but it is the world you live in, and certain writers with tough minds and a cool spirit of detachment can make very interesting patterns out of it."

————

Film noir can be subdivided into three broad phases. The first, the wartime period, 1941 to 1946 approximately, was the phase of the private eye and the lone wolf, of Chandler, Hammett, and Greene, of Bogart and Bacall, Ladd and Lake, classy directors such as Curtiz and Garnett, studio sets, and in general, more talk than action. The studio look of this period was reflected in such pictures as *The Maltese Falcon, Casablanca, Gaslight, This Gun for Hire, The Lodger, Woman in the Window, Mildred Pierce, Spellbound, The Big Sleep, Laura, The Lost Weekend, The Strange Love of Martha Ivers, To Have and To Have Not, Fallen Angel, Gilda, Murder My Sweet, The Postman Always Rings Twice, Dark Waters, Scarlet Street, So Dark the Night, The Glass Key, The Mask of Dimitrios,* and *The Dark Mirror.*

The Wilder-Chandler *Double Indemnity* provided a bridge to the postwar phase of film noir. The unflinching noir vision of *Double Indemnity* came as a shock in 1944, and the film was almost blocked by the combined efforts of Paramount, the Hays Office, and star Fred MacMurray. Three years later, however, *Double Indemnity*s were dropping off the studio assembly lines.

The second phase was the postwar realistic period from 1945 to 1949 (the dates overlap and so do the films; these are all approximate phases for which there are many exceptions). These films tended more toward the problems of crime in the streets, political corruption, and police routine. Less romantic heroes like Richard Conte, Burt Lancaster, and Charles McGraw were more suited to this period, as were proletarian directors such as Hathaway, Dassin, and Kazan. The realistic urban look of this phase is seen in such films as *The House on 92nd Street, The Killers, Raw Deal, Act of Violence, Union Station, Kiss of Death, Johnny O'Clock, Force of Evil, Dead Reckoning, Ride the Pink Horse, Dark Passage, Cry of the City, The Set-Up, T-Men, Call Northside 777, Brute Force, The Big Clock, Thieves Highway, Ruthless, Pitfall, Boomerang!,* and *The Naked City.*

The third and final phase of film noir, from 1949 to 1953, was the period of psychotic action and suicidal impulse. The noir hero,

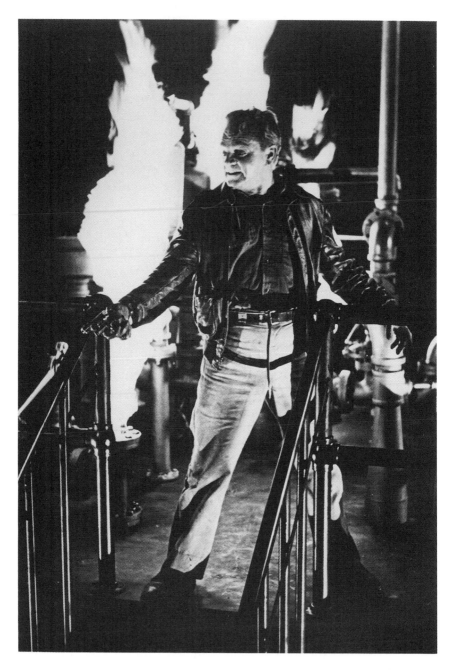

Psychotic action and suicidal impulse: James Cagney as Cody Jarrett at the top of the world in White Heat *(Walsh, 1949). Photo courtesy of Warner Bros.*

seemingly under the weight of ten years of despair, started to go bananas. The psychotic killer, who had in the first period been a subject worthy of study (Olivia de Havilland in *The Dark Mirror*) and in the second a fringe threat (Richard Widmark in *Kiss of Death*) now became the active protagonist (James Cagney in *Kiss Tomorrow Goodbye*). James Cagney made a neurotic comeback, and his instability was matched by that of younger actors such as Robert Ryan and Lee Marvin. This was the phase of the "B" noir film and of psychoanalytically inclined directors such as Ray and Walsh. The forces of personal disintegration are reflected in such films as *White Heat, Gun Crazy, D.O.A., Caught, They Live by Night, Where the Sidewalk Ends, Kiss Tomorrow Goodbye, Detective Story, In a Lonely Place, I the Jury, Ace in the Hole, Panic in the Streets, The Big Heat, On Dangerous Ground,* and *Sunset Boulevard.*

The third phase is the cream of the film noir period. Some critics may prefer the early "grey" melodramas, others the postwar "street" films, but film noir's final phase was the most aesthetically and sociologically piercing. After ten years of steadily shedding romantic conventions, the later noir films finally got down to the root causes of the period: the loss of public honour, heroic conventions, personal integrity, and finally, psychic stability. The third-phase films were painfully self-aware; they seemed to know they stood at the end of a long tradition based on despair and disintegration and did not shy away from that fact. The best and most characteristically noir films—*Gun Crazy, White Heat, Out of the Past, Kiss Tomorrow Goodbye, D.O.A., They Live by Night, The Big Heat*—stand at the end of the period and are the results of self-knowledge. The third phase is rife with end-of-the-line noir heroes: *The Big Heat* and *Where the Sidewalk Ends* are the last stops for the urban cop, *Ace in the Hole* for the newspaper man, the Victor Saville-produced Spillane series (*I the Jury, The Long Wait, Kiss Me Deadly*) for the private eye, *Sunset Boulevard* for the Black Widow, *White Heat* and *Kiss Tomorrow Goodbye* for the gangster, and *D.O.A.* for the John Doe American.

By the mid-1950s, film noir had ground to a halt. There were a few notable stragglers, *Kiss Me Deadly,* the Lewis-Alton *The Big Combo,* and film noir's epitaph, *Touch of Evil,* but for the most part, a new style of crime film had become popular.

As the rise of McCarthy and Eisenhower demonstrated, Americans were eager to see a more bourgeois view of themselves. Crime had to move to the suburbs. The criminal put on a grey flannel suit, and the footsore cop was replaced by the "mobile unit" careening down the expressway. Any attempt at social criticism had to be cloaked in ludicrous affirmations of the American way of life. Technically, television, with its demand for full lighting and close-ups, gradually undercut the German influence, and colour cinematography was, of course, the final blow to the noir look. New directors such as Siegel, Fleischer, Karlson, and Fuller and TV shows such as *Dragnet, M-Squad, Lineup,* and *Highway Patrol* stepped in to create the new crime drama.

Film noir was an immensely creative period—probably the most creative in Hollywood's history, at least if this creativity is measured not by its peaks but by its median level of artistry. Picked at random, a film noir is likely to be a better-made film than a randomly selected silent comedy, musical, Western, and so on. (A Joseph H. Lewis "B" film noir is better than a Lewis "B" Western, for example.) Taken as a whole period, film noir achieved an unusually high level of artistry.

Film noir seemed to bring out the best in everyone: directors, cameramen, screenwriters, actors. Again and again, a film noir will mark the high point on an artist's career graph. Some directors, for example, did their best work in film noir (Stuart Heisler, Robert Siodmak, Gordon Douglas, Edward Dmytryk, John Brahm, John Cromwell, Raoul Walsh, Henry Hathaway); other directors began in film noir and, it seems to me, never regained their original heights (Otto Preminger, Rudolph Maté, Nicholas Ray, Robert Wise, Jules Dassin, Richard Fleischer, John Huston, André de Toth, Robert Aldrich); and other directors who made great films in other moulds also made great films noirs (Orson Welles, Max Ophüls, Fritz Lang, Elia Kazan, Howard Hawks, Robert Rossen, Anthony Mann, Joseph Losey, Alfred Hitchcock, Stanley Kubrick). Whether or not one agrees with this particular schema, its message is irrefutable: film noir was good for practically every director's career. (Two interesting exceptions to prove the case are King Vidor and Jean Renoir.)

Film noir seems to have been a creative release for everyone involved. It gave artists a chance to work with previously forbidden themes, yet had conventions strong enough to protect the mediocre. Cinematographers were allowed to become highly mannered, and actors were sheltered by the cinematographers. It was not until years later that critics were able to distinguish between great directors and great noir directors.

———————

Film noir's remarkable creativity makes its long-time neglect the more baffling. The French, of course, have been students of the period for some time (Borde and Chaumenton's *Panorama du Film Noir* was published in 1955), but American critics until recently have preferred the Western, the musical, or the gangster film to the film noir.

Some of the reasons for this neglect are superficial: others strike to the heart of the noir style. For a long time, film noir, with its emphasis on corruption and despair, was considered an aberration of the American character. The Western, with its moral primitivism, and the gangster film, with its Horatio Alger values, were considered more American than the film noir.

This prejudice was reinforced by the fact that film noir was ideally suited to the low-budget "B" film, and many of the best noir films were "B" films. This odd sort of economic snobbery still lingers on in some critical circles: high-budget trash is considered more worthy of attention than low-budget trash, and to praise a "B" film is somehow to slight (often intentionally) an "A" film.

There has been a critical revival in the United States over the past ten years, but film noir lost out on that, too. The revival was auteur (director) oriented, and film noir was not. Auteur criticism is interested in how directors are different; film noir criticism is concerned with what they have in common.

The fundamental reason for film noir's neglect, however, is the fact that it depends more on choreography than sociology, and American critics have always been slow on the uptake when it comes to visual style. Like its protagonists, film noir is more interested in style than theme, whereas American critics have been traditionally more interested in theme than style.

American film critics have always been sociologists first and scientists second: film is important as it relates to large masses, and if a film goes awry, it is often because the theme has been somehow "violated" by the style. Film noir operates on opposite principles: the theme is hidden in the style, and bogus themes are often flaunted ("middle-class values are best") that contradict the style. Although, I believe, style determines the theme in *every* film, it was easier for sociological critics to discuss the themes of the Western and gangster film apart from stylistic analysis than it was to do for film noir.

Not surprisingly, it was the gangster film, not the film noir, that was canonized in *The Partisan Review* in 1948 by Robert Warshow's famous essay, "The Gangster as Tragic Hero." Although Warshow could be an aesthetic as well as a sociological critic, he was interested in the Western and gangster film as "popular" art rather than as style. This sociological orientation blinded Warshow, as it has many subsequent critics, to an aesthetically more important development in the gangster film—film noir.

The irony of this neglect is that in retrospect, the gangster films Warshow wrote about are inferior to film noir. The 1930s gangster was primarily a reflection of what was happening in the country, and Warshow analysed this. The film noir, although it was also a sociological reflection, went further than the gangster film. Toward the end, film noir was engaged in a life-and-death struggle with the materials it reflected; it tried to make America accept a moral vision of life based on style. That very contradiction—promoting style in a culture that valued themes— forced film noir into artistically invigorating twists and turns. Film noir attacked and interpreted its sociological conditions and, by the close of the noir period, created a new artistic world that went beyond a simple sociological reflection, a nightmarish world of American mannerism that was by far more a creation than a reflection.

Because film noir was first of all a style, because it worked out its conflicts visually rather than thematically, and because it was aware of its own identity, it was able to create artistic solutions to sociological problems. And for these reasons, films such as *Kiss Me Deadly*, *Kiss Tomorrow Goodbye*, and *Gun Crazy* can be works of art in a way that gangster films such as *Scarface*, *Public Enemy*, and *Little Caesar* can never be.

The selection of the following seven films by the Los Angeles International Film Exposition reflects a desire to select not only the best noir films but also some of the less well known.

Kiss Me Deadly. Made in 1955, *Kiss Me Deadly* comes at the end of the period and is the masterpiece of film noir. Its time delay gives it a sense of detachment and thoroughgoing seediness—it stands at the end of a long sleazy tradition.

The private-eye hero, Mike Hammer, undergoes the final stages of degradation. He is a small-time "bedroom dick," and has no qualms about it because the world around him is not much better. Ralph Meeker, in his best performance, plays Hammer, a midget among dwarfs.

Robert Aldrich's teasing direction carries noir to its sleaziest and most perversely erotic. In search of an "eternal whatsit," Hammer overturns the underworld, causing the death of his friend in the process, and when he finally finds it, it turns out to be—joke of jokes—an exploding atomic bomb. The cruelty of the individual is only a trivial matter in a world in which the bomb has the final say. Hammer can be seen struggling to safety as the bomb ejaculates, but for all practical purposes, the 1940s private-eye tradition is defunct. Written by A. I. Bezzerides. Photographed by Ernest Laszlo. Produced by Victor Saville. With Ralph Meeker, Maxine Cooper, Nick Dennis, Gaby Rodgers, Juano Hernandez, Paul Stewart, Albert Dekker, Cloris Leachman, Jack Elam.

Gun Crazy. An early Bonnie and Clyde variant, Joseph H. Lewis's *Gun Crazy* incorporates both the Black Widow and on-the-run themes. John Dall and Peggy Cummins play a winsome couple spinning at a dizzying rate into the exhilarating world of action, sex, love, and murder. Dall is confused, innocent, and passive, and Cummins is confused, vindictive, and active; together they make an irresistibly psychopathic pair. And their deadliness is sanctified by the fact that they know they are special people and will be given the right by the American ethic to act out their symbolic fantasies.

Gun Crazy's lighting is not as noir as other films of the period, but its portrayal of criminal and sexual psychopathy very much is. There are no excuses for the gun craziness—it is just crazy.

Gun Crazy has three tour de force scenes: the brilliantly executed Armour robbery, the famous one-take Hampton heist, and the meeting at the carnival, which is a ballet of sex and innuendo more subtle and teasing than the more famous sparring matches of Bogart and Bacall or Ladd and Lake. 1949. Written by Mackinlay Kantor and Millard Kaufman. Produced by the King Brothers. Photographed by Russell Harlan. With John Dall, Peggy Cummins, Barry Kroeger, Annabel Shaw, Harry Lewis, Frederick Young.

They Live by Night. Made in the same year as *Gun Crazy*, Nicholas Ray's *They Live by Night* is another Bonnie and Clyde/on-the-run film. Ray's heroes, Farley Granger and Cathy O'Donnell, as the title implies, really do live by night, and the choreography is strictly noir.

Unlike *Gun Crazy*, Granger and O'Donnell are not psychopathic; rather, the society is, as it makes them into bigger and bigger criminals and finally connives to gun down the unsuspecting Granger. There's an excellent bit by Ian Wolfe as a crooked Justice of the Peace, and Marie Bryant sings "Your Red Wagon" in the best noir tradition. Written by Charles Schnee. Photographed by George E. Diskant. Produced by John Houseman. With Farley Granger, Cathy O'Donnell, Howard Da Silva, Jay C. Flippen, Helen Craig, Will Wright, Ian Wolfe, Harry Harvey.

White Heat. There was no director better suited to portray instability than Raoul Walsh and no actor more potentially unstable than James Cagney. And when they joined forces in 1949 for *White Heat,* they produced one of the most exciting psycho-sexual crime films ever. Cagney plays an ageing Oedipal gangster who sits on his mother's lap between bouts of pistol-whipping his cohorts, planning robberies, and gunning down police.

In an exuberantly psychotic ending, Cagney stands atop an exploding oil tanker yelling, "I made it, Ma! Top of the World!" We've come a long way from *Scarface* in which Paul Muni lies in the gutter as a neon sign ironically flashes, "Cook's Tours. See the World." Cagney, now the noir hero, is not so much interested in financial gain and power as he is in suicidal showmanship. Cagney tapped the same vein the following year when he produced and starred in Gordon Douglas's *Kiss Tomorrow Goodbye*, one of the best of the late noir films. What Douglas lacked as a director, Cagney made up in just plain craziness. 1949. Written by Ivan Goff and Ben Roberts. Photographed by Sid Hickox. Produced by Louis Edelman. With James Cagney, Virginia Mayo, Edmund O'Brien, Margaret Wycherly, Steve Cochran, John Archer.

Out of the Past. Jacques Tourneur's *Out of the Past* brilliantly utilizes the noir element of narration as well as the themes of

Black Widow and on-the-run. A gangster (the young Kirk Douglas in one of his best roles) sends detective Robert Mitchum to retrieve his girlfriend, Jane Greer, who has run off with his money. Mitchum, of course, teams up with Greer, and they hide from Douglas.

Mitchum narrates his story with such pathetic relish that he obviously draws comfort from being love's perennial fool. Tourneur combines Mitchum's narration, Jane Greer's elusive beauty, and a complex chronology in such a way that there is no hope for any future; one can only take pleasure from reliving a doomed past. 1947. Written by Geoffrey Homes. Produced by Warren Duff. With Kirk Douglas, Robert Mitchum, Jane Greer, Rhonda Fleming, Steve Brodie.

Pickup on South Street. Sam Fuller's 1953 film sacks in with an odd noir bedfellow—the Red scare. The gangsters undergo a slight accent shift and become communist agents; no ideological conversion necessary.

Richard Widmark, a characteristic noir actor who has never done as well outside the period as within it, plays a two-time loser who picks the purse of a "commie" messenger and ends up with a piece of microfilm. When the State Department finally hunts him down and begins the lecture, Widmark replies, "Don't wave your flag at me."

The scenes on the waterfront are in the best noir tradition, but a dynamic fight in the subway marks Fuller as a director who would be better suited to the action-crime school of the middle 1950s. Written by Samuel Fuller. Photographed by Joe MacDonald. Produced by Jules Schermer. With Richard Widmark, Jean Peters, Thelma Ritter, Murvyn Vye, Richard Kiley.

T-Men. Anthony Mann's 1947 film was photographed by John Alton, the most characteristically noir artist of the period. Alton also photographed Joseph H. Lewis's *The Big Combo* eight years later, and the cinematography is so nearly identical that one has momentary doubts about the directorial difference between Mann and Lewis. In each film, light only enters the scene in odd slants, jagged slices, and vertical or horizontal strips.

T-Men is a bastard child of the postwar realistic school and purports to be the documented story of two Treasury agents who break a ring of counterfeiters. Complications set in when the good guys do not act any differently from the bad ones. In the end, it does not matter anyway, because they all die in the late-night shoot-outs. 1948. Written by John Higgins. Photographed by John Alton. Produced by Edward Small and Aubrey Schenck. With Dennis O'Keefe, Alfred Ryder, Mary Meade, Wallace Ford, June Lockhart, Charles McGraw, Art Smith.

Sylvia Harvey

Woman's Place: The Absent Family of Film Noir

The world view generated within the film noir entitles this group of films to be considered as a distinct and separate entity within the history of American film.[1] What this world view reflects is a series of profound changes that, although they are not yet grasped or understood, are shaking the foundations of the established and therefore normal perceptions of the social order. Like an echo chamber, film noir captures and magnifies the rumbles that preceded one of those earthquakes in human history that shift the hidden foundations of a society and that begin the displacement of its characteristic and dominant systems of values and beliefs. Like the world of Shakespeare's *King Lear,* in which the ingratitude of children toward their parents is at once the cause and effect of an immense disorder within the human universe, film noir offers us again and again examples of abnormal or monstrous behavior, which defy the patterns established for human social interaction, and which hint at a series of radical and irresolvable contradictions buried deep within the total system of economic and social interactions that constitute the known world.

Despite the presence of most of the conventions of the dominant methods of filmmaking and storytelling: the impetus toward the resolution of the plot, the diffusion of tension, the circularity of a narrative that resolves all of the problems it encounters, the successful completion of the individual's quest, these methods do not, in the end, create the most significant contours of the cultural map of film noir. The defining

Reprinted, with permission, from E. Ann Kaplan, ed., *Women in Film Noir* (London: BFI, 1978).

contours of this group of films are the product of that which is abnormal and dissonant. And the dissonances, the sense of disorientation and unease, although frequently present at the level of plot and thematic development are, more important perhaps, always a function of the visual style of this group of films. Disequilibrium is the product of a style characterised by unbalanced and disturbing frame compositions, strong contrasts of light and dark, the prevalence of shadows and areas of darkness within the frame, the visual tension created by curious camera angles, and so forth. Moreover, in film noir these strained compositions and angles are not merely embellishments or rhetorical flourishes but form the semantic substance of the film. The visual dissonances that are characteristic of these films are the mark of those ideological contradictions that form the historical context out of which the films are produced.

This principled claim that seeks to establish the importance of style and mise en scène as, materially, that which produces meaning in these movies, is not to be adequately followed up in this article.[2] The piece attempts an approach to the problem of defining the contours of this group of films from a different angle.[3] The article, that is, tries to understand the process whereby the depiction of women in these films, by a complex and circuitous network of mediation, reflects such social changes as the increasing entry of women into the labour market.

It is the representation of the institution of the family, which in so many films serves as the mechanism whereby desire is fulfilled or at least ideological equilibrium established, that in film noir serves as the vehicle for the expression of frustration. On the thematic level, one of the defining characteristics of film noir is to be found in its treatment of the family and family relations. However, there is another level of analysis beyond that of theme where things are not what they seem at the surface level of narrative and plot. One of the fundamental operations at this concealed level has to do with the nonfulfilment of desire. The way in which this underlying frustration or nonfulfilment is translated into, or expressed at, the thematic level in film noir is through the representation of romantic love relations, the family, and family relations.

The repressed presence of intolerable contradictions and the sense of uncertainty and confusion about the smooth functioning of the social environment present at the level of style in film noir can be seen also in the treatment of social institutions at the thematic level and most notably in the treatment of the family. Moreover, the kinds of tension characteristic of the portrayal of the family in these films suggest the beginnings of an attack on the dominant social values normally expressed through the representation of the family.

In so many of the major and so-called nonpolitical American films, it is the family that has served a crucial function in inserting within the film narrative the established values of competitive, repressive, and hierarchical relationships. The presence of the family has served to legitimate and naturalise these values, that is, to present them as the normal, natural and unthought premises for conducting one's life. Moreover, the representation of women has always been linked to this value-generating nexus of the family. The value of women on the market of social exchange has been to a large extent determined by the position of women within the structure of the family. Woman's place in the home determines her position in society but also serves as a reflection of oppressive social relationships generally. As Engels suggested, within the family "she is the proletarian, he the bourgeois."

All movies express social values, or the erosion of these values, through the ways in which they depict both institutions and relations between people. Certain institutions are more revealing of social values and beliefs than others, and the family is perhaps one of the most significant of these institutions. For it is through the particular representations of the family in various movies that we are able to study the processes whereby existing social relations are rendered acceptable and valid.

Through its manifestation of a whole series of customs and beliefs, the family functions as one of the ideological cornerstones of Western industrial society. It embodies a range of traditional values: love of family, love of father (father/ruler), and love of country are intertwined concepts, and we may see the family as a microcosm containing within itself all of the patterns of dominance and submission that are characteristic of the larger society.

We might summarise here some of the most important concepts that are dealt with through and in the representation of the family. First, the concepts of reproduction and socialisation: the family is the arena that is sanctified by society for the reproduction and preliminary education of the human race, for the bringing up of children. In the free labour that it requires the mother to perform in raising the child, the family serves to legitimate a whole series of practices that oppress women. Moreover, in its hierarchical structure, with the father as the head, the mother as subservient, and the children as totally dependent, it offers us a legitimating model or metaphor for a hierarchical and authoritarian society. The internal, oppressive, often violent relations within the family present a mirror image of oppressive and violent relations between classes in the larger society.

Second, the family is sanctified as the acceptable location of a sexuality defined in extremely limited terms. Western industrial society has regarded marriage, and hence the family, as the only legitimate arena for the fulfilment of sexual needs, though this legitimacy has been somewhat modified to allow for the double standard, that is, for the separate codes of sexual practice to be adhered to by male and female. What is most interesting is that in general in the movies, as in society, the family at the same time legitimates and *conceals* sexuality. Although marriage is the only place where sexual activity is to be sanctioned, oddly enough (or perhaps it is not so odd) mothers and fathers are seldom represented as sexual partners, especially in those movies of the 1940s and 1950s when censorship demanded that only bedrooms with separate beds were to be shown on the screen. So that, although married couples—that is, mothers and fathers—are the only ones allowed to engage in erotic activity, these parents or potential parents are normally presented in a totally de-eroticised way.

A final concept dealt with through the representation of the family is that of romantic love. Although so many movies go to extreme lengths to keep the two apart (a function of ideology working overtime to conceal its contradictions), romantic love and the institution of the family are logically and inevitably linked. The logical conclusion to that romantic love that seeks always the passionate and enduring love of a lifetime is the family, which must serve as the point of termination and fulfilment of romance. And if successful romantic love leads inevitably in the direction of the stable institution of marriage, the point about film noir, by contrast, is that it is structured around the destruction or absence of romantic love and the family.

Moreover, because we are engaged in analysing the ideological systems of movies and not those of novels or newspapers, it is important to note that in film noir it is not only at the level of plot and narrative resolution that lovers are not permitted to live happily ever after,[4] but it is at the additional and perhaps more important level of mise en scène or visual style that the physical environment of the lovers (whether created by landscape/set or by camera angle, framing, and lighting) is presented as threatening, disturbing, and fragmented.

The ideological significance of lovers living happily ever after lies in the unspoken, and usually invisible, metamorphosis that is implied to take place at the end of every happy ending. By means of this metamorphosis, lovers are transformed into fathers and mothers, into families. This magic circle of transformation is broken in film noir, which, in presenting family relations as broken, perverted, peripheral, or impossible, founds itself on the absence of the family.[5]

In certain ways, the representation of women in this group of films reflects the "normal" status of women within contemporary social relations. The two most common types of women in film noir are the exciting, childless whores, and the boring, potentially childbearing sweethearts. However, in other respects, the normal representation of women as the founders of families undergoes an interesting displacement. For it is the strange and compelling absence of "normal" family relations in these films that hints at important shifts in the position of women in American society. Among these changes must be listed the temporary but widespread introduction of women into the American labour force during World War II and the changing economic and ideological function of the family that parallels the changing structures and goals of an increasingly monopolistic economy. These economic changes forced certain changes in the traditional organisation of the family; and the underlying sense of horror and uncertainty in film noir may be seen, in part, as an indirect response to this forcible assault on traditional family structures and the traditional and conservative values which they embodied. The astounding Mildred Pierce (*Mildred Pierce* [1945]), woman of the world, woman of business, and only secondarily a mother, is a good example of this disruption and displacement of the values of family life. The image of Mildred, in a masculine style of dress, holding her account books and looking *away* from her lover, typifies this kind of displacement.

The appearance of the early film noir coincides with the rise and fall of nationalistic ideologies generated by the period of total war. It may be argued that the ideology of national unity, which was characteristic of the war period and which tended to gloss over and conceal class divisions, began to falter and decay, to lose its credibility, once the war was over. The encounter with a depressed peace-time economy, with its threat of high prices and rising unemployment, began a process of general disillusionment for many of those returning home after the war, in search of those values that they had fought to defend. It is this breakdown, also this erosion of expectations, that finds its way into the film noir by a series of complex transmutations. The hard facts of economic life are transmuted, in these movies, into corresponding moods and feelings.

In Double Indemnity *(Wilder, 1944), Barton Keyes (Edward G. Robinson, right) tells Walter Neff (Fred MacMurray, center) that he suspects Phyllis Dietrichson (Barbara Stanwyck) of murdering her husband, unaware that Neff helped her commit the crime. Photo courtesy of Paramount.*

Thus the feelings of loss and alienation expressed by the characters in film noir can be seen as the product both of postwar depression and of the reorganisation of the American economy.

With the increasing size of corporations, the growth of monopolies, and the accelerated elimination of small businesses, it became increasingly hard for even the petit bourgeoisie to continue to believe in certain dominant myths. Foremost among these was the dream of equality of opportunity in business and of the God-given right of every man to be his own boss. Increasingly, the petit bourgeoisie were forced into selling their labour and working for the big companies, instead of running their own businesses and working "for themselves." It is this factor of being forced to work according to the goals and purposes formulated *by someone else* that accounts in large measure for the feelings of alienation and helplessness in film noir.

It is no accident that Walter Neff in *Double Indemnity* (1944) seeks an escape from the dull routine of the insurance company that he works for in an affair with the deadly and exotic Phyllis Dietrichson. The possession of Phyllis Dietrichson, as of any of the other film noir women who function as sexual commodities, is, in the magic world of the movies, held up as a tempting means of escape from the boredom and frustration of a routinised and alienated existence. Nor is it accidental that Neff, on his way up to his office to make his final confession, encounters the elevator man who tells him that he never could buy medical insurance from the company that he has worked for all of his life because he has a bad heart. It is this feeling of being lost in a world of corporate values (represented in different films by big business, the police, the mob, etc.) that are not sensitive to the needs and desires of the individual that permeates film noir.

In the world of symbolic searches, exchanges, and satisfactions created by these movies, women are accorded the function of an ideological safety valve, but this function is ambivalent. Presented as prizes, desirable objects, they seem to offer a temporary satisfaction to the men of film noir. In the (false) satisfactions that they represent, they might be seen to prevent the mood of despondency and loss, characteristic of these films, from being translated into an understanding and analysis of the conditions that *produce* the sense of alienation and loss. However, the ideological safety valve device that operates in the offering of women as sexual commodities breaks down in probably most of these films because the women are not, finally, possessed. Walter Neff (*Double Indemnity*) summarises the position of many of the film noir men when he concludes: "I didn't get the woman and I didn't get the money." The same statement would be true for the men of *Scarlet Street* (1945), *They Live by Night* (1949), *Sunset Boulevard* (1950), *Lady From Shanghai* (1949), and *Gun Crazy* (1949).

One of the recurrent themes of film noir is concerned with the loss of those satisfactions normally obtained through the possession of a wife and the presence of a family, although this theme is manifested in different ways. At the simple level of the organisation of the plot, *Woman in the Window* (1944) is one of the most obvious examples of the multifarious evils that befall a man who is left alone without his family. At the beginning of the film, the wife and children of the professor, who is the central character of the film, depart for a summer vacation, leaving him alone with only the company of his male friends. Left to his own devices, he gets involved with a woman whose portrait, displayed in the window of a gallery, has mesmerised him. The woman turns out to be the mistress of another man, and because of his relationship with her, the professor is involved in a murder.

As he sits at home, terrified that the police are closing in on him, he is surrounded by the photographs of his family, which seem to reproach him for the life that he is leading while they are absent.

At the end of the movie, we discover that these lurid events have been enacted only in the professor's dream. But it is none the less significant that this masochistic dream is triggered by the departure of the protagonist's wife and children. Moreover in the images of this departure—the family farewells at the station—we are given certain visual clues about the operation of the marriage. The children in the foreground of the scene, engrossed in their comic books, ignore both their mother and father. The father fumbles awkwardly with his hat; the wife, with an extremely restrained gesture, touches him with one hand; both clutch at objects (the hat, the pile of glossy magazines) which prevent them from embracing each other. There is no warmth in the farewell, no hint of the erotic. Even the polished marble floor adds an element of coldness to the scene.

In the world of film noir both men and women seek sexual satisfaction outside of marriage. This is true, for example, for the characters of *Woman in the Window, Double Indemnity* and *Lady From Shanghai.* However, a fundamental ideological contradiction rises to the surface in these movies, for the noir lovers are not permitted the socially acceptable practice of quiet 'adultery' (an ideological operation which, like that of prostitution, reconfirms the primacy of monogamy), rather they are required to carry out the violent destruction of the marriage bonds. Paradoxically (and it is through this paradox that the dominant ideology attempts to reassert itself), the destruction of the sanctity of marriage, most notable in *Double Indemnity,* results in placing the relationship of the lovers under such strain, so beyond the boundaries of conventional moral law, that the relationship becomes an impossibility, and transforms itself into the locus of mutual destruction.

In *Double Indemnity* the act of killing the husband serves as the supreme act of violence against family life, and has, in some sense, to be atoned for through the mutual destruction of the lovers in the macabre shoot-out, at the family house, which ends the film. It is perhaps most clear in this movie that the expression of sexuality and the institution of marriage are at odds with one another, and that both pleasure and death lie outside the safe circle of family relations.

Moreover there is clearly an impetus in film noir to transgress the boundaries of this circle; for the presence of husbands on crutches or in wheelchairs (*Double Indemnity, Lady From Shanghai*) suggests that impotence is somehow a normal component of the married state. Other imagery in these films suggests that a routinized boredom and a sense of stifling entrapment are characteristic of marriage. A large birdcage looms in the foreground of the family home in *Scarlet Street,* separating husband and wife, and the husband hovers uncertainly at the edge of the frame, holding in one hand the paint brushes which signify for him his escape into the fantasy world of his paintings. The family home in *Double Indemnity* is the place where three people who hate each other spend endlessly boring evenings together. The husband does not merely not notice his wife, he ignores her sexually; so that it is only under Neff's gaze that her long legs become the focal point of both the room as Neff sees it and the composition of the frame. While Neff looks at her, the husband looks at the insurance papers which function as his own death warrant, in the sense that they are the device through which the lovers plan to benefit from the large insurance payments on his death. Neff is subsequently caught up in the inescapable cycle of desire, death and retribution.

By contrast, the man in *Lady From Shanghai,* Michael, does not kill, and does not die, but neither is he satisfied. He watches as husband and wife kill each other, realizing at last that she has betrayed him as well as her husband. It is at the end of the movie a condition of the lonely and frustrating freedom of Michael (as well as for the crusading private eye in *The Maltese Falcon* [1941]) that he is not married, that marriage is an impossible state for him. The men of film noir tend to be the chief protagonists, the chief movers of the plot, the locus from which the point of view of the film proceeds, and the central narrative consciousness that retells the events of the past and controls the unfolding of the tale. However, this dominance is not total. For the "Black Widow" women, for example, in *Double Indemnity* and *Lady from Shanghai,* are actively involved in the violent assault on the conventional values of family life.

If many of the films noirs depict a boredom and sterility associated with the married state, others present married couples who create a kind of antifamily. Most obviously, lovers on the run are unable to conform to the normal stereotypes of family or married behaviour. The lovers on the run of *Gun Crazy* and *They Live by Night* (1949) are, technically, married; they go through the marriage ceremony. However, their position outside the law does not permit them to function as normal couples acceptable to the dominant ideology. Their marriages function as the nexus of destruction, not as the showcase of desire fulfilled. Even the marriage ceremony has a slightly threatening quality to it in *They*

Live by Night. The left foreground of the frame is taken up by the looming figure of the man performing the ceremony; the lovers face the camera in the centre and behind them, seeming to encircle and dominate them, hover the two stern-faced witnesses. Moreover, the man who performs the ceremony appears again later in the film as the one who can most clearly foresee the rapid approach of the tragic end. In refusing with an unexpected honesty to take the money that he is offered to help the young couple across the border into Mexico, he is the one who makes clear to them, at last, the impossibility of their situation and the inevitability of a violent climax.

In *Gun Crazy*, the isolation of the couple as well as their non-conformity to certain social norms is emphasised by the way in which they are presented as outsiders to the family and family life. Taking refuge with Bart's family at the end of the film, they so clearly do not belong; they constitute a violent eruption into the ordered patterns of family life. Moreover, as in *They Live by Night*, it is through the organisation of the mise en scène that their final doom is foretold. The scene in the deserted railway shack where they plan their final heist is characterised by a series of unsettling frame compositions: by such things as the obsessive presence in the composition of a large lamp, that dwarfs the human subjects; or by the blacking out of portions of the screen, caused by the intervention of objects in the foreground. As in *Double Indemnity* and *Lady From Shanghai*, the relationship of the lovers turns to mutual destructiveness. At the end of *Gun Crazy*, in the terrible dawn scene in the marshes, with the mist rising and the police encircling the couple, Bart shoots his wife in order to stop her from shooting his male friends—the cop and the newspaper man. Destructive passion characterises the central male/female relationship, while the more protective gestures of loving are exchanged, as in *Double Indemnity*, between men.

The sterility, in conventional family terms, of the central male/female relationships in film noir (and often these relationships are unfavourably contrasted with male/male relationships) is further emphasised by the childlessness of the couples. *Sunset Boulevard* offers an interesting example of this emphasis. The absence of the family and the failure of romantic love are central thematic elements. Joe Gillis, by becoming involved in the unsanctified relationship of gigolo (the paid and kept lover) to Norma Desmond, loses whatever chances he might have had of finding a successful romantic relationship. His failure is matched by hers, and the presence of the butler (von Stroheim), her ex-husband, now her servant, ministering to her relationships with men like Joe, is a permanent reminder of the failure of romance and marriage in her life. The macabre incident in which the butler and Norma officiate at the nocturnal, candlelit burial of the chimpanzee that is Norma's substitute for a child seems to summarise the sterile state of a world that floats adrift from the normalcy of a society normally governed by the institution of marriage and the relations of family life.

The family, within a capitalist economy, has functioned both objectively and subjectively as the locus of women's particular oppression. Its internal relations have *produced* those ideological entities: daughters, wives, and mothers, that are so familiar as a part of our world. It is the absence of normal family relations (of the network of relationships between mother-father-wife-husband-daughter-son) that forms one of the distinctive parameters of film noir. If we can say that familial *entities* are the ideological fictions called into being by family relations, then the absence of these *relations*, which are by definition normal in capitalist society, creates a vacuum that ideology abhors. This terrible absence of family relations allows for the production of the *seeds* of counterideologies. The absence or disfigurement of the family both calls attention to its own lack and to its own deformity and may be seen to encourage the consideration of alternative institutions for the reproduction of social life. Despite the ritual punishment of acts of transgression, the vitality with which these acts are endowed produces an excess of meaning that cannot finally be contained. Narrative resolutions cannot recuperate their subversive significance.

NOTES

Thanks for practical assistance to David Bradley (UCLA) and the Stills Department at the British Film Institute. Thanks for intellectual stimulus to members of the doctoral seminars in film, UCLA (on the basis of which work this article was originally written in 1975): Ron Abramson, Jacoba Atlas, Joe McInerney, Bill Nichols, Janey Place, Bob Rosen, Eileen Rossi, and Alain Silver.

1. The film noir period can be taken to coincide approximately with the appearance of *The Maltese Falcon* in 1941 and of *Touch of Evil* in 1958.

2. The polemic for this position and for the primacy of this method is developed in Bill Nichols' article: "Style, Grammar and the Movies," *Film Quarterly* 28:3 (Spring 1975), 33–49.

3. The methodological inadequacy of this article lies in its failure to conceptualise the relationship between its own (only partly articulated) method and the primary hypothesis already postulated, namely, that of the primacy of visual style. Moreover, the attempt at analysing ways in which certain structures within the movies reflect certain (changing) structures within the society that is contemporary with the movies is insufficiently theorised.

4. In a few of the films noirs, for example, *Pick Up on South Street* (1953), the ending suggests that the lovers are to live happily ever after. However, it can be argued that the mood created and the knowledge produced by the visual style of the film negates or undercuts the apparent happiness of the ending.

5. The notion of a "structuring absence" is developed by the editors of *Cahiers du Cinéma* in their article on "John Ford's *Young Mr. Lincoln*"; they write:

> What will be attempted here through a re-scansion of these films
> in a process of active reading, is to make them say what they have
> to say within what they leave unsaid, to reveal their constituent
> lacks . . . they are structuring absences, always displaced . . . the
> unsaid included in the said and necessary to its constitution.

(*Cahiers du Cinéma*, No. 223 [1970] translated in *Screen* 13:3, [Autumn 1972], 5–44 and reprinted in the *Screen Reader*, No. 1 [1978].).

Mass Production, the Failure of the New, and Reaganite Cinema

Fredric Jameson

Postmodernism and Consumer Society

The concept of postmodernism is not widely accepted or even understood today. Some of the resistance to it may come from the unfamiliarity of the works it covers, which can be found in all the arts: the poetry of John Ashbery, for instance, but also the much simpler talk poetry that came out of the reaction against complex, ironic, academic modernist poetry in the 1960s; the reaction against modern architecture and in particular against the monumental buildings of the International Style, the pop buildings and decorated sheds celebrated by Robert Venturi in his manifesto, *Learning from Las Vegas*; Andy Warhol and pop art, but also the more recent Photorealism; in music, the moment of John Cage but also the later synthesis of classical and "popular" styles found in composers such as Philip Glass and Terry Riley and also punk and new-wave rock with such groups as the Clash, the Talking Heads, and the Gang of Four; in film, everything that comes out of Godard—contemporary vanguard film and video—but also a whole new style of commercial or fiction films, which has its equivalent in contemporary novels as well, in which the works of William Burroughs, Thomas Pynchon, and Ishmael Reed on the one hand and the French new novel on the other are also to be numbered among the varieties of what can be called postmodernism.

This list would seem to make two things clear at once: first, most of the postmodernisms mentioned above emerge as specific reactions against the established forms of high modernism, against this or that

Reprinted, with the permission of the author, from Hal Foster, ed., *The Anti-Aesthetic: Essays on Postmodern Culture* (Port Townsend, Wash.: Bay Press, 1983). This essay was originally a talk, portions of which were presented as a Whitney Museum Lecture in fall 1982; it is published here essentially unrevised.

185

dominant high modernism that conquered the university, the museum, the art gallery network, and the foundations. Those formerly subversive and embattled styles—Abstract Expressionism; the great modernist poetry of Pound, Eliot, or Wallace Stevens; the International Style (Le Corbusier, Frank Lloyd Wright, Mies); Stravinsky; Joyce, Proust, and Mann—felt to be scandalous or shocking by our grandparents are, for the generation that arrives at the gate in the 1960s, felt to be the establishment and the enemy—dead, stifling, canonical, the reified monuments one has to destroy to do anything new. This means that there will be as many different forms of postmodernism as there were high modernisms in place, because the former are at least initially specific and local reactions *against* those models. That obviously does not make the job of describing postmodernism as a coherent thing any easier, because the unity of this new impulse—if it has one—is given not in itself but in the very modernism it seeks to displace.

The second feature of this list of postmodernisms is the effacement in it of some key boundaries or separations, most notably the erosion of the older distinction between high culture and so-called mass or popular culture. This is perhaps the most distressing development of all from an academic standpoint, which has traditionally had a vested interest in preserving a realm of high or elite culture against the surrounding environment of philistinism, of schlock and kitsch, of TV series and *Reader's Digest* culture, and in transmitting difficult and complex skills of reading, listening, and seeing to its initiates. But many of the newer postmodernisms have been fascinated precisely by that whole landscape of advertising and motels, of the Las Vegas strip, of the late show and grade B Hollywood films, and of so-called paraliterature with its airport paperback categories of the gothic and the romance, the popular biography, the murder mystery, and the science fiction or fantasy novel. They no longer "quote" such "texts" as a Joyce might have done, or a Mahler; they incorporate them, to the point where the line between high art and commercial forms seems increasingly difficult to draw.

A rather different indication of this effacement of the older categories of genre and discourse can be found in what is sometimes called contemporary theory. A generation ago, there was still a technical discourse of professional philosophy—the great systems of Sartre or the phenomenologists, the work of Wittgenstein or analytical or common language philosophy—alongside which one could still distinguish that quite different discourse of the other academic disciplines—of political science, for example, or sociology or literary criticism. Today, increasingly, we have a kind of writing simply called "theory," which is all or none of those things at once. This new kind of discourse, generally associated with France and so-called French theory, is becoming widespread and marks the end of philosophy as such. Is the work of Michel Foucault, for example, to be called philosophy, history, social theory, or political science? It's undecidable, as they say nowadays; and I will suggest that such "theoretical discourse" is also to be numbered among the manifestations of postmodernism.

Now I must say a word about the proper use of this concept: it is not just another word for the description of a particular style. It is also, at least in my use, a periodizing concept whose function is to correlate the emergence of new formal features in culture with the emergence of a new type of social life and a new economic order—what is often euphemistically called modernization, postindustrial or consumer society, the society of the media or the spectacle, or multinational capitalism. This new moment of capitalism can be dated from the postwar boom in the United States in the late 1940s and early 1950s or, in France, from the establishment of the Fifth Republic in 1958. The 1960s are in many ways the key transitional period, a period in which the new international order (neocolonialism, the Green Revolution, computerization, and electronic information) is at one and the same time set in place and is swept and shaken by its own internal contradictions and by external resistance. I want here to sketch a few of the ways in which the new postmodernism expresses the inner truth of that newly emergent social order of late capitalism but will have to limit the description to only two of its significant features, which I will call pastiche and schizophrenia: they will give us a chance to sense the specificity of the postmodernist experience of space and time respectively.

———

One of the most significant features or practices in postmodernism today is pastiche. I must first explain this term, which people generally tend to confuse with or assimilate to that related verbal phenomenon called parody. Both pastiche and parody involve the imitation or, better still, the mimicry of other styles and particularly of the mannerisms and stylistic twitches of other styles. It is obvious that modern literature in general offers a very rich field for parody, because the great modern writers have all been defined by the invention or production of rather unique styles: think of the Faulknerian long sentence or of D. H. Lawrence's characteristic nature imagery; think of Wallace Stevens's peculiar way of using abstractions; think also of the mannerisms of the philosophers, of Heidegger, for example, or Sartre; think of the musical styles of Mahler or Prokofiev. All of these styles, however different from each other, are comparable in this: each is quite unmistakable; once one is learned, it is not likely to be confused with something else.

Now parody capitalizes on the uniqueness of these styles and seizes on their idiosyncrasies and eccentricities to produce an imitation that mocks the original. I won't say that the satiric impulse is conscious in all forms of parody. In any case, a good or great parodist has to have some secret sympathy for the original, just as a great mimic has to have the capacity to put him- or herself in the place of the person imitated. Still, the general effect of parody is—whether in sympathy or with malice—to cast ridicule on the private nature of these stylistic manner-isms and their excessiveness and eccentricity with respect to the way people normally speak or write. So there remains somewhere behind all parody the feeling that there is a linguistic norm in contrast to which the styles of the great modernists can be mocked.

But what would happen if one no longer believed in the existence of normal language, of ordinary speech, of the linguistic norm (the kind of clarity and communicative power celebrated by Orwell in his famous essay, say)? One could think of it in this way: perhaps the immense fragmentation and privatization of modern literature—its explosion into a host of distinct private styles and mannerisms—foreshadows deeper and more general tendencies in social life as a whole. Supposing that modern art and modernism—far from being a kind of specialized aes-thetic curiosity—actually anticipated social developments along these lines; supposing that in the decades since the emergence of the great modern styles society has itself begun to fragment in this way, each group coming to speak a curious private language of its own, each profession developing its private code or idiolect, and finally each individual coming to be a kind of linguistic island, separated from everyone else? But then in that case, the very possibility of any linguistic norm in terms of which one could ridicule private languages and idiosyncratic styles would vanish, and we would have nothing but stylistic diversity and heterogeneity.

That is the moment at which pastiche appears and parody has become impossible. Pastiche is, like parody, the imitation of a peculiar or unique style, the wearing of a stylistic mask, speech in a dead language: but it is a neutral practice of such mimicry, without parody's ulterior motive, without the satirical impulse, without laughter, without that still latent feeling that there exists something *normal* compared to which what is being imitated is rather comic. Pastiche is blank parody, parody that has lost its sense of humor: pastiche is to parody what that curious thing, the modern practice of a kind of blank irony, is to what Wayne Booth calls the stable and comic ironies of, say, the eighteenth century.

But now we need to introduce a new piece into this puzzle, which may help explain why classical modernism is a thing of the past and why postmodernism should have taken its place. This new component is what is generally called the "death of the subject" or, to say it in more conventional language, the end of individualism as such. The great modernisms were, as we have said, predicated on the invention of a personal, private style, as unmistakable as your fingerprint, as incomparable as your own body. But this means that the modernist aesthetic is in some way organically linked to the conception of a unique self and private identity, a unique personality and individuality, which can be expected to generate its own unique vision of the world and to forge its own unique, unmistakable style.

Yet today, from any number of distinct perspectives, the social theorists, the psychoanalysts, even the linguists, not to speak of those of us who work in the area of culture and cultural and formal change, are all exploring the notion that that kind of individualism and personal identity is a thing of the past; that the old individual or individualist subject is "dead"; and that one might even describe the concept of the unique individual and the theoretical basis of individualism as ideological. There are in fact two positions on all this, one of which is more radical than the other. The first one is content to say yes, once upon a time, in the classic age of competitive capitalism, in the heyday of the nuclear family and the emergence of the bourgeoisie as the hegemonic social class, there was such a thing as individualism, as individual subjects. But today, in the age of corporate capitalism, of the so-called organization man, of bureaucracies in business as well as in the state, of demographic explosion—today, that older bourgeois individual subject no longer exists.

Then there is a second position, the more radical of the two, what one might call the poststructuralist position. It adds, not only is the bourgeois individual subject a thing of the past, it is also a myth; it *never* really existed in the first place; there have never been autonomous subjects of that type. Rather, this construct is merely a philosophical and cultural mystification that sought to persuade people that they "had" individual subjects and possessed this unique personal identity.

For our purposes, it is not particularly important to decide which of these positions is correct (or rather, which is more interesting and productive). What we have to retain from all this is rather an aesthetic dilemma: because if the experience and the ideology of the unique self, an experience and ideology that informed the stylistic practice of classical modernism, is over and done with, then it is no longer clear what the artists and writers of the present period are supposed to be doing. What is clear is merely that the older models—Picasso, Proust, T. S. Eliot—do not work any more (or are positively harmful), because nobody has that kind of unique private world and style to express any longer. And this is perhaps not merely a "psychological" matter: we also have to take into account the immense weight of seventy or eighty years of classical modernism itself. There is another sense in which the writers and artists of the present day will no longer be able to invent new styles and worlds—they've already been invented; only a limited number of combinations are possible; the most unique ones have been thought of already. So the weight of the whole modernist aesthetic tradition—now dead—also "weighs like a nightmare on the brains of the living," as Marx said in another context.

Hence, once again, pastiche: in a world in which stylistic innovation is no longer possible, all that is left is to imitate dead styles, to speak through the masks and with the voices of the styles in the imaginary museum. But this means that contemporary or postmodernist art is going to be about art itself in a new kind of way; even more, it means that one of its essential messages will involve the necessary failure of art and the aesthetic, the failure of the new, the imprisonment in the past.

As this may seem very abstract, I want to give a few examples, one of which is so omnipresent that we rarely link it with the kinds of developments in high art discussed here. This particular practice of pastiche is not high-cultural but very much within mass culture, and it is generally known as the "nostalgia film" (what the French neatly call *la mode rétro*—retrospective styling). We must conceive of this category in the broadest way: narrowly, no doubt, it consists merely of films about the past and about specific generational moments of that past. Thus, one of the inaugural films in this new "genre" (if that's what it is) was Lucas's *American Graffiti*, which in 1973 set out to recapture all the atmosphere and stylistic peculiarities of the 1950s United States, the United States of the Eisenhower era. Polanski's great film *Chinatown* does something similar for the 1930s, as does Bertolucci's *The Conformist* for the Italian and European context of the same period, the fascist era in Italy; and so

The nostalgia film: a poster for American Graffiti *(Lucas, 1973) asks "Where were you in '62?" Photo courtesy of Universal Pictures.*

forth. We could go on listing these films for some time: why call them pastiche? Are they not rather work in the more traditional genre known as the historical film—work that can more simply be theorized by extrapolating that other well-known form that is the historical novel?

I have my reasons for thinking that we need new categories for such films. But let me first add some anomalies: supposing I suggested that *Star Wars* is also a nostalgia film. What could that mean? I presume we can agree that this is not a historical film about our own intergalactic past. Let me put it somewhat differently: one of the most important cultural experiences of the generations that grew up from the 1930s to the 1950s was the Saturday afternoon serial of the Buck Rogers type— alien villains, true American heroes, heroines in distress, the death ray or the doomsday box, and the cliffhanger at the end whose miraculous resolution was to be witnessed next Saturday afternoon. *Star Wars* reinvents this experience in the form of a pastiche: that is, there is no longer any point to a parody of such serials because they are long extinct. *Star Wars*, far from being a pointless satire of such now dead forms, satisfies a deep (might I even say repressed?) longing to experience them again: it is a complex object in which on some first-level children and adolescents can take the adventures straight, while the adult public is able to gratify a deeper and more properly nostalgic desire to return to that older period and to live its strange old aesthetic artifacts through once again. This film is thus *metonymically* a historical or nostalgia film: unlike *American Graffiti*, it does not reinvent a picture of the past in its lived totality; rather, by reinventing the feel and shape of characteristic art objects of an older period (the serials), it seeks to reawaken a sense of the past associated with those objects. *Raiders of the Lost Ark*, meanwhile, occupies an intermediary position here: on some level it is *about* the 1930s and 1940s, but in reality it too conveys that period metonymically through its own characteristic adventure stories (which are no longer ours).

Now let me discuss another interesting anomaly that may take us further toward understanding nostalgia film in particular and pastiche generally. This one involves a recent film called *Body Heat*, which, as has abundantly been pointed out by the critics, is a kind of distant remake of *The Postman Always Rings Twice* or *Double Indemnity*. (The allusive and elusive plagiarism of older plots is, of course, also a feature of pastiche.) Now *Body Heat* is technically not a nostalgia film, because it takes place in a contemporary setting, in a little Florida village near Miami. On the other hand, this technical contemporaneity is most ambiguous indeed: the credits—always our first cue—are lettered and scripted in a 1930s Art-Deco style that cannot but trigger nostalgic reactions (first to *Chinatown*, no doubt, and then beyond it to some more historical referent). Then the very style of the hero himself is ambiguous: William Hurt is a new star but has nothing of the distinctive style of the preceding generation of male superstars such as Steve McQueen or even Jack Nicholson, or rather, his persona here is a kind of mix of their characteristics with an older role of the type generally associated with Clark Gable. So here too there is a faintly archaic feel to all this. The spectator begins to wonder why this story, which could have been situated anywhere, is set in a small Florida town, despite its contemporary reference. One begins to realize after a while that the small town setting has a crucial strategic function: it allows the film to do without most of the signals and references that we might associate with the contemporary world, with consumer society—the appliances and artifacts, the high rises, the object world of late capitalism. Technically, then, its objects (its cars, for instance) are 1980s products, but everything in the film conspires to blur that immediate contemporary reference and to make it possible to receive this too as nostalgia work—as a narrative set in some indefinable nostalgic past, an eternal 1930s, say, beyond history. It seems to me exceedingly symptomatic to find the very style of nostalgia films invading and colonizing even those movies today that have contemporary settings: as though, for some reason, we were unable today to focus our own present, as though we have become incapable of achieving aesthetic representations of our own current experience. But if that is so, then it is a terrible indictment of consumer capitalism itself—or at the very least, an alarming and pathological symptom of a society that has become incapable of dealing with time and history.

So now we come back to the question of why nostalgia film or pastiche is to be considered different from the older historical novel or film (I should also include in this discussion the major literary example of all this, to my mind the novels of E. L. Doctorow—*Ragtime*, with its turn-of-the-century atmosphere, and *Loon Lake*, for the most part about our 1930s. But these are, to my mind, historical novels in appearance only. Doctorow is a serious artist and one of the few genuinely Left or radical novelists at work today. It is no disservice to him, however, to suggest that his narratives do not represent our historical past so much as they represent our ideas or cultural stereotypes about that past.) Cultural production has been driven back inside the mind, within the monadic subject: it can no longer look directly out of its eyes at the real world for the referent but must, as in Plato's cave, trace its mental images of the world on its confining walls. If there is any realism left here, it is a "realism" that springs from the shock of grasping that confinement and of realizing that, for whatever peculiar reasons, we seem condemned to seek the historical past through our own pop images and stereotypes about that past, which itself remains forever out of reach.

I now want to turn to what I see as the second basic feature of postmodernism, namely, its peculiar way with time—which one could call "textuality" or "écriture" but which I have found it useful to discuss in terms of current theories of schizophrenia. I hasten to forestall any number of possible misconceptions about my use of this word: it is meant to be descriptive and not diagnostic. I am very far indeed from believing that any of the most significant postmodernist artists—John Cage, John Ashbery, Philippe Sollers, Robert Wilson, Andy Warhol, Ishmael Reed, Michael Snow, even Samuel Beckett himself—are in any sense schizophrenics. Nor is the point some culture-and-personality diagnosis of our society and its art: there are, one would think, far more damaging things to be said about our social system than are available by the use of pop psychology. I'm not even sure that the view of schizophrenia I'm about to outline—a view largely developed in the work of the French psychoanalyst Jacques Lacan—is clinically accurate; but that doesn't matter either, for my purposes.

The originality of Lacan's thought in this area is to have considered schizophrenia essentially as a language disorder and to have linked schizophrenic experience to a whole view of language acquisition as the fundamental missing link in the Freudian conception of the formation of the mature psyche. He does this by giving us a linguistic version of the Oedipus complex in which the Oedipal rivalry is described in terms not of the biological individual who is the rival for the mother's attention but rather of what he calls the Name-of-the-Father, paternal authority now considered as linguistic function. What we need to retain from this is the idea that psychosis, and more particularly schizophrenia, emerges from the failure of the infant to accede fully into the realm of speech and language.

As for language, Lacan's model is the now orthodox structuralist one, which is based on a conception of a linguistic sign as having two (or perhaps three) components. A sign, a word, a text, is here modelled as a relationship between a signifier—a material object, the sound of a word, the script of a text—and a signified, the *meaning* of that material word or material text. The third component would be the so-called referent, the "real" object in the "real" world to which the sign refers—the real cat as opposed to the concept of a cat or the sound "cat." But for structuralism in general, there has been a tendency to feel that reference is a kind of myth, that one can no longer talk about the real in that external or objective way. So we are left with the sign itself and its two components. Meanwhile, the other thrust of structuralism has been to try to dispel the old conception of language as naming (e.g., God gave Adam language in order to name the beasts and plants in the Garden), which involves a one-to-one correspondence between a signifier and a signified. Taking a structural view, one comes quite rightly to feel that sentences don't work that way: we don't translate the individual signifiers or words that make up a sentence back into their signifieds on a one-to-one basis. Rather, we read the whole sentence, and it is from the interrelationship of its words or signifiers that a more global meaning—now called a "meaning-effect"—is derived. The signified—maybe even the illusion or the mirage of the signified and of meaning in general—is an effect produced by the interrelationships of material signifiers.

All of this puts us in the position of grasping schizophrenia as the breakdown of the relationship between signifiers. For Lacan, the experience of temporality, human time, past, present, memory, the persistence of personal identity over months and years—this existential or experiential feeling of time itself—is also an effect of language. It is because language has a past and a future, because the sentence moves in time, that we can have what seems to us a concrete or lived experience of time. But since the schizophrenic does not know language articulation in that way, he or she does not have our experience of temporal continuity either but is condemned to live a perpetual present with which the various moments of his or her past have little connection and for which there is no conceivable future on the horizon. In other words, schizophrenic experience is an experience of isolated, disconnected, discontinuous material signifiers that fail to link up into a coherent sequence. The schizophrenic thus does not know personal identity in our sense, since our feeling of identity depends on our sense of the persistence of the "I" and the "me" over time.

On the other hand, the schizophrenic will clearly have a far more intense experience of any given present of the world than we do, because our own present is always part of some larger set of projects that force us selectively to focus our perceptions. We do not, in other words, simply globally receive the outside world as an undifferentiated vision: we are always engaged in using it, in threading certain paths through it, in attending to this or that object or person within it. The schizophrenic, however, is not only "no one" in the sense of having no personal identity; he or she also does nothing, because to have a project means to be able to commit oneself to a certain continuity over time. The schizophrenic is thus given over to an undifferentiated vision of the world in the present, a by no means pleasant experience:

> I remember very well the day it happened. We were staying in the country and I had gone for a walk alone as I did now and then. Suddenly, as I was passing the school, I heard a German song; the children were having a singing lesson. I stopped to listen, and at that instant a strange feeling came over me, a feeling hard to analyze but akin to something I was to know too well later—a disturbing sense of unreality. It seemed to me that I no longer recognized the school, it had become as large as a barracks; the singing children were prisoners, compelled to sing. It was as though the school and the children's song were apart from the rest of the world. At the same time my eye encountered a field of wheat whose limits I could not see. The yellow vastness, dazzling in the sun, bound up with the song of the children imprisoned in the smooth stone school-barracks, filled me with such anxiety that I broke into sobs. I ran home to our garden and began to play "to make things seem as they usually were," that is, to return to reality. It was the first appearance of those elements which were always present in later sensations of un-reality: illimitable vastness, brilliant light, and the gloss and smoothness of material things. (Marguerite Séchehaye, *Autobiography of a Schizophrenic Girl.*)

Note that as temporal continuities break down, the experience of the present becomes powerfully, overwhelmingly vivid and "material": the world comes before the schizophrenic with heightened intensity, bearing a mysterious and oppressive charge of affect, glowing with hallucinatory energy. But what might for us seem a desirable experience—an increase in our perceptions, a libidinal or hallucinogenic intensification of our normally humdrum and familiar surroundings—is here felt as loss, as "unreality."

What I want to underscore, however, is precisely the way in which the signifier in isolation becomes ever more material—or, better still, *literal*—ever more vivid in sensory ways, whether the new experience is attractive or terrifying. We can show the same thing in the realm of language: what the schizophrenic breakdown of language does to the individual words that remain behind is to reorient the subject or the speaker to a more literalizing attention toward those words. Again, in normal speech, we try to see through the materiality of words (their strange sounds and printed appearance, my voice timbre and peculiar accent, and so forth) toward their meaning. As meaning is lost, the materiality of words becomes obsessive, as is the case when children repeat a word over and over again until its sense is lost and it becomes an incomprehensible incantation. To begin to link up with our earlier description, a signifier that has lost its signified has thereby been transformed into an image.

This long digression on schizophrenia has allowed us to add a feature that we could not quite handle in our earlier description—namely, time itself. We must therefore now shift our discussion of postmodernism from the visual arts to the temporal ones—to music, poetry, and certain kinds of narrative texts such as those of Beckett. Anyone who has listened to John Cage's music may well have had an experience similar to those just evoked: frustration and desperation—the hearing of a single chord or note followed by a silence so long that memory cannot hold on to what went before, a silence then banished into oblivion by a new strange sonorous present, which itself disappears. This experience could be illustrated by many forms of cultural production today. I have chosen a text by a younger poet, partly because his "group" or "school"—known as the Language Poets—has in many ways made the experience of temporal discontinuity—the experience described here in terms of schizophrenic language—central to their language experiments and to what they like to call the "New Sentence." This is a poem called "China" by Bob Perelman (it can be found in his recent collection *Primer*, published by This Press in Berkeley, California):

> We live on the third world from the sun. Number three. Nobody
> tells us what to do.
> The people who taught us to count were being very kind.
> It's always time to leave.
> If it rains, you either have your umbrella or you don't.
> The wind blows your hat off.
> The sun rises also.
> I'd rather the stars didn't describe us to each other; I'd
> rather we do it for ourselves.

Run in front of your shadow.
A sister who points to the sky at least once a decade is a
good sister.
The landscape is motorized.
The train takes you where it goes.
Bridges among water.
Folks straggling along vast stretches of concrete, heading
into the plane.
Don't forget what your hat and shoes will look like when you
are nowhere to be found.
Even the words floating in air make blue shadows.
If it tastes good we eat it.
The leaves are falling. Point things out.
Pick up the right things.
Hey guess what? What? *I've learned how to talk.* Great.
The person whose head was incomplete burst into tears.
As it fell, what could the doll do? Nothing.
Go to sleep.
You look great in shorts. And the flag looks great too.
Everyone enjoyed the explosions.
Time to wake up.
But better get used to dreams.

Now one may object that this is not exactly schizophrenic writing in the clinical sense; it does not seem quite right to say that these sentences are free-floating material signifiers whose signifieds have evaporated. There does seem to be some global meaning here. Indeed, insofar as this is in some curious and secret way a political poem, it does seem to capture some of the excitement of the immense and unfinished social experiment of the new China, unparalleled in world history: the unexpected emergence, between the two superpowers, of "number three"; the freshness of a whole new object-world produced by human beings in some new control over their own collective destiny; the signal event, above all, of a collectivity that has become a new "subject of history" and that, after the long subjection of feudalism and imperialism, speaks in its own voice, for itself, for the first time ("Hey guess what? . . . I've learned how to talk."). Yet such meaning floats over the text or behind it. One cannot, I think, read this text according to any of the older New Critical categories and find the complex inner relationships and texture that characterized the older "concrete universal" of classical modernisms such as Wallace Stevens's.

Perelman's work, and Language Poetry generally, owes something to Gertrude Stein and, beyond her, to certain aspects of Flaubert. So it is not inappropriate at this point to insert an old account of Flaubert's sentences by Sartre, which conveys a vivid feeling of the movement of such sentences:

> His sentence closes in on the object, seizes it, immobilizes it, and breaks its back, wraps itself around it, changes into stone and petrifies its object along with itself. It is blind and deaf, bloodless, not a breath of life; a deep silence separates it from the sentence which follows; it falls into the void, eternally, and drags its prey down into that infinite fall. Any reality, once described, is struck off the inventory. (Jean-Paul Sartre, *What Is Literature?*)

The description is a hostile one, and the liveliness of Perelman is historically rather different from this homicidal Flaubertian practice. (For Mallarmé, Barthes once observed in a similar vein, the sentence, the word, is a way of murdering the outside world.) Yet it conveys some of the mystery of sentences that fall into a void of silence so great that for a time one wonders whether any new sentence could possibly emerge to take their place.

But now the secret of this poem must be disclosed. It is a little like Photorealism, which looked like a return to representation after the antirepresentational abstractions of Abstract Expressionism, until people began to realize that these paintings are not exactly realistic either, because what they represent is not the outside world but rather only a photograph of the outside world or, in other words, the latter's image. False realisms, they are really art about other art, images of other images. In the present case, the represented object is not really China after all: what happened was that Perelman came across a book of photographs in a stationery store in Chinatown, a book whose captions and characters obviously remained dead letters (or should one say material signifiers?) to him. The sentences of the poem are *his* captions to those pictures. Their referents are other images, another text, and the "unity" of the poem is not *in* the text at all but outside it in the bound unity of an absent book.

Now I must try very rapidly in conclusion to characterize the relationship of cultural production of this kind to social life in this country today. This will also be the moment to address the principal objection to concepts of postmodernism of the type I have sketched here: namely, that all the features we have enumerated are not new at all but abundantly characterized modernism proper or what I call high-modernism. Was not Thomas Mann, after all, interested in the idea of pastiche, and are not certain chapters of *Ulysses* its most obvious realization? Did we not mention Flaubert, Mallarmé, and Gertrude Stein in our account of postmodernist temporality? What is so new about all of this? Do we really need the concept of a *post*modernism?

One kind of answer to this question would raise the whole issue of periodization and of how a historian (literary or other) posits a radical break between two henceforth distinct periods. I must limit myself to the suggestion that radical breaks between periods do not generally involve complete changes of content but rather the restructuration of a certain number of elements already given: features that in an earlier period or system were subordinate now become dominant, and features that had been dominant again become secondary. In this sense, everything we have described here can be found in earlier periods and most notably within modernism proper: my point is that until the present day those things have been secondary or minor features of modernist art, marginal rather than central, and that we have something new when they become the central features of cultural production.

But I can argue this more concretely by turning to the relationship between cultural production and social life generally. The older or classical modernism was an oppositional art; it emerged within the business society of the gilded age as scandalous and offensive to the middle-class public—ugly, dissonant, bohemian, sexually shocking. It was something to make fun of (when the police were not called in to seize the books or close the exhibitions): an offense to good taste and to common sense, or, as Freud and Marcuse would have put it, a provocative challenge to the reigning reality and performance principles of early twentieth-century middle-class society. Modernism in general did not go well with overstuffed Victorian furniture, with Victorian moral taboos, or with the conventions of polite society. This is to say that whatever the explicit political content of the great high modernisms, the latter were always in some mostly implicit ways dangerous and explosive, subversive within the established order.

If then we suddenly return to the present day, we can measure the immensity of the cultural changes that have taken place. Not only are Joyce and Picasso no longer weird and repulsive, they have become classics and now look rather realistic to us. Meanwhile, there is very little in either the form or the content of contemporary art that contemporary society finds intolerable and scandalous. The most offensive forms of this art—punk rock, say, or what is called sexually explicit material—are all taken in stride by society, and they are commercially successful, unlike the productions of the older high-modernism. But this means that even if contemporary art has all the same formal features as the older modernism, it has still shifted its position fundamentally within our culture. For one thing, commodity production and in particular our clothing, furniture, buildings, and other artifacts are now intimately tied in with styling changes that derive from artistic experimentation; our advertising, for example, is fed by postmodernism in all the arts and inconceivable without it. For another, the classics of high-modernism are now part of the so-called canon and are taught in schools and universities—which at once empties them of any of their older subversive power. Indeed, one way of marking the break between the periods and of dating the emergence of postmodernism is precisely to be found there: in the moment (the early 1960s, one would think) in which the position of high-modernism and its dominant aesthetics become established in the academy and are henceforth felt to be academic by a whole new generation of poets, painters, and musicians.

But one can also come at the break from the other side and describe it in terms of periods of recent social life. As I have suggested, non-Marxists and Marxists alike have come around to the general feeling that at some point following World War II a new kind of society began to emerge (variously described as postindustrial society, multinational capitalism, consumer society, media society, and so forth). New types of consumption; planned obsolescence; an ever more rapid rhythm of fashion and styling changes; the penetration of advertising, television, and the media generally to a hitherto unparalleled degree throughout society; the replacement of the old tension between city and country, center and province, by the suburb and by universal standardization; the growth of the great networks of superhighways and the arrival of automobile culture—these are some of the features that would seem to mark a radical break with that older prewar society in which high-modernism was still an underground force.

I believe that the emergence of postmodernism is closely related to the emergence of this new moment of late, consumer or multinational capitalism. I believe also that its formal features in many ways express the deeper logic of that particular social system. I will only be able, however, to show this for one major theme: namely, the disappearance of a sense of history, the way in which our entire contemporary social system has little by little begun to lose its capacity to retain its own past, has begun to live in a perpetual present and in a perpetual change that obliterates traditions of the kind that all earlier social formations have had in one way or another to preserve. Think only of the media exhaustion of news: of how Nixon and, even more so, Kennedy are figures from a now distant past. One is tempted to say that the very function of the news media is to relegate such recent historical experiences as rapidly as possible into the past. The informational function of the media would thus be to help us forget, to serve as the very agents and mechanisms for our historical amnesia.

But in that case the two features of postmodernism on which I have dwelt here—the transformation of reality into images, the fragmentation of time into a series of perpetual presents—are both extraordinarily consonant with this process. My own conclusion here must take the form of a question about the critical value of the newer art. There is some agreement that the older modernism functioned against its society in ways that are variously described as critical, negative, contestatory, subversive, oppositional, and the like. Can anything of the sort be affirmed about postmodernism and its social moment? We have seen that there is a way in which postmodernism replicates or reproduces— reinforces—the logic of consumer capitalism; the more significant question is whether there is also a way in which it resists that logic. But that is a question we must leave open.

Robin Wood

Papering the Cracks:
Fantasy and Ideology
in the Reagan Era

The Lucas-Spielberg Syndrome

The crisis in ideological confidence of the 1970s, visible on all levels of American culture and variously enacted in Hollywood's "incoherent texts," has not been resolved: within the system of patriarchal capitalism, no resolution of the fundamental conflicts is possible. Instead, it has been forgotten, although its specter, masquerading as idealized nostalgia for lost radicalism, still intermittently haunts the cinema (*The Big Fix, The Big Chill, Return of the Secaucus Seven*). Remembering can be pleasant when it is accompanied by the sense that there is really nothing you can do any more ("Times have changed"). Vietnam ends, Watergate comes to seem an unfortunate aberration (with a film such as *All The President's Men* actually feeling able, although ambiguously, to celebrate the democratic system that can expose and rectify such anomalies); the Carter administration, promising the sense of a decent and reassuring liberalism, makes possible a huge ideological sigh of relief in preparation for an era of recuperation and reaction. *Rocky* and *Star Wars*—the two seminal works of what Andrew Britton (in an article in *Movie* 31/32 to which the present chapter is heavily indebted) has termed "Reaganite

From *Hollywood from Vietnam to Reagan.* Copyright © 1986 by Columbia University Press, New York. Reprinted with permission of the publisher.

203

entertainment"—appear a few years before Reagan's election, and are instant overwhelming commercial successes. Their respective progenies are still very much with us.

Reassurance is the keynote, and one immediately reflects that this is the era of sequels and repetition. The success of *Raiders of the Lost Ark, E.T.,* and the *Star Wars* movies is dependent not only on the fact that so many people go to see them but also that so many see them again and again. The phenomenon develops a certain irony in conjunction with Barthes' remarks on "rereading," in *S/Z:* "Rereading [is] an operation contrary to the commercial and ideological habits of our society, which would have us 'throw away' the story once it has been consumed ('devoured'), so that we can then move on to another story, buy another book, and which is tolerated only in certain marginal categories of readers (children, old people, and professors)."

Clearly, different kinds of rereading occur (children and professors do not reread in quite the same way or for the same purpose): it is possible to "read" a film such as *Letter from an Unknown Woman* or *Late Spring* twenty times and still discover new meanings, new complexities, ambiguities, possibilities of interpretation. It seems unlikely, however, that this is what takes people back, again and again, to *Star Wars.*

Young children require not-quite-endless repetition—the same game played over and over. When at last they begin to weary of exact repetition, they demand slight variation: the game still easily recognizable but not entirely predictable. It can be argued that this pattern forms the basis for much of our adult pleasure in traditional art. Stephen Neale, in one of the very few useful works on the subject (*Genre,* British Film Institute, 1980), discusses the Hollywood genres in such terms. The distinction between the great genre movies and the utterly uncreative hack work (between, say, *Rio Bravo* and *The Man Who Shot Liberty Valance,* on the one hand and the Roy Rogers or Hopalong Cassidy series on the other) lies very largely in the relationship between the familiar and the surprising—in the length of the leap the spectator is asked to make from generic expectations to specific transformations, the transformations being as much ideological as conventional. The repetition-and-sequel pattern of the 1980s is obviously of a very different order: despite the expensiveness of the films and their status as "cultural event," it is closer to Roy Rogers than to Ford and Hawks. The satisfactions of *Star Wars* are repeated until a sequel is required: same formula, with variations. But instead of a leap, only an infant footstep is necessary, and never one that might demand an adjustment on the level of ideology.

Hence the ironic appositeness of Barthes' perception that rereading is tolerated in children. The category of children's films has, of course, always existed. The 1980s variant is the curious and disturbing phenomenon of children's films conceived and marketed largely for adults—films that construct the adult spectator as a child, or more precisely, as a childish adult, an adult who would like to be a child. The child loses him- or herself in fantasy, accepting the illusion; the childish adult both does and does not, simultaneously. The characteristic response to *E.T.* (heard, with variations, over and over again) was "Wasn't it *wonderful?*" followed instantly by a nervously apologetic "But of course, it's pure fantasy." In this way, the particular satisfactions the films offer—the lost breast repeatedly rediscovered—can be at once indulged and laughed off. That the apology (after all, the merest statement of the obvious) has to be made at all testifies to the completeness of the surrender on another level to the indulgence.

It remains to define just what those satisfactions are, the kinds of reassurance demanded and so profitably supplied. It will be scarcely surprising that they—as it were, incidentally and obliquely—diminish, defuse, and render safe all the major radical movements that gained so much impetus, became so threatening, in the 1970s: radical feminism, black militancy, gay liberation, the assault on patriarchy. Before cataloguing them, however, it is as well to foreground certain problems that arise in discussing (and attacking) the films. It is, in fact, peculiarly difficult to discuss them seriously. The films themselves set up a deliberate resistance: they are so insistently not serious, so knowing about their own escapist fantasy/pure entertainment nature, and they consistently invite the audience's complicity in this. To raise serious objections to them is to run the risk of looking a fool (they're "just entertainment," after all) or, worse, a spoilsport (they're "such fun"). Pleasure is indeed an important issue. I had better confess at once that I enjoy the *Star Wars* films well enough: I get moderately excited, laugh a bit, even brush back a tear at the happy endings, all right on cue: they work, they are extremely efficient. But just what do we mean when we say "they work"? They work because their workings correspond to the workings of our own social construction. I claim no exemption from this: I enjoy being reconstructed as a child, surrendering to the reactivation of a set of values and structures my adult self has long since repudiated, I am not immune to the blandishments of reassurance. Pleasure itself, in fact, is patently ideological. We may be born with the desire for pleasure, but the actual gratifications of the desire are of necessity culturally determined, a product of our social conditioning. Pleasure, then, can never be taken for granted while we wish to remain adult; it isn't sacrosanct, purely natural and spontaneous, beyond analysis which spoils it (on many levels, it is imperative that our pleasure be spoiled). The pleasure offered by the *Star Wars* films corresponds very closely to our basic conditioning; it is extremely reactionary, as all mindless and automatic pleasure tends to be. The finer pleasures are those we have to work for.

I do not want to argue that the films are intrinsically and uniquely harmful: they are no more so than the vast majority of artifacts currently being produced by capitalist enterprise for popular consumption within a patriarchal culture. In many ways they resemble the old serials (Buck Rogers, Superman, Batman, etc.) that used to accompany feature films in weekly installments as program fillers, or get shown at children's matinees. What I find worrying about the Spielberg-Lucas syndrome is the enormous importance our society has conferred on the films, an importance not at all incompatible with their not being taken seriously ("But of course, it's pure fantasy"): indeed, the apparent contradiction is crucial to the phenomenon. The old serials were not taken seriously on *any* level (except perhaps by real children, and then only young ones); their role in popular culture was minor and marginal; they posed no threat to the coexistence of challenging, disturbing, or genuinely distinguished Hollywood movies, which they often accompanied in their lowly capacity. Today it is becoming difficult for films that are not like *Star Wars* (at least in the general sense of dispensing reassurance, but increasingly in more specific and literal ways, too) to get made, and when they do get made, the public and often the critics reject them: witness the box office failure of *Heaven's Gate*, *Blade Runner*, and *King of Comedy*.

These, then, are what seem to me the major areas in which the films provide reassurance. I have centered the argument in the *Star Wars* films (*E.T.* is dealt with separately afterward), but it will be obvious that most of my points apply, to varying degrees, over a much wider field of contemporary Hollywood cinema.

1. *Childishness.* I cannot abandon this theme without somewhat fuller development. It is important to stress that I am not positing some diabolical Hollywood-capitalist-Reaganite conspiracy to impose mindlessness and mystification on a potentially revolutionary populace, nor does there seem much point in blaming the filmmakers for what they are doing (the critics are another matter). The success of the films is only comprehensible when one assumes a

widespread *desire* for regression to infantilism, a populace who wants to be constructed as mock children. Crucial here, no doubt, is the urge to evade responsibility—responsibility for actions, decisions, thought, responsibility for changing things: children do not have to be responsible, there are older people to look after them. That is one reason why these films must be intellectually undemanding. It is not exactly that one doesn't have to think to enjoy *Star Wars* but rather that thought is strictly limited to the most superficial narrative channels: "What will happen? How will they get out of *this?*" The films are obviously very skillful in their handling of narrative, their resourceful ceaseless interweaving of actions and enigmas, their knowing deployment of the most familiar narrative patterns: don't worry, Uncle George (or Uncle Steven) will take you by the hand and lead you through Wonderland. Some dangers will appear on the way, but never fear, he'll also see you safely home; home being essentially those "good old values" that Sylvester Stallone told us *Rocky* was designed to reinstate: racism, sexism, "democratic" capitalism; the capitalist myths of freedom of choice and equality of opportunity, the individual hero whose achievements somehow "make everything all right," even for the millions who never make it to individual heroism (but every man can be a hero—even, such is the grudging generosity of contemporary liberalism, every woman).

2. *Special effects.* These represent the essence of Wonderland Today (Alice never needed reassurance about technology) and the one really significant way in which the films differ from the old serials. Again, one must assume a kind of automatic doublethink in audience response: we both know and don't know that we are watching special effects, technological fakery. Only thus can we respond simultaneously to the two levels of "magic": the diegetic wonders within the narrative and the extradiegetic magic of Hollywood (the best magic that money can buy), the technology on screen, the technology off. Spectacle—the sense of reckless prodigal extravagance, no expense spared—is essential: the unemployment lines in the world outside may get longer and longer, we may even have to go out and join them, but if capitalism can still throw out entertainments such as *Star Wars* (the films' very uselessness an aspect of the prodigality), the system must be basically OK, right? Hence, as capitalism approaches its ultimate breakdown, through that series of escalating economic crises prophesied by Marx well over a

century ago, its entertainments must become more dazzling, more extravagant, more luxuriously unnecessary.

3. *Imagination/Originality.* A further seeming paradox (actually only the extension of the "But of course, it's pure fantasy" syndrome) is that the audiences who wish to be constructed as children also wish to regard themselves as extremely sophisticated and "modern." The actual level of this sophistication can be gauged from the phenomenon (not unfamiliar to teachers of first-year film studies in universities) that the same young people who sit rapt through *Star Wars* find it necessary to laugh condescendingly at, say, a von Sternberg/Dietrich movie or a Ford Western in order to establish their superiority to such passé simple-mindedness. "Of course, it's pure fantasy—but what imagination!"—the flattering sense of one's own sophistication depends on the ability to juggle such attitudes, an ability the films constantly nurture. If we are to continue using the term *imagination* to apply to a William Blake, we have no business using it of a George Lucas. Imagination and what is popularly referred to as pure fantasy (actually there is no such thing) are fundamentally incompatible. Imagination is a force that strives to grasp and transform the world, not restore "the good old values." What we can justly credit Lucas with (I use the name, be it understood, to stand for his whole production team) is facility of invention, especially on the level of special effects and makeup and the creation of a range of cute or sinister or grotesque fauna (human and nonhuman).

The "originality" of the films goes very precisely with their "imagination": window dressing to conceal—but not entirely—the extreme familiarity of plot, characterization, situation, and character relations. Again, doublethink operates: even while we relish the originality, we must also retain the sense of the familiar, the comforting nostalgia for the childish repetitive pleasures of comic strip and serial (if we can't find the lost breast, we can at least suck our thumbs). Here doublethink becomes almost a synonym for sophistication. The fanciful trimmings of the *Star Wars* saga enable us to indulge in satisfactions that would have us writhing in embarrassment if they were presented naked. The films have in fact largely replaced Hollywood genres that are no longer viable without careful "it's pure fantasy" disguise, but for whose basic impulses there survives a need created and sustained by the dominant ideology of imperialist capitalism. Consider their relation to the 1940s war movie, of which Hawks's *Air Force* might stand as both representative and superior example: the group (bomber crew, infantry platoon, etc.) constructed as a microcosm of multiracial democracy. The war movie gave us various ethnic types (Jew, Polack, etc.) under the leadership of a WASP American; the Lucas films substitute fantasy figures (robots, Chewbacca) fulfilling precisely the same roles, surreptitiously permitting the same indulgence in WASP superiority. *Air Force* culminates in an all-out assault on the Japanese fleet, blasted out of the sea by "our boys": a faceless inhuman enemy getting its just deserts. Today, the Japanese can no longer be called Japs ("One fried Jap going down"— *Air Force*'s most notorious line) and are also no longer available for fulfilling that function (we are too "sophisticated"). However, dress the enemy in odd costumes (they remain faceless and inhuman, perhaps even totally metallic) and we can still cheer our boys when they blast them out of the sky as in the climax of *Star Wars*, etc.: the same indoctrinated values of patriotism, racism, and militarism are being indulged and celebrated.

Consider also the exotic adventure movie: our white heroes, plus comic relief, encounter a potentially hostile tribe; but the natives turn out to be harmless, childlike, innocent—they have never seen a white man before, and they promptly worship our heroes as gods. You can't do that any more: such movies (mostly despised "B" movies anyway) don't get shown now, and if we saw one on late-night television, we would have to laugh at it. But dress the natives as koala bears, displace the god identity on to a robot so that the natives appear even stupider, and you can still get away with it: the natives can still be childlike, lovable, and ready to help the heroes out of a fix; the nature of the laughter changes from repudiation to complicity.

4. *Nuclear anxiety.* This is central to Andrew Britton's thesis, and for an adequately detailed treatment I refer readers to the article cited above. The fear of nuclear war—at least, of indescribable suffering, at most, of the end of the world, with the end of civilization somewhere between—is certainly one of the main sources of our desire to be constructed as children, to be reassured, to evade responsibility and thought. The characteristic and widespread sense of helplessness—that it's all out of our hands, beyond all hope of effective intervention, perhaps already predetermined—for which there is unfortunately a certain degree of rational justification, is

continually fostered both by the media and by the cynicism of politicians: whether we *can* actually do anything (and to escape despair and insanity, we must surely cling to any rational belief that we can), it is clearly in the interests of our political/economic system for us to believe we can't. In terms of cinema, one side of this fear is the contemporary horror film, centered on the unkillable and ultimately inexplicable monster, the mysterious and terrible destructive force we can neither destroy, nor communicate with, nor understand. The Michael of *Halloween* and the Jason of the later *Friday the 13th* films are the obvious prototypes, but the indestructible psychopath of Michael Miller's *Silent Rage* is especially interesting because he is actually signified as the product of scientific experimentation with nuclear energy. The other side is the series of fantasy films centered on the struggle for possession of an ultimate weapon or power: the Ark of the Covenant of *Raiders of the Lost Ark*, the Genesis project of *Star Trek II*, "the Force" of *Star Wars*. The relationship of the two cycles (which developed simultaneously and are both extremely popular with, and aimed at, young audiences) might seem at first sight to be one of diametrical opposition (hopelessness vs. reassurance), yet their respective overall messages—"There's nothing you can do, anyway" and "Don't worry"—can be read as complements rather than opposites: both are deterrents to action. The pervasive, if surreptitious, implication of the fantasy films is that nuclear power is positive and justified as long as it is in the right (i.e., American) hands. *Raiders* is particularly blatant on the subject, offering a direct invitation to deliberate ignorance: you'll be all right, and all your enemies will be destroyed, as long as you "don't look"; nuclear power is synonymous with the power of God, who is, by definition, on our side. The film is also particularly blatant in its racism: non-Americans are in general either evil or stupid. The disguise of comic strip is somewhat more transparent than the disguise of pure fantasy. Nonetheless, it can scarcely escape notice that the arch-villain Khan of *Star Trek II* is heavily signified as foreign (and played by a foreign actor, Ricardo Montalban), as against the American-led crew of the spaceship (with its appropriate collection of fantasy-ethnic subordinates). The younger generation of *Star Wars* heroes is also conspicuously American.

The question has been raised as to whether the *Star Wars* films really fit this pattern: if they contain a fantasy embodiment of nuclear power, it is surely not the Force but the Death Star, which the Force, primarily signified in terms of moral rectitude and discipline rather than physical or technological power, is used to destroy. Can't they then be read as *anti*-nuclear films? Perhaps an ambiguity can be conceded (I concede it without much conviction). But moral rectitude has always been an attribute of Americans in the Hollywood war movie; the Death Star was created by the Force (its "dark side," associated with the evil non-Americans); and the use of the Force by Luke Skywalker in *Star Wars* is undeniably martial, violent, and destructive (although *Return of the Jedi* raises some belated qualms about this). Given the context—both generic and social-political—it seems to me that the same essential message, perhaps more covert and opaque, can be read from the *Star Wars* trilogy as from *Raiders* and *Star Trek II*.

5. *Fear of fascism.* I refer here not to the possibility of a Fascist threat from outside but from *inside:* the fear, scarcely unfounded, that continually troubles the American (un-)consciousness that democratic capitalism may not be cleanly separable from Fascism and may carry within itself the potential to become Fascist, totalitarian, a police state. The theme has been handled with varying degrees of intelligence and complexity in a number of overtly political films— supremely, *Meet John Doe;* but also a range of films from *All the King's Men* through *Advise and Consent* and *The Parallax View* to *The Dead Zone,* the theme particularly taking the form of the demagogue-who-may-become-dictator by fooling enough of the people enough of the time. The fear haunts the work of Hitchcock: the U-Boat commander of *Lifeboat* is, of course, German and explicitly Fascist, but he is not clearly distinguishable in his ruthlessness, his assumption of superiority, and his insidious charm from the American murderers of *Shadow of a Doubt* and *Rope.* More generally, how does one distinguish between the American individualist hero and the Fascist hero? Are the archetypes of westerner and gangster opposites or complements? The quandary becomes ever more pressing in the Reagan era, with the resurgence of an increasingly militant, vociferous, and powerful Right, the Fascist potential forcing itself to recognition. It would be neither fair nor accurate to describe *Rocky* and *Raiders of the Lost Ark* as Fascist films; yet they are precisely the kinds of entertainment that a potentially Fascist culture would be expected to produce and enjoy (what exactly are we applauding as we cheer on the exploits of Indiana Jones?).

The most positively interesting aspect of the *Star Wars* films (their other interests being largely of the type we call symptomatic) seems to me their dramatization of this dilemma. There is the ambiguity of the Force itself, with its powerful, and powerfully seductive, dark side to which the all-American hero may succumb: the Force, Obi One informs Luke, "has a strong influence on the weak-minded," as had Nazism. There is also the question (introduced early in *Star Wars*, developed as the dominant enigma in *The Empire Strikes Back*, and only resolved in the latter part of *Return of the Jedi*) of Luke's parentage: is the father of our hero *really* the prototypical Fascist beast Darth Vader? By the end of the third film, the dilemma has developed quasi-philosophical dimensions: as Darth Vader represents rule-by-force, if Luke resorts to force (*the* Force) to defeat him, doesn't he become Darth Vader? The film can extricate itself from this knot only by the extreme device of having Darth Vader abruptly redeem himself and destroy the unredeemable Emperor.

The trilogy's simple but absolutely systematic code of accents extends this theme in the wider terms of the American heritage. All the older-generation Jedi knights, both good and evil, and their immediate underlings (e.g., Peter Cushing) have British accents, in marked contrast to the American accents of the young heroes. The contradictions in the origins of America are relevant here: a nation founded in the name of freedom by people fleeing oppression, the founding itself an act of oppression (the subjugation of the Indians), the result an extremely oppressive civilization based on the persecution of minorities (e.g., the Salem witch hunts). Britain itself has, of course, markedly contradictory connotations—a democracy as well as an imperialist power ("the Empire"), which America inherited. It is therefore fitting that both Obi One and Darth Vader should be clearly signified as British and that doubt should exist as to which of them is Luke Skywalker's father, whether literal or moral/political. Hence the films' unease and inability satisfactorily to deal with the problem of lineage: what will the rebels against the Empire create if not another empire? The unease is epitomized in the final sequence of *Star Wars*, with its visual reference (so often pointed out by critics) to *Triumph of the Will*. A film buff's joke? Perhaps. But Freud showed a long time ago that we are often most serious when we joke. From the triumph of the Force to the Triumph of the Will is but a step.

Parenthetically, it is worth drawing brief attention here to John Milius' *Conan the Barbarian,* perhaps the only one of these 1980s fantasy films to dispense with a liberal cloak, parading its Fascism shamelessly in instantly recognizable popular signifiers: it opens with a quotation from Nietsche, has the spirit of its dead heroine leap to the rescue at the climax as a Wagnerian Valkyrie, and in between unabashedly celebrates the Aryan male physique with a singlemindedness that would have delighted Leni Riefenstahl. Its token gay is dispatched with a kick in the groin, and its arch-villain is black. There is an attempt, it is true, to project Fascism on to *him* (so that he can be allotted the most gruesome of the film's many grisly deaths), but it is difficult to imagine a more transparent act of displacement.

6. *Restoration of the father.* One might reasonably argue that this constitutes—and logically enough—the dominant project, ad infinitum and post nauseam, of the contemporary Hollywood cinema, a veritable thematic metasystem embracing all the available genres and all the current cycles, from realist drama to pure fantasy, taking in en route comedy and film noir and even in devious ways infiltrating the horror film. The father must here be understood in all senses, symbolic, literal, potential: patriarchal authority (the Law), which assigns all other elements to their correct, subordinate, allotted roles; the actual heads of families, fathers of recalcitrant children, husbands of recalcitrant wives, who must either learn the virtue and justice of submission or pack their bags; the young heterosexual male, father of the future, whose eventual union with the "good woman" has always formed the archetypal happy ending of the American film, guarantee of the perpetuation of the nuclear family and social stability.

The restoration of the father has many ramifications, one of the most important of which is, of course, the corresponding restoration of women, after a decade of feminism and "liberation." The 1980s have seen the development (or, in many cases, the resurrection) of a number of strategies for coping with this project. There is the plot about the liberated woman who proves she's as good as the man but then discovers that this doesn't make her happy and that what she really wanted all the time was to serve him. Thus Debra Winger in *Urban Cowboy* proves that she can ride the mechanical bull as well as John Travolta but withdraws from competition in order to spend the future washing his socks. Or

Sondra Locke in *Bronco Billy* demonstrates that she can shoot as well as Clint Eastwood but ends up spread out on a wheel as his target/object-for-the-gaze. (The grasp of feminist principle implicit in this—that what women want is to be able to do the same things men do because they envy them so much—is obviously somewhat limited.) The corollary of this is the plot that suggests that men, if need arises, can fill the woman's role just as well if not better (*Kramer vs. Kramer, Author! Author!, Mr. Mom*). It's the father, anyway, who has all the real responsibility, women being by nature irresponsible, as in the despicable *Middle Age Crazy*, which asks us to shed tears over the burden of "being the daddy," the cross that our patriarchs must bear.

If the woman can't accept her subordination, she must be expelled from the narrative altogether, such as Mary Tyler Moore in *Ordinary People* or Tuesday Weld and Dyan Cannon in *Author! Author!*, leaving the father to develop his beautiful relationship with his offspring untrammeled by female complications. *Ordinary People* makes particularly clear the brutality to the woman of the Oedipal trajectory our culture continues to construct: from the moment in the narrative when our young hero takes the decisive step of identification with the father/ acquisition of his own woman, the mother becomes superfluous to Oedipal/patriarchal concerns, a mere burdensome redundancy. The father, on the other hand, must be loved, accepted, and respected, even if he is initially inadequate (*Kramer vs. Kramer*) or generally deficient, unpleasant, or monstrous (*Tribute, The Great Santini*). Even a nonfamily movie such as *Body Heat* can be read as another variant on the same pattern. Its purpose in reviving the film noir woman of the 1940s so long after (one had innocently supposed) her cultural significance had become obsolete seems to be to suggest that, if women are so perverse as to want power and autonomy, men are better off without them: at the end of the film, William Hurt is emotionally "with" his male buddies even though ruined and in prison, while Kathleen Turner is totally isolated and miserable even though rich and free on a Mexican beach. Clearly, what she really needed was the love of a good man, and as she willfully rejected it, she must suffer the consequences. Seen like this, *Body Heat* is merely the *Ordinary People* of film noir.

Back in the world of pure fantasy (but we have scarcely left it), we find precisely the same patterns, the same ideological project, reiterated. Women are allowed minor feats of heroism and aggression (in deference to the theory that what they want is to be able to behave like men): thus Karen Allen can punch Harrison Ford in the face near the beginning of *Raiders*, and Princess Leia has intermittent outbursts of activity, usually in the earlier parts of the movies. Subsequently, the woman's main function is to be rescued by the men, involving her reduction to helplessness and dependency. Although Princess Leia is ultimately revealed to be Luke Skywalker's sister, there is never any suggestion that *she* might inherit the Force or have the privilege of being trained and instructed by Obi One and Yoda. In fact, the strategy of making her Luke's sister seems largely a matter of narrative convenience: it renders romance with Luke automatically unthinkable and sets her free, without impediments, for union with Han Solo. Nowhere do the films invite us to take any interest in *her* parentage. They play continually on the necessity for Luke to confirm his allegiance to the "good father" (Obi One) and repudiate the "bad father" (Darth Vader), even if the latter proves to be his *real* father. With this set up and developed in the first two films, *Return of the Jedi* manages to cap it triumphantly with the redemption of Darth Vader. The trilogy can then culminate in a veritable Fourth of July of Fathericity: a grandiose firework display to celebrate Luke's coming through, as he stands backed by the ghostly figures of Obi One, Darth, and Yoda, all smiling benevolently. The mother, here, is so superfluous that she doesn't figure in the narrative at all—except, perhaps, at some strange, deeply sinister, unconscious level, disguised as the unredeemably evil Emperor who, as so many people have remarked, seems modeled on the witch in *Snow White* (the heroine's stepmother). Her male disguise makes it permissible to subject her to the most violent expulsion from the narrative yet. Read like this, *Return of the Jedi* becomes the *Ordinary People* of outer space, with Darth Vader as Donald Sutherland and Obi One and Yoda in tandem as the psychiatrist.

If the *Star Wars* films—like the overwhelming majority of 1980s Hollywood movies—put women back where they belong (subordinate or nowhere), they do the same, in a casual incidental way, for blacks and gays. The token black (Billy Dee Williams) is given a certain token autonomy and self-assertiveness, but he has a mere supporting role, in all senses of the term, on the right side and raises no question of threat or revolution. Gays are handled more surreptitiously. Just as the 1940s war movie generously included various ethnics in its platoon/bomber crew, so its 1980s equivalent has its subordinate, subservient (and comic and timid) gay character, in the entirely unchallenging form of an asexual robot: C3PO, with his affected British accent, effeminate mannerisms, and harmlessly pedophile relationship with R2D2 (after all, what can robots do?). On the other hand, there is the *Star Wars* rendering of a gay bar, the clientele exclusively male, and all grotesque freaks.

Thus the project of the *Star Wars* films and related works is to put everyone back in his or her place, reconstruct us as dependent children, and reassure us that it will all come right in the end: trust father.*

Spielberg and E.T.

Although it is in many respects permissible to speak of a Lucas-Spielberg syndrome—films catering to the desire for regression to infantilism, the doublethink phenomenon of pure fantasy—Spielberg and, especially, *E.T.* also demand some separate consideration. The *Star Wars* films are knowing concoctions, the level of personal involvement (that facility of invention that I have granted them) superficial. *Raiders of the Lost Ark* belongs with them, but with *Close Encounters of the Third Kind* and *E.T.*, there is a certain sense of pressure, of personal necessity. Semiologists would call this the inscription of the author in the film; the popular response is to applaud Spielberg's "sincerity." However one takes it—as evidence of a genuine creative drive or as simply one further level of signification—I am not arguing that it necessarily makes the films better than the *Star Wars* movies. Sincerity is a difficult concept (Spielberg's, in conjunction with the films' extraordinary efficiency, makes him a lot of money) and in itself carries no connotations of value; popularly, it tends to get confused with "giving us a nice feeling," but logically there is no more reason to credit Spielberg with it than, say, Mickey Spillane, whose novels also carry a charge of personal investment. If the Spielberg films are in some ways more interesting than the

---

*It is striking that, since this chapter was written, the essential ugliness of the 1980s science fiction/comic strip project—hitherto concealed beneath the sweetness-and-light of patriarchal morality—has risen to the surface: witness the obsessive violence of *Indiana Jones and the Temple of Doom* and the pervasively sick imagery of *Gremlins* (which Spielberg "presented"). *Dune* is the culmination of the exposure of rottenness. It is the most obscenely homophobic film I have ever seen, managing to associate with homosexuality in a single scene physical grossness, moral depravity, violence, and disease. It shows no real interest in its bland young lovers or its last-minute divine revelation, all its energies being devoted to the expression of physical and sexual disgust. Much of the imagery strongly recalls David Lynch's earlier *Eraserhead*, but the film seems only partly explicable in auteurist terms; the choice of Lynch as writer-director would also need to be explained, and the film must be seen in the wider context as a product of the 1980s Hollywood machine.

Star Wars trilogy, it is because the personal investment has as its corollary, or perhaps its source, a certain disturbance; the sincerity seems in large part the need to cover over that disturbance, a *personal* need for reassurance (which the *Star Wars* films peddle as a commodity), the desire to "believe." Another way of saying this is to suggest that the patriarchal/Oedipal trajectory is never quite as simple, direct, or untroubled and takes more curious and deviant routes in the Spielberg movies. That the films fail to be more interesting than they are testifies to the success of the fantasy: the disturbance is covered over very effectively, almost obliterated. Illuminating comparisons might be made with two of *E.T.*'s thematic antecedents: Lewton's *Curse of the Cat People* and Cohen's *It's Alive* movies.

One needs to distinguish carefully between the childlike and the childish (just as one needs to distinguish the true innocence of childhood from the sentimental, sanitized, desexualized version of bourgeois ideology). Peter Coveney's admirable *The Image of Childhood* undertakes just such a distinction, examining the differences between the Romantic concept of the child (Blake, Wordsworth) as symbol of new growth and regeneration (of ourselves, of civilization) and the regressive Victorian sentimentalization of children as identification figures for "childish adults," the use of the infantile as escape from an adult world perceived as irredeemably corrupt, or at least bewilderingly problematic.* Both models persist, intermittently, in our culture: within the modern cinema, one might take as an exemplary reference point the Madlyn of *Celine and Julie Go Boating* and the multiple suggestions of growth and renewal she develops in relation to the four women of the film. Spielberg in *E.T.* seems to hesitate between the two concepts (Elliott's freshness and energy are seen in relation to a generally oppressive civilization, although he is never Blake's "fiend hid in a cloud") before finally committing himself to the childish. If Spielberg is the ideal director for the 1980s, it is because his "sincerity" (the one quality that the *Star Wars* films are vaguely felt to lack) expresses itself as an emotional investment in precisely that form of regression that appears to be so generally desired.

The attitude to the patriarchal family implicit in Spielberg's films is somewhat curious. In *Jaws* the family is tense and precarious; in *Close Encounters* it disintegrates; in *E.T.* it has already broken up

---

*It is peculiarly appropriate that a new version of *Peter Pan* should be among Spielberg's current projects.

Spielberg's characters, like his audiences, typically look up in childlike wonder at the spectacle he provides them. Here, Jillian (Melinda Dillon) and her son Barry (Cary Guffey) enjoy Close Encounters of the Third Kind *(Spielberg, 1977). Photo courtesy of Columbia Pictures.*

before the film begins. The first part of *E.T.* quite vividly depicts the oppressiveness of life in the nuclear family: incessant bickering, mean-mindedness, one-upmanship. This state of affairs is the result of the father's defection, perhaps: the boys have no one to imitate, as Roy Scheider's son in *Jaws* had. But he has defected only recently, and the *Close Encounters* family is scarcely any better. Yet Spielberg seems quite incapable of thinking beyond this: all he can do is reassert the "essential" goodness of family life in the face of all the evidence he himself provides. Hence the end of *E.T.* surreptitiously reconstructs the image of the nuclear family. Spielberg is sufficiently sophisticated to realize that he can't bring Dad home from Mexico for a last-minute repentance and reunion (it would be too corny, not realistic, in a film that for all its status as pure fantasy has a great stake in the accumulated connotations of "real life"). But he produces a paternal scientist in Dad's place (an even better father who can explicitly identify himself with Elliott—"When I was ten I was just like you," or words to that effect). A climactic image groups him with mother and daughter in an archetypal family composition, like a posed photograph. For Spielberg it doesn't really matter that the scientist has no intimate relationship with the mother, as his imagination is essentially pre-sexual: it is enough that he stands in for Elliott's missing father.

It follows that the position of women in Spielberg's work is fairly ignominious. Largely denied any sexual presence, they function exclusively as wives and mothers (especially mothers), with no suggestion that they might reasonably want anything beyond that. The two women in *Close Encounters* typify the extremely limited possibilities. On the one hand, there is the wife of Richard Dreyfuss (Teri Garr), whom the film severely criticizes for not standing staunchly by her husband even when his behavior suggests that he is clearly certifiable: she has to be dismissed from the narrative to leave him free to depart in the spaceship. On the other hand, there is the mother (Melinda Dillon) whose sole objective is to regain her child (a male child, inevitably). No suggestion is made that *she* might go off in the spaceship or even that she might want to. The end of *E.T.* offers the precise complement to this: the extraterrestrial transmits his wisdom and powers to the male child, Elliott, by applying a finger to his forehead, then instructs the little girl to "be good": like Princess Leia, she will never inherit the Force.

As for men, Spielberg shows an intermittent desire to salute Mr. Middle America, which is not entirely incompatible with his basic project, given the way in which serious (read subversive) thought is repressed by the media: at the end of *Jaws*, Roy Scheider destroys the shark after both the proletarian and the intellectual have failed. By inclination, however, he gravitates toward the infantile presexual male, a progression obviously completed by Elliott. (No one, of course, is really presexual; yet the myth of the presexuality of children remains dominant, and it is logical that the desire for regression to infantilism should incorporate this myth.) Roy Neary in *Close Encounters* is an interesting transitional figure. As he falls under the influence of the extraterrestrial forces, his behavior becomes increasingly infantile (given the dirt he deposits all over the house, one might see him as regressing to the pre-toilet training period). Divested of the encumbrances of wife and family, he proceeds to erect a huge phallus in the living room; but, before he can achieve the actual revelation of its meaning, he must learn to slice off its top. As with the mother and the scientist of *E.T.*, the film contradicts generic expectations by conspicuously not developing a sexual relationship, although Neary's alliance with Melinda Dillon makes this more than feasible—generically speaking, almost obligatory. Instead, the symbolic castration makes possible the desexualized sublimation of the ending: Neary led into the spaceship by frail, little, asexual, childlike figures, to fly off with a display of bright lights the Smiths of *Meet Me in St. Louis* never dreamed of. The logical next step (leaving aside the equally regressive comic strip inanities of *Raiders of the Lost Ark*) is to a literal, but still necessarily male, child as hero.

Spielberg's identification with Elliott (that there is virtually no distance whatever between character and director is clearly the source of the film's seductive suspect charm) makes possible the precise nature of the fantasy *E.T.* offers: not so much a child's fantasy as an adult's fantasy about childhood. It is also essentially a male fantasy: apart from Pauline Kael (whose feminist consciousness is so undeveloped one could barely describe it as embryonic), I know of no women who respond to the film the way so many men do (although not without embarrassment), as, in Kael's term, a "bliss-out." The film caters to the wish—practically universal, within our culture—that what W. B. Yeats so evocatively called "the ignominy of boyhood" might have been a little less ignominious. It is the fulfillment of this wish that most male adults find so irresistible. It is, however, always worth examining what precisely it is that we have failed to resist. The film does for the problems of childhood exactly what Spielberg's contribution to *Twilight Zone* did for the problem of old age: it raises them in order to dissolve them in fantasy, so that we are lulled into feeling they never really existed. Meanwhile, boyhood (not to mention girlhood) remains, within the patriarchal nuclear family, as ignominious as ever.

Such a view of family life, male/female relations, and compensatory fantasy is obviously quite curious and idiosyncratic, always verging on the exposure of contradictions that only the intensity of the commitment to fantasy conceals. The essential flimsiness and vulnerability of the fantasy are suggested by the instability of E.T. himself as a realized presence in the film. Were it not for Spielberg's sincerity (a sincerity unaccompanied by anything one might reasonably term intelligence, and in fact incompatible with it)—his evident investment in the fantasy—one might describe the use of E.T. as shamelessly opportunistic. From scene to scene, almost moment to moment, he represents whatever is convenient to Spielberg and to Elliott: helpless/potent, mental defective/intellectual giant, child figure/father figure.

The film's central theme is clearly the acceptance of Otherness (that specter that haunts, and must continue to haunt, patriarchal bourgeois society)—by Elliott, initially, then by his siblings, eventually by his mother, by the benevolent scientist, by the schoolboys. On the surface level—"E.T." as an e.t.—this seems quite negligible, a nonissue. This is not to assert that there are no such things as extraterrestrials, but simply that, as yet, they haven't constituted a serious social problem. They have a habit of turning up at convenient moments in modern history: in the 1950s, with the cold war and the fear of Communist infiltration, everyone saw hostile flying saucers, and Hollywood duly produced movies about them; at a period when (in the aftermath of Vietnam and Watergate, and with a new Vietnam in Central America hovering over American heads) we need reassurance, Hollywood produces *nice* extraterrestrials. (The 1950s produced some benevolent ones, too—*It Came from Outer Space*, for example—but they proved less profitable; contrariwise, the hostile, totally intractable kind are still with us—witness Carpenter's *The Thing*, released almost simultaneously with *E.T.*—but the model is definitely not popular.)

Unfortunately, on a less literal level, as a more general representation of Otherness, E.T. almost totally lacks resonance ("zero charisma," one might say). All the Others of white patriarchal bourgeois culture—workers, women, gays, blacks—are in various ways threatening, and their very existence represents a demand that society transform itself. E.T. isn't threatening at all: in fact, he's just about as cute as a little rubber Martian could be. This, it seems to me, is what makes the film (for all its charm, for all the sincerity) in the last resort irredeemably smug: a nation that was founded on the denial of Otherness now—after radical feminism, after gay liberation, after black militancy—complacently produces a film in which Otherness is something we can all love and cuddle and cry over, without unduly disturbing the nuclear family and the American way of life. E.T. is one of us; he just looks a bit funny.

Poltergeist requires a brief postscript here. It is tempting to dismiss it simply as Tobe Hooper's worst film, but it clearly belongs to the Spielberg *oeuvre* rather than to Hooper's. Its interest and the particular brand of reassurances it offers both lie in its relation to the 1970s family horror film—in the way in which Spielberg enlists the genre's potential radicalism and perverts it into 1980s conservatism. One can discern two parallel and closely related projects: first, the attempt (already familiar from *Jaws*) to separate the American family from "bad" capitalism, to pretend the two are without connection: there are a few greedy people, putting profit before human concerns, who bring on catastrophes, whether by keeping open dangerous beaches or not removing the bodies before converting cemeteries into housing developments. The project has a long history in the American cinema (its inherent tensions and contradictions wonderfully organized by Capra, for example, in *It's a Wonderful Life*). With Spielberg, it becomes reduced merely to a blatant example of what Barthes calls "inoculation," where ideology acknowledges a minor, local, reformable evil in order to divert attention from the fundamental ones. Second is the attempt to absolve the American family from all responsibility for the horror. In short, a cleansing job: in the 1970s, the monster was located within the family, perceived as its logical product. *Poltergeist* appears at first to be toying with this concept, before declaring the family innocent and locating the monstrous elsewhere: it is defined in terms of either meaningless superstition (corpses resent having swimming pools built over them) or some vague metaphysical concept of eternal evil ("the Beast"—superstition on a more grandiose scale), the two connected by the implication that the latter is evoked by, or is working through, the former. In any case, as in *E.T.*, the suburban bourgeois nuclear family remains the best of all possible worlds, if only because any other is beyond Spielberg's imagination. One might suggest that the overall development of the Hollywood cinema from the late 1960s to the 1980s is summed up in the movement from Romero's use of the Star-Spangled Banner (the flag) at the beginning of *Night of the Living Dead* to Spielberg's use of it (the music) at the beginning of *Poltergeist*.

Blade Runner

Blade Runner was released in the United States simultaneously with *E.T.* and for one week was its serious challenger at the box office; then receipts for *Blade Runner* dropped disastrously while those for *E.T.* soared. The North American critical establishment was generally ecstatic about *E.T.* and cool or ambivalent about *Blade Runner*. *E.T.* was nominated for a great many Academy Awards and won a few; *Blade Runner* was nominated for a few and won none. I take these facts as representing a choice made in conjunction by critics and public, ratified by the Motion Picture Academy—a choice whose significance extends far beyond a mere preference for one film over another, expressing a preference for the reassuring over the disturbing, the reactionary over the progressive, the safe over the challenging, the childish over the adult, spectator passivity over spectator activity.

Admirers of the original novel (Philip Dick's *Do Androids Dream of Electric Sheep?*) tend to regard the film with some hostility. But *Blade Runner* is not really an adaptation: rather, the film is built on certain ideas and motifs selected from the novel. Its aim, argument, and tone are so different that it is best to regard it as an autonomous work. Gone or played down are most of the novel's major structuring premises: the nuclear war that has rendered the earth unsafe for the support of life and health; the use of animals as rare, expensive, coveted status symbols; the pseudoreligion of "Mercerism." One might define the fundamental difference thus: the concerns of the novel are predominantly metaphysical, those of the film predominantly social. Some of the features discussed here derive (in most cases, rather loosely) from the book; others do not. They are so well integrated that it seems unnecessary to spell out the distinction in each individual case.

Fantasy, by and large, can be used in two ways—as a means of escaping from contemporary reality, or as a means of illuminating it. Against the Spielbergian complacency of *E.T.* can be set *Blade Runner's* vision of capitalism, which is projected into the future, yet intended to be clearly recognizable. It is important that the novel's explanation of the state of the world (the nuclear war) is withheld from the film: the effect is to lay the blame on capitalism directly. The society we see is our own writ large, its present excesses carried to their logical extremes: power and money controlled by even fewer, in even larger monopolies; worse poverty, squalor, degradation; racial oppression; a polluted planet, from which those who can emigrate to other worlds. The film opposes to Marx's view of inevitable collapse a chilling vision of capitalism hanging on, by the maintenance of power and oppression, in the midst of an essentially disintegrated civilization.

The depiction of the role played in this maintenance by the media is a masterly example of the kind of clarification—a complex idea compressed into a single image—advocated by Brecht: the mystified poor are mostly Asians; the ideal image they are given, therefore, dominating the city in neon lights, is that of a beautiful, richly dressed, exquisitely made-up female oriental, connected in the film (directly or indirectly) with emigration, Coca-Cola and pill popping, various forms of consumption, pacification, and flight.

The central interest of the film lies in the relationship between the hero, Deckard, and the "replicants"; the hero, one might add, is interesting *only* in relation to the replicants. The relationship is strange, elusive, multileveled, inadequately worked out (the failure of the film is as striking as its evident successes): the meeting of Raymond Chandler and William Blake is not exactly unproblematic. The private eye/film noir aspect of the movie is strongly underlined by Deckard's voice-over narration, demanded by the studio after the film's completion because someone felt that audiences would have difficulty in following the narrative (justifiably, alas: our own conditioning by the contemporary media is centered on, and continually reinforces, the assumption that we are either unable or unwilling to do any work). But that aspect is clearly there already in the film, which draws not only on the Chandler ethos but also on the rethinking of it in 1970s cinema (Altman's *The Long Goodbye,* more impressively Penn's *Night Moves*): the moral position of Chandler's knight walking the "mean streets" can no longer be regarded as uncompromised. Deckard's position as hero is compromised, above all, by the way the film draws on another figure of film noir (and much before it), the figure of the double—which brings us to the replicants.

If *Blade Runner*'s attitude to American capitalism is at the opposite pole to Spielberg's, the logical corollary is that the film's representation of the Other is at the opposite pole to that of E.T., although without falling into the alternative trap embodied by Carpenter's "Thing." The replicants (I am thinking especially of Roy and Pris) are dangerous but fascinating, frightening but beautiful, other but not totally and intractably alien; they gradually emerge as the film's true emotional center and certainly represent its finest achievement. Their impressiveness depends partly on their striking visual presence, but more on the multiple connotations they accrue as the film proceeds, through processes of suggestion, association, and reference.

The central defining one is that established by the near-quotation from Blake with which Roy Batty introduces himself (it has no equivalent in the novel):

> Fiery the angels fell; deep thunder rolled
> Around their shores, burning with the fires
> of Orc
> (*America: A Prophecy,* lines 115–16)

Blake's poem is a celebration of the American Revolution, a narrative about the founding of modern America, interpreted on a spiritual/symbolic plane. Orc leads the revolt against oppression; he is one of Blake's devil-angels, descendant of Milton's Lucifer as reinterpreted by Blake ("Milton was of the devil's party without knowing it"), the spirit of freedom, "Lover of wild rebellion and transgression of God's law," consistently associated with fire ("the fiery joy"). Roy, however, misquotes: Blake's original reads "Fiery the angels rose," the rising of the angels signifying the beginning of the revolt that is to found the free democratic state that, 200 years ago, could be viewed idealistically as a step in humanity's progress toward the New Jerusalem. The change from "rose" to "fell" must be read, then, in terms of the *end* of the American democratic principle of freedom, its ultimate failure: the shot that introduces Roy, the rebel angel, links him in a single camera movement to the imagery of urban squalor and disintegration through which he is moving. Clearly, in the context of 1980s Hollywood, such an implication could be suggested only in secret, concealed in a particularly esoteric reference. Subsequently, Roy's identification with the Blake revolutionary hero is rendered visually: stripped to the waist for the final combat with Deckard, he could have stepped straight out of one of Blake's visionary paintings.

The other connotations are less insistent, more a matter of suggestion, but (grouping themselves around the allusion to Blake) they add up to a remarkably complex and comprehensive definition of the Other. First, the replicants are identified as an oppressed and exploited proletariat: produced to serve their capitalist masters, they are discarded when their usefulness is over and "retired" (i.e., destroyed) when they rebel against such usage. Roy tells Deckard: "Quite an experience to live in fear. That's what it is to be a slave." They are also associated with racial minorities: when Deckard's boss refers to them by the slang term *skin-jobs*, Deckard immediately connects this to the term *niggers*. Retaining a certain sexual mystery, they carry suggestions of sexual ambiguity: Rachael's response to one of Deckard's questions in the interrogation scene is "Are you trying to find out if I'm a replicant or if I'm a lesbian?"; the climatic Roy/Deckard battle accumulates marked homoerotic overtones (made explicit in Roy's challenge "You'd better get it up"), culminating in his decision to save Deckard's life. The replicants have no families: they have not been through the bourgeois patriarchal process known euphemistically as socialization. They appear to be of two kinds—those who are not supposed to know they are replicants (Rachael) and have accordingly been supplied with "memory banks," false family photographs, etc., and who are therefore more amenable to socialization, and those who know they are other (Roy/Pris) and live by that knowledge. Roy and Pris are also associated with childhood, not only by the fact that they are literally only 4 years old, but by their juxtaposition with the toys in J. F. Sebastian's apartment, an environment in which they are so at home that Pris can be assimilated into it, becoming one of Sebastian's creations when she hides from Deckard. Pris, made up as a living doll, irresistibly evokes punk and the youth rebellion associated with it. As in Blake, the revolution is ultimately against the father, the symbolic figure of authority, oppression, and denial ("Thou shalt not"); it is therefore appropriate that the film should move toward Roy's murder of Tyrell, his creator, owner, and potential destroyer.

The parallels that seek to establish Roy as Deckard's double are fairly systematic but not entirely convincing, the problem lying partly in the incompatibility of the film's literary sources (Philip Marlowe can scarcely look into the mirror and see Orc as his reflection). Rachael's question (never answered) "Did you ever take that test yourself?" suggests that Deckard could be a replicant; Deckard's own line, "Replicants weren't supposed to have feelings, neither were blade runners," develops the parallel. The crosscutting in the battle with Roy repeatedly emphasizes the idea of the mirror image with the injured hands, the cries of pain. The relationship is above all suggested in Roy's contemptuously ironic "Aren't you 'the good man'?": hero and villain change places, all moral certainties based on the status quo collapse.

The more often I see *Blade Runner*, the more I am impressed by its achievement and the more convinced of its failure. The problem may be that the central thrust of the film, the source of its energy, is too revolutionary to be permissible: it *has* to be compromised. The unsatisfactoriness comes to a head in the ludicrous, bathetic ending, apparently tacked on in desperation at the last minute. But how should the film end? In the absence of any clear information, two possibilities come to mind, the choice depending, one might say, on whether Philip Marlowe or Orc is to have the last word. The first scenario involves the film noir ending in which Rachael is retired by Deckard's superior who is then killed in turn by Deckard (himself mortally wounded, perhaps) in a final gun battle. In the second, Deckard joins the replicant revolution. The former is probably too bleak for 1980s Hollywood, the latter too explicitly subversive for *any* Hollywood. Either would, however, make some sense and would be the outcome of a logical progression within the film, whereas the ending we have makes no sense at all: Deckard and Rachael fly off to live happily ever after (where?—the film has clearly established that there is nowhere on earth to go). The problem partly lies in the added voice-over commentary, the only evidence we are given that Rachael has been constructed without a "determination date": were she about to die, the notion of a last desperate fling in the wilderness would make slightly more sense, and we would not be left with the awkward question of how they are going to survive.

The film's problems, however, are not confined to its last couple of minutes: just as its strengths are centered in the replicants, so too are its weaknesses. If Roy is the incarnation of the Blakean revolutionary hero, he also, especially in association with Pris, carries other connotations that are much more dubious, those of an Aryan master race. This is very strongly suggested by the characters' physical attributes (blondness, beauty, immense strength), but it is also, more worryingly, signified in their ruthlessness: the offscreen murder of J. F. Sebastian (not in the novel) seems completely arbitrary and unmotivated, put in simply to discredit the replicants so that they cannot be mistaken for the film's true heroes. The problem is rooted in the entire tradition of the Gothic, of horror literature and horror film: the problem of the positive monster, who, insofar as he becomes positive, ceases to be monstrous, hence no longer frightening. It is the problem that Cohen confronted in the *It's Alive* movies (and failed to resolve in the second) and that Badham confronted in *Dracula* (a film that, like *Blade Runner*, develops disturbing Fascist overtones in its movement toward the monster's rehabilitation).

The central problem, however, is Rachael and her progressive humanization. The notion of what is human is obviously very heavily weighted ideologically; here, it amounts to no more than becoming the traditional "good object," the passive woman who willingly submits to the dominant male. What are we to make of the moment when, to save Deckard's life, Rachael shoots a fellow replicant? Not, clearly, what other aspects of this confused movie might powerfully suggest: the tragic betrayal of her class and race.

The film is in fact defeated by the overwhelming legacy of classical narrative. It succumbs to one of its most firmly traditional and ideologically reactionary formulas: the elimination of the bad couple (Roy, Pris) in order to construct the good couple (Deckard, Rachael). The only important difference is that in classical narrative the good couple would then settle down ("I'll take you home now"), whereas here they merely fly away to nowhere. Long ago, *Stagecoach* had its couple drive off, "saved from the blessings of civilization," to start a farm over the border; *The Chase* was perhaps the first Hollywood film to acknowledge, ahead of its time, that there was no longer any home to go to. Seventeen years later, *Blade Runner* can manage no more than an empty repetition of this—with the added cynicism of presenting it as if it were a happy ending.

Blade Runner belongs with the incoherent texts of the 1970s: it is either ten years behind its time or hopefully a few years ahead of it. If the human race survives, we may certainly hope to enter, soon, another era of militancy, protest, rage, disturbance, and radical questioning, in which context *Blade Runner* will appear quite at home.

Against the Grain

Clyde Taylor

New U.S. Black Cinema

The best approach to black cinema as art is to see it in intimate relation to the full range of Afro-American art expression. The urgent need at this point is to recognize that black cinema has arrived to take its natural place beside black music, literature, dance, and drama. By black cinema, I am speaking of the independent films made since the late 1960s by determined, university-trained filmmakers who owe Hollywood nothing at all.

If the Harlem Renaissance or, better yet, the New Negro Movement that began in the 1920s were to take place under today's conditions, many of its major creative talents would be filmmakers. They would celebrate and join a contemporary black renaissance in films. Consider: Paul Robeson's struggle to bring dignity to the Afro-American screen image is well documented. Richard Wright's interest in films extended beyond the filming of *Native Son* (1951) to include his search for work as a screenwriter for the National Film Board of Canada and the drafting of unused film scripts. Langston Hughes coauthored the script for *Way Down South* (1939) with Clarence Muse and continually sought creative opportunities in Hollywood. In 1941, he wrote with great clarity to his friend Arna Bontemps, "Have been having some conferences with movie producers, but no results. I think only a subsidized Negro Film Institute, or the revolution, will cause any really good Negro pictures to be made in America."[1] In 1950, Arna Bontemps tried to stir up interest in the production of black films in the manner of Italian neorealism.[2] About this same time, the Committee for Mass Education in Race Relations was set up with the intent to "produce films that combine entertain-

Reprinted, with permission, from *Jump Cut* 28 (1983).

ment and purposeful mass education in race relations." Among the consultants and members of this committee were Katherine Dunham, Paul Robeson, Richard Wright, Eslanda Robeson, Langston Hughes, and Countee Cullen.[3]

I pinpoint the film involvement of some of the central artist-intellectuals of the New Negro era in order to contrast the lack, with some important exceptions, of a comparable interest among their successors. This short-sightedness is both ironic and painful, for over the past decade, a body of Afro-American films has emerged comparable to the flowering of the "Harlem Renaissance" in their cultural independence, originality, and boldness—their appearance marking perhaps the most significant recent development in Afro-American art.

This body of films, which I call the new black cinema, is distinct from four prior episodes of filmmaking about Afro-Americans: Hollywood films portraying blacks before World War II, Hollywood films after that war, films made by black independents such as Oscar Micheaux and Spencer Williams before WWII, and the black exploitation movies of the late 1960s and early 1970s. What separates the new black cinema from these other episodes is its freedom from the mental colonization that Hollywood tries to impose on all its audiences, black and white.

The new black cinema was born out of the black arts movement of the 1960s, out of the same concerns with a self-determining black cultural identity. This film phenomenon drew inspiration from black-subject films made by white directors in the 1960s such as *Nothing but a Man* (1964), *Cool World* (1963), *Shadows* (1959), and *Sweet Love, Bitter* (1967) but was also fired by the creative heresies of Italian neorealism (following Arna Bontemps's early interest) and ultimately by an expanding international film culture, with a particularly deep impression being scored by African and other Third World filmmakers.

The new black cinema is a movement with many separate beginnings in the late 1960s. One was the gathering of a nucleus of young black filmmakers at "Black Journal," a weekly television magazine aired on PBS under the leadership of Bill Greaves in New York. Another was the tragically brief career of Richie Mason, who, without training, took cameras into the streets of New York to make dramatic street films (*You Dig It?; Ghetto*). Still another was a path-breaking exhibition of historical and contemporary independent black films in New York organized by Pearl Bowser. By the time films of great innovation and energy began emerging from UCLA in the early 1970s from Haile Gerima, Larry Clark, and Charles Burnett, it was clear that a new path had been broken toward a liberated black screen image.

What gives this new cinema its particular unifying character? In truth, little more than its determined resistance to the film ideology of Hollywood—but that, as we shall see, is a great deal. Under that broad umbrella of kinship, these filmmakers have produced work of considerable diversity, pursuing various goals of aesthetic individualism, cultural integrity, or political relevance. Despite this diversity, some core features, or defining aesthetic principles, can be seen to underlie many works of the new black cinema in three directions: its realness dimension, its relation to Afro-American oral tradition, and its connections with black music.

The Realness Dimension

Indigenous Afro-American films project onto a social space, as UCLA film scholar Teshome Gabriel observes, noting the difference between it and the privatistic, individualistic space of Hollywood's film theater. It is a space carrying a commitment, in echoes and connotations, to the particular social experience of Afro-American people. It establishes only the slightest, if any, departure from the contiguous offscreen reality.

While shooting *Bush Mama* (Haile Gerima, 1976), for instance, one camera crew was accosted by the Los Angeles police. What was there in the sight of black men with motion picture cameras filming in the streets of southcentral Los Angeles (Watts) that prompted the police to pull their guns, spread-eagle these filmmakers against cars, and frisk them? Did they mistake the cameras for weapons—did they sense a robbery in progress, a misappropriation of evidence? Did they suspect the cameras were stolen, being in the inappropriate hands of the intended victims of cinema?

The paranoia of such questions belongs to the mentality of the Los Angeles Police Department. The evidence of their actions is recorded objectively in cinema verite as the establishing shots of the film. These shots make a fitting prologue because *Bush Mama* is about the policing of the black community by school officials, in and out of uniform, who intrude their behavioral directives into the most intimate reaches of its residents. From such a documentary beginning, one is more easily convinced that the daily actions of its inhabitants are constantly policed in the sense that all actions are regarded with hostility and suspicion except those that reproduce the cycles of victimization and self-repression.

The social space of many new black films is saturated with contingency. Simply, it is the contingency of on-location shooting. But what a location. It is a space in which invasion is imminent. A street scene in these films is a place where anything can happen, any bizarre or brutal picaresque eventuality, as in *A Place in Time* (Charles Lane, 1976). An interior location attracts the feeling of prison or refuge. A door is a venue through which an intruder may suddenly burst, either police or madman. The folklore surrounding this school of adventuresome film-making is replete with art-life ironies: a film about a black man trying to live his life without going to jail is interrupted when the actor interpreting the role is put in jail for nonsupport.

The intensities of such dilemmas, sometimes the events themselves, become interwoven into the text of the film. Everyone knows that the anthropologist with a camera alters the village reality he or she records. Similarly, "reality" arranges itself differently in America for an independent black filmmaker. Nor does this filmmaker always maintain a cool detachment in the face of these rearrangements. The hot rage that suffuses *Sweet Sweetback's Baadasssss Song* (Melvin Van Peebles, 1971) is one clue that the film itself is allegorical of the furious ordeal of a black person trying to make a mentally independent film against the resistances the society will mount in reaction. By Larry Clark's testimony, the sharp-edged racial portrayals in *Passing Through* (1977) reflect his frustrations in getting his film completed against such resistances.

So the space occupied by an independent black film is frequently tempered by the values of social paranoia, volatility, and contingency and by a more knowing acquaintance with these values than the stable tranquility and predictable unpredictability of an American movie set, even when that set is background for a commercial black movie.

The screen and theatrical space of the new black cinema is one the spectator can enter and exit in without carrying away the glazed eyes and the afterglow of erotic-egotistic enchantment that identifies the colonized moviegoer. In it, both filmmakers and spectators can move easily and interchangeably before and behind the camera without drastic alterations of character. This is a rare circumstance for Afro-Americans, for as Walter Benjamin notes of another cinema,

> Some of the players whom we meet in Russian films are not actors in
> our sense but people who portray themselves—and primarily in their

own work process. In Western Europe the capitalistic exploitation of the film denies consideration to modern man's legitimate claim to being reproduced.[4]

It is a space open to wide-ranging possibilities, yet free of the illusionism whose effects make mainstream commercial films so superficially enchanting. To take one convention of the Hollywood cinematic code, for example, consider the double pyramid that describes the individualistic perspective. One of these imaginary pyramids extends from the four corners of the screen toward a vanishing point within the scene, reproductive of the depth perception of Renaissance painting. The other perspectual pyramid extends from these same points, converging on the eye-screen of the single observer. Such a perspective has great potential for focusing attention at hierarchically staged points of meaning, which seem to the individual observer to be channeled directly to his or her mind-screen, a chamber of privileged voyeurism.

The camera of the new black cinema is not similarly obsessed. The focus of its attention is wider, more open to diverse, competing, even accidental impressions. The basic palette of the indigenous Afro screen is closer to that of Italian neorealism and Third World cinema than to southern California. Charlie Burnett, in *Killer of Sheep* (1977), for instance, makes effective use of the open frame, in which characters walk in and out of the frame from top, bottom, and sides—a forbidden practice in the classical code of Hollywood (but common in European and Japanese films he saw as a UCLA student). One further encounters fewer close-ups, suggesting less preoccupation with the interior emotions of individual personages.

The techniques of the new directors do not exclude inventive camera movements and placements, but these are dictated more often by the need of social reflection than the demands of individual fascination. The treatment of space generally reminds us that linear perspective was an invention and once the exclusive preoccupation of postmedieval Western art. By contrast, in Afro cinema one often finds the nonlinear, psychic space of medieval paintings, oriental scrolls, and other non-Western media. In *Child of Resistance* (1972), to take another example from the prolific Haile Gerima, the camera follows the central figure, a woman dressed in a robe, hands bound, being transported through a barroom into a jail cell, directly outside of which later appears a jury box filled with jurors. Linearity is rejected as space is treated poetically, following the coordinates of a propulsive social idea—the social imprisonment of black women.

Director Charles Burnett. Photo courtesy of the Samuel Goldwyn Company.

The goals of the new cinema frequently cause it to invade territory familiar to documentary films, although this is an observation that may be misleading. What is shared with documentary is reality orientation. This reality dimension is present even in Afro films of the most intensively dramatic or fantastic content, of which there are several examples, and even in scenes of exquisite visual beauty.

Despite this shared orientation, the term *docudrama* is too loosely employed in discussion of Afro films. Two recent films by Woodie King, for instance, *The Torture of Mothers* (1980) and *Death of a Prophet* (1981), deal with events of recent history, the police frame-up of several black youths in New York in 1964, and the last day in the life of Malcolm X. They aim to be accurate to the historical record, they use actors and nonactors, but their intent is far more to dramatize than document.

Techniques associated with nonfictional cinema appear frequently in indigenous Afro films. One of the most piercing scenes in Ben Caldwell's poetic and literary *I and I* (1978) is staged as a documentary interview. Similarly, the dramatic action of *Torture of Mothers* is launched from the setting of a group pooling testimony before a tape recorder. An off-camera voice track supplants dialogue in *Child of Resistance*. And Larry Clark, in making *Passing Through*, goes beyond the typical use of archival footage as historical flashback by inventing a documentary-looking sequence that places his hero, Womack, in the midst of the eruption at Attica.

In effect, the responsibility to social reality that presides over the space of the new black cinema has led to a number of films that not only arise out of a "documentary" setting but continue to unfold in a world articulated by the techniques and strategies of nonfictional cinema, as in Italian neorealism, but with an Afro sensibility.

Another support of the realness dimension in Afro cinema is its use of cultural-historical time. The cultural identity of the people in these films may be expressed as that of a people with a certain history. Dramatic time is never wholly divorced from historic time. What time is it is a question that is inseparable from the texture of the scene.

Both black and white independent filmmakers sometimes foresake explicit cultural and historical reference but usually for different reasons. It has been said of the affecting documentary, *The Quiet One* (1948), made by Sidney Meyers, that "the boy's blackness was not given any special significance."[5] And *Nothing but a Man* (1964), directed by Michael Roemer, omitted reference to the civil rights movement taking place at the time and place of the film's action. In these respects, the themes of these two films, both respected by black cineastes, would probably have received different treatment by indigenous filmmakers. For example, when Haile Gerima downplays the particulars of the legal case in *Wilmington 10, USA Ten Thousand* (1978), it is to subsume that travesty within a broader historical framework, that of the continuous struggle of Afro-Americans for liberation, in which 10,000 have been victimized in the manner dealt to the Wilmington freedom fighters.[6]

Even where concrete historical reference is absent, where the action is set in an unspecified present tense, the idea of who black people are historically is implicitly reflected in every communicative action and reflected most consistently with the self-understanding of the cultural group portrayed. This is true despite variations in the sense of history among individual filmmakers.

In Hollywood portrayals of blacks, there is also a historical dimension, but this sense of history is "vaudevillainous"—the play history of musical comedy, costume spectaculars, and sentimentalized biographies. It is not noted often enough that the liberties taken with history for the sake of a more entertaining story in this vaudevillainous cinema have an important connection with ethnic distortions. For when a people are distorted on screen, their history, their collective cultural memory, is disfigured at the same moment.

The subtly implanted sense of who these people are and where they are coming from is thus a major source of the greater internal authority of the new black cinema—because it is a cinema in which Afro-Americans are both the subject and the object of consideration, and the relations of those considerations are least tempered with by extraneous manipulations.

Oral Tradition

In one of the most rudimentary film situations, the "talking head" sequence of nonfiction film, lies a key to another source of the character of indigenous Afro films. When our attention is riveted by the information given by the speaker, as in television newscasts, we may think of the speaker as an interviewee. When this attention is split between the information imparted and the personality of the speaker, the manner of speech, the cultural resonance of the words and images, the social and cultural connotations, the art of the message spoken, when, in short, speech takes on the character of *performance,* we may likely think of the speaker as an oral historian.

One finds oral historians in all segments of American cinema, from the Appalachian coal miners of *Harlan County, USA* to the interviews inserted in *Reds.* But the Afro speaker in films is more likely to speak as an oral historian, if only because of inadequate assimilation of the bourgeois broadcast orientation that leaves one voice interchangeable with another. The significant contrast is between the Afro-American oral tradition, easily the most vital vernacular tradition surviving in America, and the linearized speech dominated by Western literacy. In Afro oral tradition, filmmakers of the new black cinema find one of their most invaluable resources.

Because it brashly transgresses the barriers of standardized communication, Afro oral tradition is also a magnet for those inclined to vaudevillize, minstrelize, or sensationalize it. *Cotton Comes to Harlem* (1970) is typical of the exploitative use of black speech with its gratuitous vaudeville jokes that harken back to the slack-mouthed asides of Willie Best. The humor of *Putney Swope* (1969) relies mainly on a leering treatment of black hipspeech and profanity. And the supposedly left-radical documentary slide show *American Pictures* miserably distorts and dehumanizes its black (and white) informants by framing them within its condescending, self-indulgent liberalism.

But the real thing is abundantly available in documentaries and ethnographic films made by black and white filmmakers about the Afro oral tradition or its related expressions—in films such as *No Maps on my Taps* (1980) (tapdancing), *American Shoeshine* (1976), *Ephesus* (1965), and *Let the Church Say Amen* (1972) (folk preaching), *The Facts of Life* (1981) (blues), and *The Day the Animals Talked* (1981) (folktales), both by Carol Lawrence and the southern folklore films of William Ferris and particularly in jazz films like *But Then She's Betty Carter* (1981), *Mingus* (1966), and *The Last of the Blue Devils* (1980). In such films one might find a saturation of black values and therefore an edge toward the definition of black identity in films after Stephen Henderson's approach to black poetry.[7]

Contrasting postures toward the representation of Afro oral history are seen in two carefully positioned nonfiction films, Warrington Hudlin's *Street Corner Stories* (1978) and Haile Gerima's *Wilmington 10, USA Ten Thousand*. The orientation of *Street Corner Stories* is *observational*. Hudlin used cinema-verite techniques, exposing his films in and around a New Haven corner store where black men congregate before going to work, catching their practice of black storytelling and uninhibited rapping, not entirely unobserved, as their occasional straining for effects reveals. The orientation of *Wilmington 10* is *committed*. This is nowhere more apparent than in the powerful impassioned speeches of the women who dominate its text, the wives and mothers of some of the Wilmington defendants who recount chapter and verse of liberation struggles past and present together with their uncensored opinions, directly into the camera.

It is not simply the case of one approach being more political than the other, for both are necessarily ideological and reflective of the ideological diversity and oppositions *within* the indigenous Afro film movement . . . Nor is it narrowly a question of technique: neither film, for instance, uses a voice of God narration. Finally, as is usual with nonfiction cinema, it is a question of selectivity. *Street Corner Stories* derives its Afro oral energies from the witty irreverence of black crackerbarrel humor, its rimes and jibes merely transposed from the porch of the country store to the city. *Wilmington 10* is much like an updated escaped-slave narrative, with all of the intense political sermonizing familiar to that genre. Both films are valid, essentially successful deployments of black verbal creativity in different occasional modes.

Yet what they have to tell us about the ideological tendencies they reflect is communicated by the hazards of their respective orientations. Hudlin's film was intended as a response to the superficial sociology of works such as Elliot Liebow's book *Talley's Corner*, in which black streetmen are portrayed as defeated moral opportunists, sexual chauvinists, and exploiters and compensatory dreamers. Yet Hudlin's own portrait reflects communal self-hatred without interpreting its source in an oppressive society. One cannot contest the reportorial accuracy of his portrayal nor the achievement in his film of a look of unmanipulated realness. Still Hudlin's streetmen impress one much like those on Talley's corner. *Street Corner Stories* does not overcome the danger of distortion arising from "objectivity" without explanation or the danger of distorting Afro oral tradition by exploiting it voyeuristically while presenting it as pure anthropology.

As black oral history, many of the scenes in *Wilmington 10* are unsurpassed in the projection of strong committed black speech and personality, offered straight from the soul with earthy articulateness. The folk songs and prison blues of its sound track are hauntingly supportive of the film's eloquence. Yet the film is excessively rhetorical, specifically in its last sequences, in which unidentified black activists of no clear connection with the Wilmington struggle make political speeches while sitting in abstract isolation on pedestals. Their inclusion is gratuitous, an inorganic code to the Wilmington scene from which the earlier speakers drew their spontaneous vitality. Ironically, the ideological tendencies of both films are pushed toward enervation by their urging too much of one kind of text without sufficient balancing context.

In Afro-American "orature," one can generally find many distinctive and richly expressive characteristics, including a tolerance for semantic ambiguity, a fascination with bold extravagant metaphor, a "cool" sensibility, a funky explicitness, and a frequently prophetic mode of utterance. The centrality of this tradition to the new black cinema is only understood when we realize its presence not only in the speech and "performance" of the participants in nonfiction films but within the total configuration of both nonfiction and dramatic works, in characterization, camera strategies, principles of montage, tempo, narrative structure, and so forth. One can even find its features in Charles Lane's wittily silent tragi-comedy *A Place in Time.* As in Afro orature, narrative structure in the new films is often more episodic and nonsequential than the well-made plot dear to Western popular drama and more concerned with tonal placement and emphasis. In its search for its own voice, for a film language uncompromised by the ubiquitous precedents of the dominant cinema, the new black cinema is making productive explorations into the still undominated speech of black people.

The Influence of Black Music

To turn from black oral tradition to black music is really not to turn at all but only to allow one's attention to glide from the words to the melody of a people's indivisible cultural expression. But what has been said about the influence of oral tradition has been inferential; the impact of black music on the new black cinema is clearly intentional and well documented. Of about twenty black filmmakers I have interviewed recently, roughly three-fourths of them stressed black music as a formative and fundamental reference for their art.

The involvement with black music probes deeper than laying a rhythmic sound track beneath images of black people (tom-toms for the rising redemptive energies of the collective), although the musical sound track is a good place to begin.

Western music will menace a non-Western film with cultural compromise. Not intrinsically, not inevitably, Charles Lane, for one, uses "classical" music effectively in his silent farce, *A Place in Time,* with no loss to its Afro character. But who can have escaped the subsidized imposition of European superiority as communicated by its musical "classics," which are hawked and hustled everywhere, underwriting, for instance, the insistent Europeanness of so many, say, French new-wave films with their Bached and Mozartized scores or not noticed the introduction of nonclassical music for comic or pastoral diversion? For the new black filmmaker, the technical invention and development of the art of cinema in the West poses a burden and challenge to his or her creative independence that is lifted once he or she turns to the question of music. Being artists, living under cultural domination, they will be privy to the open secret that the definitive musical sound of the twentieth century originates from their people.

What is more revealing is the way music is used. Ousmane Sembene, Africa's most independent film innovator, accurately observes that "the whites have music for everything in their films—music for rain, music for the wind, music for tears, music for moments of emotion, but they don't know how to make these elements speak for themselves."[8] But recognizing in their music an invaluable precedent of cultural liberation, Afro filmmakers have not pursued, with Sembene, a "cinema of silence." (Although Woodie King effectively omits music from *The Torture of Mothers*, a taut reliving of a series of brutal racist incidents.)

Instead, their use of music in films is less sentimental and less literary than conventional Western practice. To get to the core of the difference, we should recall Richard Wright's contrast between the false sentiment of tin-pan-alley songs and lyrics, with their twittering about *moon, croon, June,* and the more adult, realistic directness of the blues. Mass film entertainment in America has never outgrown the musical shadow work of the silent film era when piano or organ sententiously telegraphed the appropriate emotion to the viewer regarding the character, place, and event on the screen, channeling the viewer's aural responses toward a self-pitying individualism, much as the visual cinematic code cultivates egocentric perspective.

In Afro film, music relates to screen action more like the relation of guitar accompaniment to sung blues, broadening the primary narrative statement with commentary that sometimes modulates its directness but just as frequently establishes an ironic, parallel, or distancing realism. When used as sympathetic accompaniment, the music in Afro cinema frequently shares connotations with its audience of collective, cultural-historic significance, in contrast to the music of bourgeois, commercial egoism. Although subject to abuse, the motif of tom-tom signifying communal resurgence nevertheless illustrates this less privatistic musical intention.

The deeper possibilities of black music for furnishing a creative paradigm for Afro cinema have been advanced in Warrington Hudlin's film concept of "blues realism," a defining attitude and style of life.

> It seems to me that if black films are to continue to be called black films, they will have to develop an aesthetic character that will distinguish

them in the same way that Japanese films, Italian neo-realist films, or even the French new wave films are distinct. I think the blues provides an aesthetic base and direction. At the risk of sounding pretentious, I feel my efforts in *Street Corner Stories* and the achievement of Robert Gardner in his exceptional short film *I Could Hear You All the Way Down the Hall* (1976) are the beginnings of a new school of filmmaking, a new wave, if you will.[9]

In retrospect, Hudlin's formulation of blues realism betrays the adventitiousness of artistic theory developed in the course of resolving particular aesthetic problems, then promoted too broadly as a vehicle of self-definition. Blues realism relied too narrowly on the blues concept of novelist Ralph Ellison and was applied too strictly to too few films. Perhaps recognizing this, Hudlin has since distanced himself from the concept, partly, I think, because his subsequent films *Capoeria* (1980) and *Color* (video, 1982), have moved away from the cinema-verite technique of *Street Corner Stories* that he associated with blues realism and partly because, at the time of its formulation, he had not seen several Afro films, particularly West Coast films, that might have modified or challenged his definitions.

Blues realism as articulated by Hudlin needs to be respected, nevertheless, as a premature sally onto sound grounds. We do not need to discard it but to amplify and extend it to many different blues sensibilities and many different registers of black musical sensibility which help us realize an understanding of Afro films in their variety. *Street Corner Stories*, for instance, captures the tonal reference of an amoral, all-male blues world moving from country to city on a trajectory roughly parallel to the course from Lightin' Hopkins to Jimmie Witherspoon. Alternatively, *Wilmington 10*, as already noted, vibrates most completely to the blues of the southern prison farm but also realizes on the screen the equivalent of its sound-track employment of the woman-supportive, a capella country/folk singing of "Sweet Honey in the Rock."

Many of the new filmmakers attempt to transpose the tonal/structural register and cognitive framework of several varieties of black music. The works of others seem attached to specific black musical worlds by virtue of their having tapped dimensions of black experience congruent with certain musical precedents. (One must understand music in Afro-American culture as a constituent element of thought, perception, and communication[10]) Hugh Hill's *Light Opera* (1975) offers an example from the "pure" end of the visual music spectrum with his exposures and editing of light and images in New York's Times Square, orchestrated nonnarratively to the music of Ornette Coleman and to the more abstract explorations of New Jazz. The fictive-emotional world of Bill Gunn's *Ganja and Hess* (1973) is embedded in the resonances of a literary, self-conscious form of gospel music. The visual imagery of Barbara McCullough's experimental *Water Ritual #1* (1979) emerges out of a funky New Jazz, saturated in African cosmology.

Ben Caldwell's *I and I*, another film deeply implicated in black music, is best understood as a meditation in blues mode on identities of Africa in America. Its title further notes a debt to reggae-Rastafarian consciousness. Framed by the passage of a spirit-woman protagonist from Africa through experiences and revelations in America, its structure rests principally on three "stanzas" or "choruses." First, the protagonist becomes a black man mourning/cursing his coffined white father. Next, she witnesses the oral narration of an old black woman, recounting the lynch-murder of her grandfather. Finally, she metamorphoses into a contemporary black woman, imparting a cosmological heritage to her son.

The distinct contribution of *I and I* to the repertory of music-based black cinema is its impact on improvisation. Still photos of urban and rural black life are interspersed among explicitly funky dramatic vignettes and lyrical prophetic stagings in an order hovering between narrative closure and abstract association, one idea or image giving birth to another in the manner of an instrumental jazz soloist's far flung, highly colored variations on a traditional blues theme. The semantics of this film are akin to those of the instrumental jazz theater in which the performer calls the audience to gather to celebrate shared passages of life through his/her voicing of a familiar tune. In *I and I*, blues realism is extended to blues prophetism in a register my ears would place close to the spiritualized, Africanized blues of John Coltrane or Coltrane-Ellington.

The idea of black film as music is also given wide syntactical exploration in Larry Clark's dramatic feature, *Passing Through*. Here, the dramatic theme is black music, the struggle of musicians against the exploitations of gangster entrepreneurs. More subtly fulfilled than its story is its visual exposition through musical montage. Each sequence is introduced or segmented by music. Musical cues dominate its architecture. Typically, in the middle of a tenor saxophone solo played by the protagonist, Womack, the camera closes in on the bell of the horn, which becomes an iris perspective, framing the documentary flashbacks mentioned earlier, the dogs of Birmingham, black nationalist/police shootout in Cleveland, Attica. Clark's montage suggests visual references for the solo's nonverbal expression, offering a visual exegesis of the way improvised jazz solos reflect individual and group experience.

I and I and *Passing Through*, together with the briefer explorations of Barbara McCullough and Hugh Hill, offer the widest, most far-reaching illustrations of the integral relation of black music and film. In these works, we recognize the representative palette of the new black filmmaker as a keyboard. The greater dimension of performance in the identity of the African and Afro-American artist also extends to the new black filmmakers. We should visualize them as shaping their compositions by selectively *playing*, with more or less emphasis, the available elements of documentary realism, the several modes of Afro oral tradition, musical structure and coloration, and dramatic intention.

Two useful perspectives can be gained by viewing the new black cinema as a creative "renaissance." Some fruitful bearings can be found in considering the recent film movement alongside the Harlem Renaissance, the best-known art movement launched by black Americans. One is then further drawn to the fundamental relatedness between this body of films and other forms of black art.

The independent films of Afro-Americans since the late 1960s, it should be clear by now, have made a departure from all prior examples of black imagery sharp enough to be considered a distinct aesthetic phenomenon. History has not favored the new film movement with a reverberating social and artistic era in which it might achieve its full resonance. Many Afro-Americans have lamented the virtual adoption as pets of the writers of the 1920s by white patrons and faddists, yet ironically remain mute when an indigenous film movement emerges without benefit of such dubious blessings.

Without the buoyancy of a vogue or the nostalgia of an era consecrated in popular mythology, the new black cinema has managed a transformation of imaginative possibilities comparable in scope, diversity, and creative verve to the literary 1920s. Over the past decade, Afro independents have produced more than 200 films of varied length, including a score of dramatic features and an equal number of documentary features—an output rivaling the literary output of the Harlem Renaissance.

The singular accomplishment of the literary awakening of the 1920s was to establish an Afro-American voice for literary art, the recreation of a cultural identity in literary form, more solidly in poetry than prose, and principally through the reappropriation of Afro vernacular in speech and music. The writers of that period advanced a fertile decolonization from Western aesthetic norms. Almost without notice, the contemporary filmmakers have gone further toward decolonization of a more blatantly colonized medium. They have not only planted a new body of Afro-American art, they have done this while freeing that art of colonial imitation, apology, or deference. And although the observations made here fall far short of exhausting the characteristics that give these films their cultural identity, they might point the way to the realization that the new cinema, unlike any other, is a representative expression of Afro-American life.

NOTES

1. Charles H. Nichols, ed., *Arna Bontemps—Langston Hughes Letters, 1925–1967* (New York: Dodd, Mead & Co., 1980), p. 89.

2. Ibid., p. 273.

3. From a brochure in the files of the Schomburg Library, New York City.

4. Walter Benjamin, *Illuminations* (New York: Harcourt, Brace & World, 1968), p. 232.

5. Lewis Jacobs, *The Documentary Tradition* (New York: Norton, 1979), p. 187.

6. The Wilmington 10 were defendants in a celebrated case of official misjustice. The 10 North Carolina political activists were charged with firebombing a grocery store during a time of racial tension in 1971 and convicted on the basis of pressured testimony, later recanted by some of the supposed witnesses. They were given unusually harsh sentences. At the time of the film, all but the Reverend Ben Chavis had been released. Chavis himself is now free.

7. *Understanding the New Black Poetry* (New York: Morrow, 1973). By saturation, Henderson means a density of reference and tone by which the observer can recognize the cultural Afro-ness of a work, even in the absence of explicit verbal clues. Henderson finds saturation, for instance, in Aretha Franklin's "Spirits in the Dark."

8. "Film-Makers Have a Great Responsibility to Our People: An Interview with Ousmane Sembene," *Cineaste* 6:1, (Fall 1975), 29.

9. "Interview: Warrington Hudlin," by Oliver Franklin, program brochure for Black Films and Film Makers, Afro-American Historical and Cultural Museum, Philadelphia, Pa.

10. See Clyde Taylor, "Salt Peanuts: Sound and Sense in African/American Oral/Musical Creativity," *Callaloo* (June 1982).

bell hooks

The Oppositional Gaze:
Black Female Spectators

When thinking about black female spectators, I remember being punished as a child for staring, for those hard intense direct looks children would give grown-ups, looks that were seen as confrontational, as gestures of resistance, challenges to authority. The "gaze" has always been political in my life. Imagine the terror felt by the child who has come to understand through repeated punishments that one's gaze can be dangerous. The child who has learned so well to look the other way when necessary. Yet, when punished, the child is told by parents, "Look at me when I talk to you." Only, the child is afraid to look. Afraid to look, but fascinated by the gaze. There is power in looking.

Amazed the first time I read in history classes that white slaveowners (men, women, and children) punished enslaved black people for looking, I wondered how this traumatic relationship to the gaze had informed black parenting and black spectatorship. The politics of slavery, of racialized power relations, were such that the slaves were denied their right to gaze. Connecting this strategy of domination to that used by grown folks in southern black rural communities where I grew up, I was pained to think that there was no absolute difference between whites who had oppressed black people and ourselves. Years later, reading Michel Foucault, I thought again about these connections, about the ways power as domination reproduces itself in different locations employing similar apparatuses, strategies, and mechanisms of control. Since I knew as a child that the dominating power adults exercised over me

Reprinted, with permission, from *Black Looks: Race and Representation* (Boston: South End Press, 1992).

and over my gaze was never so absolute that I did not dare to look, to sneak a peep, to stare dangerously, I knew that the slaves had looked. That all attempts to repress our/black peoples' right to gaze had produced in us an overwhelming longing to look, a rebellious desire, an oppositional gaze. By courageously looking, we defiantly declared: "Not only will I stare. I want my look to change reality." Even in the worse circumstances of domination, the ability to manipulate one's gaze in the face of structures of domination that would contain it, opens up the possibility of agency. In much of his work, Michel Foucault insists on describing domination in terms of "relations of power" as part of an effort to challenge the assumption that "power is a system of domination which controls everything and which leaves no room for freedom." Emphatically stating that in all relations of power "there is necessarily the possibility of resistance," he invites the critical thinker to search those margins, gaps, and locations on and through the body where agency can be found.

Stuart Hall calls for recognition of our agency as black spectators in his essay "Cultural Identity and Cinematic Representation." Speaking against the construction of white representations of blackness as totalizing, Hall says of white presence:

> The error is not to conceptualize this 'presence' in terms of power, but to locate that power as wholly external to us—as *extrinsic* force, whose influence can be thrown off like the serpent sheds its skin." What Franz Fanon reminds us, in *Black Skin, White Masks*, is how power is inside as well as outside: "The movements, the attitudes, the glances of the Other fixed me there, in the sense in which a chemical solution is fixed by a dye. I was indignant; I demanded an explanation. Nothing happened. I burst apart. Now the fragments have been put together again by another self." This "look," from—so to speak—the place of the Other, fixes us, not only in its violence, hostility and aggression, but in the ambivalence of its desire.

Spaces of agency exist for black people, wherein we can both interrogate the gaze of the Other but also look back, and at one another, naming what we see. The "gaze" has been and is a site of resistance for colonized black people globally. Subordinates in relations of power learn experientially that there is a critical gaze, one that "looks" to document, one that is oppositional. In resistance struggle, the power of the dominated to assert agency by claiming and cultivating "awareness" politicizes "looking" relations—one learns to look a certain way in order to resist.

When most black people in the United States first had the opportunity to look at film and television, they did so fully aware that mass media was a system of knowledge and power reproducing and maintaining white supremacy. To stare at the television, or mainstream movies, to engage its images, was to engage its negation of black representation. It was the oppositional black gaze that responded to these looking relations by developing independent black cinema. Black viewers of mainstream cinema and television could chart the progress of political movements for racial equality via the construction of images, and did so. Within my family's southern black working-class home, located in a racially segregated neighborhood, watching television was one way to develop critical spectatorship. Unless you went to work in the white world, across the tracks, you learned to look at white people by staring at them on the screen. Black looks, as they were constituted in the context of social movements for racial uplift, were interrogating gazes. We laughed at television shows such as *Our Gang* and *Amos 'n' Andy*, at these white representations of blackness, but we also looked at them critically. Before racial integration, black viewers of movies and television experienced visual pleasure in a context in which looking was also about contestation and confrontation.

Writing about black looking relations in "Black British Cinema: Spectatorship and Identity Formation in Territories," Manthia Diawara identifies the power of the spectator: "Every narration places the spectator in a position of agency; and race, class and sexual relations influence the way in which this subjecthood is filled by the spectator." Of particular concern for him are moments of "rupture" when the spectator resists "complete identification with the film's discourse." These ruptures define the relation between black spectators and dominant cinema prior to racial integration. Then, one's enjoyment of a film wherein representations of blackness were stereotypically degrading and dehumanizing coexisted with a critical practice that restored presence where it was negated. Critical discussion of the film while it was in progress or at its conclusion maintained the distance between spectator and the image. Black films were also subject to critical interrogation. Because they came into being in part as a response to the failure of white-dominated cinema to represent blackness in a manner that did not reinforce white supremacy, they too were critiqued to see if images were seen as complicit with dominant cinematic practices.

Critical interrogating black looks were mainly concerned with issues of race and racism, the way racial domination of blacks by whites overdetermined representation. They were rarely concerned with gender. As spectators, black men could repudiate the reproduction of racism in cinema and television, the negation of black presence, even as they could feel as though they were rebelling against white supremacy by daring to look, by engaging phallocentric politics of spectatorship. Given the real-life public circumstances wherein black men were murdered/ lynched for looking at white womanhood, where the black male gaze was always subject to control and/or punishment by the powerful white Other, the private realm of television screens or dark theaters could unleash the repressed gaze. There they could "look" at white woman-hood without a structure of domination overseeing the gaze, interpreting, and punishing. That white supremacist structure that had murdered Emmet Till after interpreting his look as violation, as "rape" of white womanhood, could not control black male responses to screen images. In their role as spectators, black men could enter an imaginative space of phallocentric power that mediated racial negation. This gendered relation to looking made the experience of the black male spectator radically different from that of the black female spectator. Major early black male independent filmmakers represented black women in their films as objects of male gaze. Whether looking through the camera or as spectators watching films, whether mainstream cinema or "race" movies such as those made by Oscar Micheaux, the black male gaze had a different scope from that of the black female.

Black women have written little about black female spectator-ship, about our moviegoing practices. A growing body of film theory and criticism by black women has only begun to emerge. The pro-longed silence of black women as spectators and critics was a response to absence, to cinematic negation. In "The Technology of Gender," Teresa de Lauretis, drawing on the work of Monique Wittig, calls attention to "the power of discourses to 'do violence' to people, a violence which is material and physical, although produced by ab-stract and scientific discourses as well as the discourses of the mass media." With the possible exception of early race movies, black female spectators have had to develop looking relations within a cinematic context that constructs our presence as absence, that denies the "body" of the black female so as to perpetuate white supremacy and with it a phallocentric spectatorship where the woman to be looked at and desired is "white." (Recent movies do not conform to this paradigm, but I am turning to the past with the intent to chart the development of black female spectatorship.)

Talking with black women of all ages and classes, in different areas of the United States, about their filmic looking relations, I hear again and again ambivalent responses to cinema. Only a few of the black women I talked with remembered the pleasure of race movies, and even those who did, felt that pleasure interrupted and usurped by Hollywood. Most of the black women I talked with were adamant that they never went to movies expecting to see compelling representations of black femaleness. They were all acutely aware of cinematic racism—its violent erasure of black womanhood. In Anne Friedberg's essay "A Denial of Difference: Theories of Cinematic Identification," she stresses that "identification can only be made through recognition, and all recognition is itself an implicit confirmation of the ideology of the status quo." Even when representations of black women were present in film, our bodies and being were there to serve—to enhance and maintain white womanhood as object of the phallocentric gaze.

Commenting on Hollywood's characterization of black women in *Girls on Film*, Julie Burchill describes this absent presence:

> Black women have been mothers without children (Mammies—who can ever forget the sickening spectacle of Hattie McDaniel waiting on the simpering Vivien Leigh hand and foot and enquiring like a ninny, "What's ma lamb gonna wear?") . . . Lena Horne, the first black performer signed to a long term contract with a major (M-G-M), looked gutless but was actually quite spirited. She seethed when Tallulah Bankhead complimented her on the paleness of her skin and the non-Negroidness of her features.

When black women actresses such as Lena Horne appeared in mainstream cinema, most white viewers were not aware that they were looking at black females unless the film was specifically coded as being about blacks. Burchill is one of the few white women film critics who has dared to examine the intersection of race and gender in relation to the construction of the category "woman" in film as object of the phallocentric gaze. With characteristic wit she asserts: "What does it say about racial purity that the best blondes have all been brunettes (Harlow, Monroe, Bardot)? I think it says that we are not as white as we think." Burchill could easily have said "we are not as white as we want to be," for clearly the obsession to have white women film stars be ultra-white was a cinematic practice that sought to maintain a distance, a separation between that image and the black female Other; it was a way to perpetuate white supremacy. Politics of race and gender were inscribed into mainstream cinematic narrative from *The Birth of a Nation* on. As a seminal work, this film identified what the place and function of white womanhood would be in cinema. There was clearly no place for black women.

Remembering my past in relation to screen images of black womanhood, I wrote a short essay, "Do You Remember Sapphire?" which explored both the negation of black female representation in cinema and television and our rejection of these images. Identifying the character of "Sapphire" from *Amos 'n' Andy* as that screen representation of black femaleness I first saw in childhood, I wrote:

> She was even then backdrop, foil. She was bitch—nag. She was there to soften images of black men, to make them seem vulnerable, easygoing, funny, and unthreatening to a white audience. She was there as man in drag, as castrating bitch, as someone to be lied to, someone to be tricked, someone the white and black audience could hate. Scapegoated on all sides. *She was not us.* We laughed with the black men, with the white people. We laughed at this black woman who was not us. And we did not even long to be there on the screen. How could we long to be there when our image, visually constructed, was so ugly. We did not long to be there. We did not long for her. We did not want our construction to be this hated black female thing—foil, backdrop. Her black female image was not the body of desire. There was nothing to see. She was not us.

Grown black women had a different response to Sapphire; they identified with her frustrations and her woes. They resented the way she was mocked. They resented the way these screen images could assault black womanhood, could name us bitches, nags. And in opposition they claimed Sapphire as their own, as the symbol of that angry part of themselves white folks and black men could not even begin to understand.

Conventional representations of black women have done violence to the image. Responding to this assault, many black women spectators shut out the image, looked the other way, accorded cinema no importance in their lives. Then there were those spectators whose gaze was that of desire and complicity. Assuming a posture of subordination, they submitted to cinema's capacity to seduce and betray. They were cinematically "gaslighted." Every black woman I spoke with who was/is an ardent moviegoer, a lover of the Hollywood film, testified that to experience fully the pleasure of that cinema they had to close down critique, analysis; they had to forget racism. And mostly they did not think about sexism. What was the nature then of this adoring black female gaze—this look that could bring pleasure in the midst of negation? In her first novel, *The Bluest Eye*, Toni Morrison constructs a portrait of the black female spectator; her gaze is the masochistic look of victimization. Describing her looking relations, Miss Pauline Breedlove, a poor working woman, maid in the house of a prosperous white family, asserts:

> The onliest time I be happy seem like was when I was in the picture show. Every time I got, I went, I'd go early, before the show started. They's cut off the lights, and everything be black. Then the screen would light up, and I's move right on in them picture. White men taking such good care of they women, and they all dressed up in big clean houses with the bath tubs right in the same room with the toilet. Them pictures gave me a lot of pleasure.

To experience pleasure, Miss Pauline sitting in the dark must imagine herself transformed, turned into the white woman portrayed on the screen. After watching movies, feeling the pleasure, she says, "But it made coming home hard."

We come home to ourselves. Not all black women spectators submitted to that spectacle of regression through identification. Most of the women I talked with felt that they consciously resisted identification with films—that this tension made moviegoing less than pleasurable; at times it caused pain. As one black woman put, "I could always get pleasure from movies as long as I did not look too deep." For black female spectators who have "looked too deep," the encounter with the screen hurt. That some of us chose to stop looking was a gesture of resistance, turning away was one way to protest, to reject negation. My pleasure in the screen ended abruptly when I and my sisters first watched *Imitation of Life*. Writing about this experience in the "Sapphire" piece, I addressed the movie directly, confessing:

> I had until now forgotten you, that screen image seen in adolescence, those images that made me stop looking. It was there in *Imitation of Life,* that comfortable mammy image. There was something familiar about this hard-working black woman who loved her daughter so much, loved her in a way that hurt.

Indeed, as young southern black girls watching this film, Peola's mother reminded us of the hardworking, churchgoing, Big Mamas we knew and loved. Consequently, it was not this image that captured our gaze; we were fascinated by Peola. Addressing her, I wrote:

You were different. There was something scary in this image of young sexual sensual black beauty betrayed—that daughter who did not want to be confined by blackness, that "tragic mulatto" who did not want to be negated. "Just let me escape this image forever," she could have said. I will always remember that image. I remembered how we cried for her, for our unrealized desiring selves. She was tragic because there was no place in the cinema for her, no loving pictures. She too was absent image. It was better then, that we were absent, for when we were there it was humiliating, strange, sad. We cried all night for you, for the cinema that had no place for you. And like you, we stopped thinking it would one day be different.

When I returned to films as a young woman, after a long period of silence, I had developed an oppositional gaze. Not only would I not be hurt by the absence of black female presence, or the insertion of violating representation, I interrogated the work, cultivated a way to look past race and gender for aspects of content, form, language. Foreign films and U.S. independent cinema were the primary locations of my filmic looking relations, even though I also watched Hollywood films.

From "jump," black female spectators have gone to films with awareness of the way in which race and racism determined the visual construction of gender. Whether it was *Birth of a Nation* or Shirley Temple shows, we knew that white womanhood was the racialized sexual difference occupying the place of stardom in mainstream narrative film. We assumed white women knew it too. Reading Laura Mulvey's provocative essay, "Visual Pleasure and Narrative Cinema," from a standpoint that acknowledges race, one sees clearly why black women spectators not duped by mainstream cinema would develop an oppositional gaze. Placing ourselves outside that pleasure in looking, Mulvey argues, was determined by a "split between active/male and passive/female." Black female spectators actively chose not to identify with the film's imaginary subject because such identification was disenabling.

Looking at films with an oppositional gaze, black women were able to critically assess the cinema's construction of white womanhood as object of phallocentric gaze and choose not to identify with either the victim or the perpetrator. Black female spectators, who refused to identify with white womanhood, who would not take on the phallocentric gaze of desire and possession, created a critical space where the binary opposition Mulvey posits of "woman as image, man as bearer of the look" was continually deconstructed. As critical spectators, black women looked from a location that disrupted, one akin to that described by Annette Kuhn in *The Power of The Image:*

> The acts of analysis, of deconstruction, and of reading "against the grain" offer an additional pleasure—the pleasure of resistance, of saying "no"; not to "unsophisticated" enjoyment, by ourselves and others, of culturally dominant images, but to the structures of power which ask us to consume them uncritically and in highly circumscribed ways.

Mainstream feminist film criticism in no way acknowledges black female spectatorship. It does not even consider the possibility that women can construct an oppositional gaze via an understanding and awareness of the politics of race and racism. Feminist film theory rooted in an ahistorical psychoanalytic framework that privileges sexual difference actively suppresses recognition of race, reenacting and mirroring the erasure of black womanhood that occurs in films, silencing any discussion of racial difference—of racialized sexual difference. Despite feminist critical interventions aimed at deconstructing the category "woman," which highlight the significance of race, many feminist film critics continue to structure their discourse as though it speaks about "women" when in actuality it speaks only about white women. It seems ironic that the cover of the recent anthology *Feminism and Film Theory* edited by Constance Penley has a graphic that is a reproduction of the photo of white actresses Rosalind Russell and Dorothy Arzner on the 1936 set of the film *Craig's Wife*, yet there is no acknowledgment in any essay in this collection that the woman "subject" under discussion is always white. Even though there are photos of black women from films reproduced in the text, there is no acknowledgment of racial difference.

It would be too simplistic to interpret this failure of insight solely as a gesture of racism. Importantly, it also speaks to the problem of structuring feminist film theory around a totalizing narrative of woman as object whose image functions solely to reaffirm and reinscribe patriarchy. Mary Ann Doane addresses this issue in the essay "Remembering Women: Psychical and Historical Construction in Film Theory":

> This attachment to the figure of a degeneralizible Woman as the product of the apparatus indicates why, for many, feminist film theory seems to have reached an impasse, a certain blockage in its theorization . . . In focusing upon the task of delineating in great detail the attributes of woman as effect of the apparatus, feminist film theory participates in the abstraction of women. The concept "woman" effaces the difference

between women in specific socio-historical contexts, between women defined precisely as historical subjects rather than as *a* psychic subject (or nonsubject).

Although Doane does not focus on race, her comments speak directly to the problem of its erasure. For it is only as one imagines "woman" in the abstract, when woman becomes fiction or fantasy, can race not be seen as significant. Are we really to imagine that feminist theorists writing only about images of white women, who subsume this specific historical subject under the totalizing category "woman," do not "see" the whiteness of the image? It may very well be that they engage in a process of denial that eliminates the necessity of revisioning conventional ways of thinking about psychoanalysis as a paradigm of analysis and the need to rethink a body of feminist film theory that is firmly rooted in a denial of the reality that sex/sexuality may not be the primary and/or exclusive signifier of difference. Doane's essay appears in a very recent anthology, *Psychoanalysis and Cinema* edited by E. Ann Kaplan, in which, once again, none of the theory presented acknowledges or discusses racial difference, with the exception of one essay, "Not Speaking with Language, Speaking with No Language," which problematizes notions of orientalism in its examination of Leslie Thornton's film *Adynata*. Yet in most of the essays, the theories espoused are rendered problematic if one includes race as a category of analysis.

Constructing feminist film theory along these lines enables the production of a discursive practice that need never theorize any aspect of black female representation or spectatorship. Yet the existence of black women within white supremacist culture problematizes, and makes complex, the overall issue of female identity, representation, and spectatorship. If, as Friedberg suggests, "identification is a process which commands the subject to be displaced by an other; it is a procedure which breeches the separation between self and other, and, in this way, replicates the very structure of patriarchy." If identification "demands sameness, necessitates similarity, disallows difference"—must we then surmise that many feminist film critics who are "overidentified" with the mainstream cinematic apparatus produce theories that replicate its totalizing agenda? Why is it that feminist film criticism, which has most claimed the terrain of woman's identity, representation, and subjectivity as its field of analysis, remains aggressively silent on the subject of blackness and specifically representations of black womanhood? Just as mainstream cinema has historically forced aware black female spectators not to look, much feminist film criticism disallows the possibility of a theoretical dialogue that might include black women's voices. It is difficult to talk when you feel no one is listening, when you feel as though a special jargon or narrative has been created that only the chosen can understand. No wonder then that black women have for the most part confined our critical commentary on film to conversations. And it must be reiterated that this gesture is a strategy that protects us from the violence perpetuated and advocated by discourses of mass media. A new focus on issues of race and representation in the field of film theory could critically intervene on the historical repression reproduced in some arenas of contemporary critical practice, making a discursive space for discussion of black female spectatorship possible.

When I asked a black woman in her twenties, an obsessive moviegoer, why she thought we had not written about black female spectatorship, she commented: "We are afraid to talk about ourselves as spectators because we have been so abused by 'the gaze.'" An aspect of that abuse was the imposition of the assumption that black female looking relations were not important enough to theorize. Film theory as a critical "turf" in the United States has been and continues to be influenced by and reflective of white racial domination. Because feminist film criticism was initially rooted in a women's liberation movement informed by racist practices, it did not open up the discursive terrain and make it more inclusive. Recently, even those white film theorists who include an analysis of race show no interest in black female spectatorship. In her introduction to the collection of essays *Visual and Other Pleasures*, Laura Mulvey describes her initial romantic absorption in Hollywood cinema, stating:

> Although this great, previously unquestioned and unanalyzed love was put in crisis by the impact of feminism on my thought in the early 1970s, it also had an enormous influence on the development of my critical work and ideas and the debate within film culture with which I became preoccupied over the next fifteen years or so. Watched through eyes that were affected by the changing climate of consciousness, the movies lost their magic.

Watching movies from a feminist perspective, Mulvey arrived at that location of disaffection that is the starting point for many black women approaching cinema within the lived harsh reality of racism. Yet her account of being a part of a film culture whose roots rest on a founding relationship of adoration and love indicates how difficult it would have been to enter that world from "jump" as a critical spectator whose gaze had been formed in opposition.

Given the context of class exploitation, and racist and sexist domination, it has only been through resistance, struggle, reading, and looking "against the grain" that black women have been able to value our process of looking enough to publicly name it. Centrally, those black female spectators who attest to the oppositionality of their gaze deconstruct theories of female spectatorship that have relied heavily on the assumption that, as Doane suggests in her essay "Woman's Stake: Filming the Female Body," "woman can only mimic man's relation to language, that is assume a position defined by the penis-phallus as the supreme arbiter of lack." Identifying with neither the phallocentric gaze nor the construction of white womanhood as lack, critical black female spectators construct a theory of looking relations where cinematic visual delight is the pleasure of interrogation. Every black woman spectator I talked to, with rare exception, spoke of being "on guard" at the movies. Talking about the way being a critical spectator of Hollywood films influenced her, black woman filmmaker Julie Dash exclaims, "I make films because I was such a spectator!" Looking at Hollywood cinema from a distance, from that critical politicized standpoint that did not want to be seduced by narratives reproducing her negation, Dash watched mainstream movies over and over again for the pleasure of deconstructing them. And, of course, there is that added delight if one happens, in the process of interrogation, to come across a narrative that invites the black female spectator to engage the text with no threat of violation.

Significantly, I began to write film criticism in response to the first Spike Lee movie, *She's Gotta Have It*, contesting Lee's replication of mainstream patriarchal cinematic practices that explicitly represents woman (in this instance, black woman) as the object of a phallocentric gaze. Lee's investment in patriarchal filmic practices that mirror dominant patterns makes him the perfect black candidate for entrance to the Hollywood canon. His work mimics the cinematic construction of white womanhood as object, replacing her body as text on which to write male desire with the black female body. It is transference without transformation. Entering the discourse of film criticism from the politicized location of resistance, of not wanting, as a working-class black woman I interviewed stated, "to see black women in the position white women have occupied in film forever," I began to think critically about black female spectatorship.

For years I went to independent and/or foreign films where I was the only black female present in the theater. I often imagined that in

Black looks: Eula Peazant (Alva Rodgers, left), Yellow Mary (Barbara O, center), and Nana Peazant (Cora Lee Day, right) in Julie Dash's Daughters of the Dust *(1992). Photo courtesy of Kino International.*

every theater in the United States there was another black woman watching the same film wondering why she was the only visible black female spectator. I remember trying to share with one of my five sisters the cinema I liked so much. She was "enraged" that I brought her to a theater where she would have to read subtitles. To her it was a violation of Hollywood notions of spectatorship, of coming to the movies to be entertained. When I interviewed her to ask what had changed her mind over the years, led her to embrace this cinema, she connected it to coming to critical consciousness, saying, "I learned that there was more to looking than I had been exposed to in ordinary (Hollywood) movies." I shared that though most of the films I loved were all white, I could engage them because they did not have in their deep structure a subtext reproducing the narrative of white supremacy. Her response was to say that these films demystified "whiteness," because the lives they depicted seemed less rooted in fantasies of escape. They were, she suggested, more like "what we knew life to be, the deeper side of life as well." Always more seduced and enchanted with Hollywood cinema than me, she stressed that unaware black female spectators must "break out," no longer be imprisoned by images that enact a drama of our negation. Although she still sees Hollywood films, because "they are a major influence in the culture"—she no longer feels duped or victimized.

Talking with black female spectators, looking at written discussions either in fiction or academic essays about black women, I noted the connection made between the realm of representation in mass media and the capacity of black women to construct ourselves as subjects in daily life. The extent to which black women feel devalued, objectified, dehumanized in this society determines the scope and texture of their looking relations. Those black women whose identities were constructed in resistance, by practices that oppose the dominant order, were most inclined to develop an oppositional gaze. Now that there is a growing interest in films produced by black women and those films have become more accessible to viewers, it is possible to talk about black female spectatorship in relation to that work. So far, most discussions of black spectatorship that I have come across focus on men. In "Black Spectatorship: Problems of Identification and Resistance," Manthia Diawara suggests that "the components of 'difference'" among elements of sex, gender, and sexuality give rise to different readings of the same material, adding that these conditions produce a "resisting" spectator. He focuses his critical discussion on black masculinity.

The recent publication of the anthology *The Female Gaze: Women as Viewers of Popular Culture* excited me, especially as it included an essay, "Black Looks," by Jacqui Roach and Petal Felix that attempts to address black female spectatorship. The essay posed provocative questions that were not answered: Is there a black female gaze? How do black women relate to the gender politics of representation? Concluding, the authors assert that black females have "our own reality, our own history, our own gaze—one which sees the world rather differently from 'anyone else.'" Yet, they do not name/describe this experience of seeing "rather differently." The absence of definition and explanation suggests they are assuming an essentialist stance wherein it is presumed that black women, as victims of race and gender oppression, have an inherently different field of vision. Many black women do not "see differently" precisely because their perceptions of reality are so profoundly colonized, shaped by dominant ways of knowing. As Trinh T. Minh-ha points out in "Outside In, Inside Out": "Subjectivity does not merely consist of talking about oneself . . . be this talking indulgent or critical."

Critical black female spectatorship emerges as a site of resistance only when individual black women actively resist the imposition of dominant ways of knowing and looking. Although every black woman I talked to was aware of racism, that awareness did not automatically correspond with politicization, the development of an oppositional gaze. When it did, individual black women consciously named the process. Manthia Diawara's "resisting spectatorship" is a term that does not adequately describe the terrain of black female spectatorship. We do more than resist. We create alternative texts that are not solely reactions. As critical spectators, black women participate in a broad range of looking relations, contest, resist, revise, interrogate, and invent on multiple levels. Certainly when I watch the work of black women filmmakers Camille Billops, Kathleen Collins, Julie Dash, Ayoka Chenzira, Zeinabu Davis, I do not need to "resist" the images even as I still choose to watch their work with a critical eye.

Black female critical thinkers concerned with creating space for the construction of radical black female subjectivity, and the way cultural production informs this possibility, fully acknowledge the importance of mass media, film in particular, as a powerful site for critical intervention. Certainly Julie Dash's film *Illusions* identifies the terrain of Hollywood cinema as a space of knowledge production that has enormous power. Yet, she also creates a filmic narrative wherein the black female protagonist subversively claims that space. Inverting the "real-life" power structure, she offers the black female spectator representations that challenge stereotypical notions that place us outside the realm of filmic discursive practices. Within the film she uses the strategy of Hollywood suspense films to undermine those cinematic practices that deny black women a place in this structure. Problematizing the question of "racial" identity by depicting passing, suddenly it is the white male's capacity to gaze, define, and know that is called into question.

When Mary Ann Doane describes in "Woman's Stake: Filming the Female Body" the way in which feminist filmmaking practice can elaborate "a special syntax for a different articulation of the female body," she names a critical process that "undoes the structure of the classical narrative through an insistence upon its repressions." An eloquent description, this precisely names Dash's strategy in *Illusions,* even though the film is not unproblematic and works within certain conventions that are not successfully challenged. For example, the film does not indicate whether the character Mignon will make Hollywood films that subvert and transform the genre or whether she will simply assimilate and perpetuate the norm. Still, subversively, *Illusions* problematizes the issue of race and spectatorship. White people in the film are unable to "see" that race informs their looking relations. Although she is passing to gain access to the machinery of cultural production represented by film, Mignon continually asserts her ties to black community. The bond between her and the young black woman singer Esther Jeeter is affirmed by caring gestures of affirmation, often expressed by eye-to-eye contact, the direct unmediated gaze of recognition. Ironically, it is the desiring objectifying sexualized white male gaze that threatens to penetrate her "secrets" and disrupt her process. Metaphorically, Dash suggests the power of black women to make films will be threatened and undermined by that white male gaze that seeks to reinscribe the black female body in a narrative of voyeuristic pleasure where the only relevant opposition is male/female, and the only location for the female is as a victim. These tensions are not resolved by the narrative. It is not at all evident that Mignon will triumph over the white supremacist capitalist imperialist dominating "gaze."

Throughout *Illusions,* Mignon's power is affirmed by her contact with the younger black woman whom she nurtures and protects. It is this process of mirrored recognition that enables both black women to define their reality, apart from the reality imposed on them by structures of domination. The shared gaze of the two women reinforces their solidarity. As the younger subject, Esther represents a potential audience for films that Mignon might produce, films wherein black females will be the narrative focus. Julie Dash's recent feature-length film *Daughters of the Dust* dares to place black females at the center of its narrative. This focus caused critics (especially white males) to critique the film negatively or to express many reservations. Clearly, the impact of racism and sexism so overdetermine spectatorship—not only what we look at but who we identify with—that viewers who are not black females find it hard to empathize with the central characters in the movie. They are adrift without a white presence in the film.

Another representation of black females nurturing one another via recognition of their common struggle for subjectivity is depicted in Sankofa's collective work *Passion of Remembrance*. In the film, two black women friends, Louise and Maggie, are from the onset of the narrative struggling with the issue of subjectivity, of their place in progressive black liberation movements that have been sexist. They challenge old norms and want to replace them with new understandings of the complexity of black identity and the need for liberation struggles that address that complexity. Dressing to go to a party, Louise and Maggie claim the "gaze." Looking at one another, staring in mirrors, they appear completely focused on their encounter with black femaleness. How they see themselves is most important, not how they will be stared at by others. Dancing to the tune "Let's Get Loose," they display their bodies not for a voyeuristic colonizing gaze but for that look of recognition that affirms their subjectivity—that constitutes them as spectators. Mutually empowered they eagerly leave the privatized domain to confront the public. Disrupting conventional racist and sexist stereotypical representations of black female bodies, these scenes invite the audience to look differently. They act to critically intervene and transform conventional filmic practices, changing notions of spectatorship. *Illusions, Daughters of the Dust*, and *A Passion of Remembrance* employ a deconstructive filmic practice to undermine existing grand cinematic narratives even as they retheorize subjectivity in the realm of the visual. Without providing "realistic" positive representations that emerge only as a response to the totalizing nature of existing narratives, they offer points of radical departure. Opening up a space for the assertion of a critical black female spectatorship, they do not simply offer diverse representations, they imagine new transgressive possibilities for the formulation of identity.

In this sense they make explicit a critical practice that provides us with different ways to think about black female subjectivity and black female spectatorship. Cinematically, they provide new points of re-cognition, embodying Stuart Hall's vision of a critical practice that acknowledges that identity is constituted "not outside but within repre-sentation," and invites us to see film "not as a second-order mirror held up to reflect what already exists, but as that form of representation which is able to constitute us as new kinds of subjects, and thereby enable us to discover who we are." It is this critical practice that enables production of feminist film theory that theorizes black female spectatorship. Look-ing and looking back, black women involve ourselves in a process whereby we see our history as countermemory, using it as a way to know the present and invent the future.

Select Bibliography

Allen, Robert, and Douglas Gomery. *Film History: Theory and Practice.* New York: Alfred A. Knopf, 1985.

Balio, Tino, ed. *The American Film Industry,* rev. ed. Madison: University of Wisconsin Press, 1985.

———, ed. *Hollywood in the Age of Television.* Boston: Unwin Hyman, 1990.

———. *Grand Design: Hollywood as a Modern Business Enterprise, 1930–1939.* New York: Scribners, 1993.

Belton, John. *Widescreen Cinema.* Cambridge: Harvard University Press, 1992.

———. *American Cinema/American Culture.* New York: McGraw-Hill, 1994.

Bergman, Andrew. *We're in the Money: Depression America and Its Films.* New York: New York University Press, 1971.

Biskind, Peter. *Seeing Is Believing: How Hollywood Taught Us to Stop Worrying and Love the Fifties.* New York: Pantheon, 1983.

Black, Gregory D. *Hollywood Censored: Morality Codes, Catholics, and the Movies.* New York: Cambridge University Press, 1994.

Bogle, Donald. *Toms, Coons, Mulattoes, Mammies, and Bucks: An Interpretive History of Blacks in American Films* (new expanded edition). New York: Continuum, 1989.

Bordwell, David, Janet Staiger, and Kristin Thompson. *The Classical Hollywood Cinema: Film Style & Mode of Production to 1960.* New York: Columbia University Press, 1985.

Bowser, Eileen. *The Transformation of Cinema: 1907–1915.* New York: Scribners, 1990.

Britton, Andrew. "Blissing Out: The Politics of Reaganite Entertainment," *Movie* 31/32 (1984), 1–42.

Brownlow, Kevin. *Behind the Mask of Innocence.* New York: Knopf, 1990.

Buscombe, Ed, ed. *The BFI Companion to the Western.* London: Andre Deutsch, 1988.

Butsch, Richard, ed. *For Fun and Profit: The Transformation of Leisure into Consumption.* Philadelphia: Temple University Press, 1990.

Cagin, Seth, and Philip Dray. *Hollywood Films of the Seventies: Sex, Drugs, Violence, Rock n' Roll and Politics.* New York: Harper & Row, 1984.

Carroll, Noel. "The Future of Allusion: Hollywood in the Seventies (and Beyond)," *October* 20 (Spring 1982), 51–81.

Ceplair, Larry, and Steven Englund. *The Inquisition in Hollywood: Politics in the Film Community, 1930–1960.* Berkeley: University of California Press, 1983.

Combs, James E. *American Political Movies: An Annotated Filmography of Feature Films.* New York: Garland, 1990.

Cordova, Richard de. *Picture Personalities: The Emergence of the Star System in America.* Urbana: University of Illinois Press, 1990.

Cripps, Thomas. *Slow Fade to Black, The Negro in American Film, 1900–1942.* New York: Oxford University Press, 1977.

———. *Black Film as Genre.* Bloomington: Indiana University Press, 1978.

Diawara, Manthia, ed. *Black American Cinema.* New York: Routledge, 1993.

Dittmar, Linda, and Gene Michaud, eds. *From Hanoi to Hollywood: The Vietnam War in American Film.* New Brunswick: Rutgers University Press, 1990.

Doane, Mary Ann. *The Desire to Desire: The Woman's Film of the 1940s.* Bloomington: Indiana University Press, 1987.

Doherty, Thomas. *Teenagers & Teenpics: The Juvenilization of American Movies in the 1950s.* Boston: Unwin Hyman, 1988.

———. *Projections of War: Hollywood, American Culture, and World War II.* New York: Columbia University Press, 1993.

Douglas, Ann. *The Feminization of American Culture.* New York: Knopf, 1977.

Dowdy, Andrew. *Movies Are Better Than Ever: Widescreen Memories of the Fifties.* New York: Morrow, 1973.

Dyer, Richard. *Stars.* London: British Film Institute, 1979.

———. *Heavenly Bodies: Film Stars and Society.* New York: St. Martin's Press, 1986.

Elsaesser, Thomas, ed. (with Adam Barker). *Early Cinema: Space, Frame, Narrative.* London: British Film Institute, 1990.

Everson, William, K. *American Silent Film.* New York: Oxford, 1978.

Foster, Hal, ed. *The Anti-Aesthetic: Essays on Postmodern Culture.* Port Townsend, Wash.: Bay Press, 1983.

Gabler, Neal. *An Empire of Their Own: How the Jews Invented Hollywood.* New York: Crown, 1988.

Gledhill, Christine, ed. *Stardom: Industry of Desire.* New York: Routledge, 1991.

Gomery, Douglas. *The Hollywood Studio System.* New York: St. Martin's Press, 1986.

———. *Shared Pleasures: A History of Movie Presentation in the United States.* Madison: University of Wisconsin Press, 1992.

Gorbman, Claudia. *Unheard Melodies: Narrative Film Music.* Bloomington: Indiana University Press, 1987.

Grant, Barry K., ed. *Film Genre Reader.* Austin: University of Texas Press, 1986.

Guerrero, Edward. *Framing Blackness: The Politics and Culture of the Black Image in American Cinema.* Philadelphia: Temple University Press, 1993.

Gunning, Tom. *D. W. Griffith and the Origins of American Narrative Film: The Early Years at Biograph.* Urbana: University of Illinois Press, 1991.

Hall, Ben M. *The Best Remaining Seats: The Story of the Golden Age of the Movie Palace.* New York: Bramhall House, 1961.

Hall, Stuart, and Paddy Whannel. *The Popular Arts: A Critical Guide to the Mass Media.* Boston: Beacon Press, 1964.

Handel, Leo A. *Hollywood Looks at Its Audience.* Urbana: University of Illinois Press, 1950.

Hansen, Miriam. *Babel & Babylon: Spectatorship in American Silent Film.* Cambridge: Harvard University Press, 1991.

Haskell, Molly. *From Reverence to Rape: The Treatment of Women in the Movies.* New York: Holt, 1973.

hooks, bell. *Black Looks: Race and Representation.* Boston: South End Press, 1992.

Huettig, Mae. *Economic Control of the Motion Picture Industry.* Philadelphia: University of Pennsylvania Press, 1944.

Jacobs, Lea. *The Wages of Sin: Censorship and the Fallen Woman Film, 1928–1942.* Madison: University of Wisconsin Press, 1991.

James, David E. *Allegories of Cinema: American Film in the Sixties.* Princeton: Princeton University Press, 1989.

Jameson, Fredric. "Reification and Utopia in Mass Culture," *Social Text* 1 (1979), 130–49.

Jarvie, Ian. *Hollywood's Overseas Campaign: The North Atlantic Movie Trade, 1920–1950.* New York: Cambridge University Press, 1992.

Jenkins, Henry. *What Made Pistachio Nuts? Early Sound Comedy and the Vaudeville Aesthetic.* New York: Columbia University Press, 1992.

Jowett, Garth. *Film, the Democratic Art: A Social History of American Film.* Boston: Little, Brown, 1976.

Kanfer, Stefan. *A Journal of the Plague Years.* New York: Atheneum, 1973.

Kaplan, E. Ann, ed. *Women in Film Noir.* London: British Film Institute, 1978.

Kellner, Douglas, and Michael Ryan, eds. *Camera Politica: The Politics and Ideology of Contemporary Hollywood Film.* Bloomington: Indiana University Press, 1988.

Kindem, Gorham. *The American Movie Industry: The Business of Motion Pictures.* Carbondale: University of Illinois Press, 1982.

Klotman, Phyllis. *Frame by Frame: A Black Filmography.* Bloomington: Indiana University Press, 1979.

Koszarski, Richard. *An Evening's Entertainment: The Age of the Silent Feature Picture, 1915–1928.* New York: Scribners, 1990.

Lang, Robert. *American Film Melodrama: Griffith, Vidor, Minnelli.* Princeton: Princeton University Press, 1989.

Lebergott, Stanley. *Pursuing Happiness: American Consumers in the Twentieth Century.* Princeton: Princeton University Press, 1993.

Lhamon, W. T., Jr. *Deliberate Speed: The Origins of a Cultural Style in the American 1950s.* Washington, D.C.: Smithsonian Press, 1990.

Maland, Charles. *Chaplin and American Culture: The Evolution of a Star Image.* Princeton: Princeton University Press, 1989.

Maltby, Richard. *Harmless Entertainment: Hollywood and the Ideology of Consensus.* Metuchen, N.J.: Scarecrow Press, 1983.

May, Lary. *Screening Out the Past: The Birth of Mass Culture and the Motion Picture Industry.* New York: Oxford University Press, 1980.

Mayne, Judith. "Immigrants and Spectators," *Wide Angle* 5:2 (1982), 32–41.

Miller, Mark Crispin, ed. *Seeing through Movies*. New York: Pantheon, 1990.

Modleski, Tania. *Feminism without Women: Culture and Criticism in a "Post-feminist" Age*. New York: Routledge, 1991.

Mordden, Ethan. *Medium Cool: The Movies of the 1960s*. New York: Knopf, 1990.

Musser, Charles. *The Emergence of Cinema: The American Screen to 1907*. New York: Scribners, 1990.

———. *Before the Nickelodeon: Edwin S. Porter and the Edison Manufacturing Co*. Berkeley: University of California, 1991.

Paul, William. *Laughing Screaming: Modern Hollywood Horror & Comedy*. New York: Columbia University Press, 1994.

Peiss, Kathy. *Cheap Amusements: Working Women and Leisure in Turn-of-the-Century New York*. Philadelphia: Temple University Press, 1986.

Pines, Jim. *Blacks in Film: A Study of Racial Themes and Images in the American Film*. London: Cassell & Collier Macmillan, 1975.

Polan, Dana. *Power & Paranoia: History, Narrative, and the American Cinema, 1940–1950*. New York: Columbia University Press, 1986.

Prince, Stephen. *Visions of Empire: Political Imagery in Contemporary American Film*. New York: Praeger, 1992.

Purdy, Jim, and Peter Roffman. *The Hollywood Social Problem Film: Madness, Despair, and Politics from the Depression to the Fifties*. Bloomington: Indiana University Press, 1981.

Pye, Michael, and Lynda Myles. *The Movie Brats: How the Film Generation Took Over Hollywood*. New York: Holt, 1979.

Ray, Robert. *A Certain Tendency in the Hollywood Cinema, 1930–1980*. Princeton: Princeton University Press, 1985.

Richards, Jeffrey. *Visions of Yesterday*. London: Routledge & Kegan Paul, 1973.

Roddick, Nick. *A New Deal in Entertainment: Warner Bros. in the 1930s*. London: British Film Institute, 1983.

Rogin, Michael. *Ronald Reagan, the Movie, and Other Episodes in Political Demonology*. Berkeley: University of California Press, 1987.

Rosenberg, Bernard, and David Manning White, eds. *Mass Culture: The Popular Arts in America*. Glencoe, Ill.: The Free Press, 1957.

Ross, Andrew. *No Respect: Intellectuals & Popular Culture*. New York: Routledge, 1989.

Rubin, Martin. *Showstoppers: Busby Berkeley and the Tradition of Spectacle*. New York: Columbia University Press, 1993.

Russo, Vito. *The Celluloid Closet: Homosexuality in the Movies*. New York: Harper & Row, 1981.

Sarris, Andrew. *The American Cinema: Directors and Directions, 1929–1968*. New York: Dutton, 1968.

———. "Sex Comedy without the Sex," *American Film* III:5 (March 1978), 8–15.

Sayre, Nora. *Running Times: Films of the Cold War*. New York: Dial, 1982.

Schatz, Thomas. *The Genius of the System: Hollywood Filmmaking in the Studio Era*. New York: Pantheon, 1988.

Sikov, Ed. *Screwball: Hollywood's Madcap Romantic Comedies*. New York: Crown, 1989.

————. *Laughing Hysterically: American Screen Comedies of the 1950s.* New York: Columbia University Press, 1994.

Sklar, Robert. *Movie-Made America: A Cultural History of American Movies.* New York: Random House, 1975.

Slotkin, Richard. *Gunfighter Nation: The Myth of the Frontier in Twentieth-Century America.* New York: Atheneum, 1992.

Staiger, Janet. *Interpreting Films: Studies in the Historical Reception of American Cinema.* Princeton: Princeton University Press, 1992.

Thorp, Margaret. *America at the Movies.* New Haven: Yale University Press, 1939.

Warshow, Robert. *The Immediate Experience: Movies, Comics, Theatre and Other Aspects of Popular Culture.* New York: Atheneum, 1979.

Whitfield, Stephen J. *The Culture of the Cold War.* Baltimore: Johns Hopkins, 1991.

Wood, Robin. *Hollywood from Vietnam to Reagan.* New York: Columbia University Press, 1986.

Wright, Will. *Sixguns & Society: A Structural Study of the Western.* Berkeley: University of California Press, 1975.

Contributors

JOHN BELTON is Professor of English at Rutgers University and is author of *Widescreen Cinema* (winner of the 1993 Kraszna Krausz Prize for books on the moving image) and *American Cinema/American Culture.*

MARY ANN DOANE is Professor of English and Modern Culture and Media at Brown University and is the author of *The Desire to Desire* and *Femmes Fatales.*

CHARLES ECKERT taught film at Indiana University and wrote for *Jump Cut, Film Comment,* and the *Quarterly Review of Film Studies.*

SYLVIA HARVEY is Senior Lecturer in Critical Studies and Film at Sheffield City Polytechnic and the author of *May 1968 and Film Culture.*

BELL HOOKS (Gloria Watkins) teaches feminism and cultural studies at The Graduate Center, City University of New York, and is the author of *Ain't I a Woman: Black Women and Feminism; Yearning: Race, Gender, and Culture; Black Looks: Race and Representation; Sisters of the Yam: Black Women and Self-Recovery,* and other books.

FREDRIC JAMESON is Professor of French and Comparative Literature at Duke University and the author of *Signatures of the Visible, The Geopolitical Aesthetic: Cinema and Space in the World System,* and other books.

LARY MAY is Associate Professor of American Studies at the University of Minnesota. He is the author of *Screening Out the Past: The Birth of Mass Culture and the Motion Picture Industry* and the editor of *Recasting America: Culture and Politics in the Age of the Cold War.*

MARTIN RUBIN is the author of *Showstoppers: Busby Berkeley and the Tradition of Spectacle.* He has taught at the State University of New York at Purchase, Wright State University, and the University of California at Santa Barbara.

Contributors

PAUL SCHRADER has written screenplays for *Taxi Driver, Obsession, Raging Bull, The Mosquito Coast, The Last Temptation of Christ*, and other films and is the director of *Blue Collar, Hardcore, American Gigolo, Cat People, Mishima, Light of Day, Patty Hearst*, and other films.

CLYDE TAYLOR teaches film and cultural studies at Tufts University and is the author of *Breaking the Aesthetic Contract*.

Index